Understanding Artificial Intelligence

Fundamentals and Applications

Understanding Artificial Intelligence

Fundamentals and Applications

Mr. Sameer Awasthi

Dr. Gaurav Kumar Srivastava

Dr. Arun Kumar Yadav

Ms. Ranjana Rajput

ACADEMIC ENCLAVE

First Edition, 2025

ISBN: 978-93-48642-10-3

Published by
ACADEMIC ENCLAVE™
House No. 10/15, Ground Floor,
Block-A, Street No. 14/3, Kamal Vihar,
Kamal Pur, Burari, Delhi-110084
Email: info@academicenclave.com
Mobile: +91-7042423166
Website: www.academicenclave.com

Printed at Replika Press Pvt. Ltd.

Preface

Artificial Intelligence (AI) has become one of the most transformative and revolutionary fields in contemporary science and technology, aiming to develop systems capable of mimicking human intelligence, solving complex problems, and learning from data and experiences. The book, "Concept of Artificial Intelligence," offers a comprehensive introduction to AI, thoroughly examining its fundamental principles, advanced techniques, and practical applications. It is designed as a valuable resource for students, researchers, and practitioners interested in understanding the core methodologies and concepts driving this rapidly evolving domain. Structured progressively, the book begins with an introductory overview in Chapter 1, providing foundational insights into AI's historical evolution, objectives, and societal impacts. Chapter 2 covers problem-solving and search techniques, detailing algorithms and strategies essential for navigating intricate decision-making scenarios. Chapter 3 explores knowledge representation, emphasizing methods of structuring information to facilitate reasoning and effective decision-making. Natural language understanding is addressed in Chapter 4, highlighting the processes by which AI systems interpret, analyze, and generate human language. Chapter 5 discusses current and future trends in AI, including prominent applications and critical ethical considerations. Finally, Chapter 6 delves into learning and adaptation within AI, examining key learning paradigms such as supervised, unsupervised, and reinforcement learning, along with advanced topics in optimization and evaluation.

Whether you're just starting out or already an experienced professional, this book provides a balanced blend of theoretical knowledge and practical insights. By the end of this journey, readers will develop a deeper appreciation of AI's capabilities and challenges, as well as its immense potential to shape the future of humanity

Mr. Sameer Awasthi

Dr. Gaurav Kumar Srivastava

Dr. Arun Kumar Yadav

Ms. Ranjana Rajput

Authors

Mr. Sameer Awasthi is currently working in Bansal Institute of Engineering and Technology, Lucknow as an Assistant Professor and Head in Department of Computer Science & Engineering (Artificial Intelligence & Artificial Intelligence and Machine Learning). He is having 21 years of teaching experience. He is completed his MTech. (CSE) from Amity University, Lucknow and B.Tech.(IT) from BBDNITM Lucknow. He has published 12 Journal Papers and 10 conference paper in various reputed international journals. He has published 3 Indian patent and 2 International patents. His area of interest is Artificial Intelligence, Machine Learning, Cloud Computing and Ad-Hoc networks.

Dr. Gaurav Kumar Srivastava is currently working in Pranveer Singh Institute of Technology Kanpur, Uttar Pradesh India. as an Associate Professor in the department of Computer Science and Engineering. He is having 14 year of teaching and research experience. He has completed his Ph.D. from MUIT Lucknow, M.Tech (SE) from BBDU Lucknow and B.Tech (IT) From AKTU, Lucknow His area of research is Artificial Intelligence and Machine Learning. He has given valuable inputs as a guide to 2+ PhD. 4+M.Tech students and 20+ B.Tech students in his career so far. He has published 1 Indian patents and 1 International Patents with Grants. He has published 03 Conferences Papers and 16 Journal Papers in which 7 are in Scopus journal and some are in reputed journals. He is the reviewer of reputed conference and journals.

Dr. Arun Kumar Yadav is currently working in Bansal Institute of Engineering and Technology, Lucknow as an Associate Professor in Department of Electrical Engineering. He is having 16 year of teaching and research experience. He has completed his Ph.D. from Sri Venkateswara University, Gajurla Uttar Pradesh, M.Tech. from NIT Patna Bihar and B.Tech from PIT Jaunpur. He has published various journal and conference papers and his area of interest is Power System.

Ms. Ranjana Rajput is an Assistant Professor at St. Andrews Institute of Technology and Management in Gurugram, where she teaches and researches in the field of computer science. She holds an M.Tech in CSE and has over four years of academic and industry experience. Her favorite subjects include Python programming, Machine Learning, and Data Science, which she is passionate about making accessible and engaging for students and readers alike. Ranjana Rajput is committed to bridging the gap between academic theory and real-world application through her work in artificial intelligence.

Contents

CHAPTER-1
INTRODUCTION

Introduction & Objective

This chapter provides a comprehensive foundation for understanding Artificial Intelligence (AI) by exploring its historical evolution, core concepts, and wide-ranging applications. It begins by examining the origins of AI, including pivotal ideas such as the Turing Test, which serves as a method for evaluating a machine's ability to exhibit human-like intelligence. A key focus is the classification of AI into various forms: Weak AI, which is designed to handle specific tasks, and Strong AI, which aspires to emulate the full range of human cognitive abilities. Further distinctions are drawn between Narrow AI, Artificial General Intelligence (AGI), and Super AI, highlighting the continuum from task-specific systems to hypothetical constructs that surpass human intellect. An essential component of the chapter is the introduction of rational agents—entities capable of perceiving their environment, reasoning about it, and taking goal-directed actions. The structure, behavior, and interaction of these agents within diverse task environments are discussed in detail, emphasizing how AI systems operate and make intelligent decisions in practical scenarios. By examining these foundational principles, this chapter aims to equip readers with a clear understanding of AI's underlying mechanisms and its transformative potential across fields such as healthcare, finance, robotics, and beyond.

Overview of Artificial Intelligence

The goal of the computer science discipline known as artificial intelligence (AI) is to build machines that are able to carry out operations that are commonly associated with human intelligence, such as language comprehension, learning, reasoning, problem-solving, and perception. AI aims to create machines that can think, act, and adapt similarly to humans by mimicking human cognitive processes. AI has developed from theoretical study into real-world applications in recent decades, radically changing a number of industries and how people use technology. A crucial branch of artificial intelligence, machine learning enables systems to learn from data on their own without explicit programming.

Machine learning algorithms use statistical methods to identify trends and arrive at well-informed conclusions. Applications like recommendation engines on websites like Netflix and Amazon are prime examples of how machine learning can accurately forecast user preferences. By examining large datasets, deep learning, a subfield of machine learning, uses neural networks that are modeled after the human brain to perform complex tasks like speech synthesis and image recognition.

There are two types of AI: general AI and narrow AI. Although it lacks broader cognitive abilities, narrow AI, also known as weak AI, is already widely used and specialized for particular tasks like voice recognition or autonomous driving. Strong AI, also known as general AI, attempts to mimic human intelligence in a variety of tasks but is still primarily theoretical and faces significant ethical and technical obstacles. AI's wide range of applications in industries like healthcare, finance, education, and agriculture demonstrate how it can be used to solve global issues. Governments and organizations must create regulatory frameworks to ensure responsible AI development and implementation, though, because ethical concerns like algorithmic bias, privacy concerns, and job displacement demand transparent, accountable, and equitable AI systems.

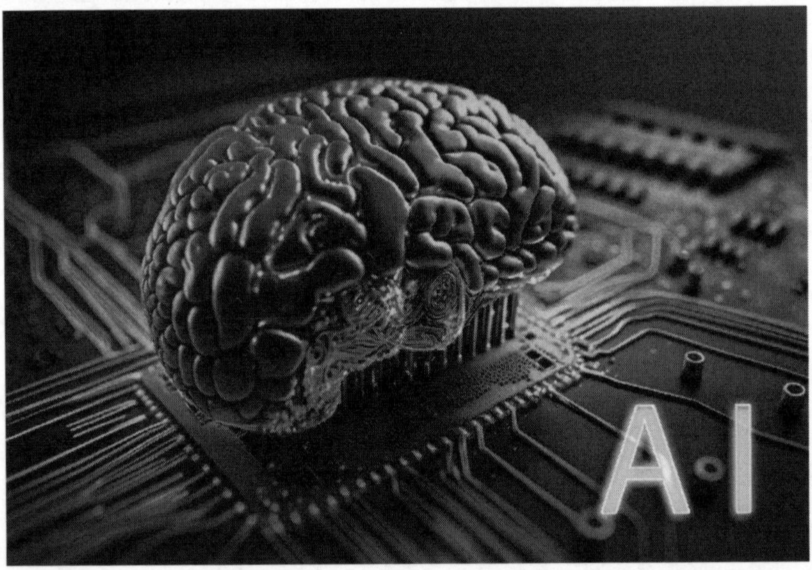

Figure 1.1: Concept of Artificial Intelligence. Source (Business Incubation Program)

A visually appealing depiction of artificial intelligence (AI) is shown in Figure 1.1, which vividly displays some of its many uses, including sophisticated neural networks and futuristic interfaces. The illustration effectively conveys the dynamic character of AI, highlighting its revolutionary potential to spur creativity, improve productivity, and tackle pressing worldwide issues in a range of fields, such as sustainability, healthcare, and education. It is becoming more and more important to approach AI development with ethical mindfulness as it develops further and its capabilities grow exponentially. AI can fairly benefit humanity without escalating current inequalities or ethical quandaries if technological advancement is balanced with responsible application. As we all work to navigate the complexities and promises of this ground-breaking field, it is crucial to promote a thorough understanding of AI's principles, opportunities, and related challenges for both technology experts and the general public.

Categories of AI

The goal of this classification is to evaluate an AI system's level of sophistication and ability to carry out tasks and replicate human intelligence (Figure 1.2). Narrow AI, General AI, and Super AI are among the capabilities-based categories, each of which represents varying degrees of complexity and problem-solving flexibility. Super AI completely outperforms human cognitive capacities, General AI can reason and adapt broadly like a human, and Narrow AI is limited to specific tasks with predetermined parameters. Furthermore, AI systems are divided into four categories based on their functionalities: Theory of Mind, Limited Memory, Self-Aware AI, and Reactive Machines. Reactive machines don't remember previous interactions; they only work with current inputs. AI with limited memory can make snap decisions by taking into account prior experiences. The most sophisticated type of AI, known as Self-Aware AI, has consciousness, self-awareness, and a profound comprehension of its own existence. Theory of Mind AI would comprehend and react to human emotions and thoughts.

1. Narrow AI (Weak AI)

Narrow AI refers to systems that are made especially to carry out specific tasks with remarkable efficiency, working strictly within predefined parameters and not being able to apply their knowledge to unrelated fields. Virtual assistants like Siri and Alexa, Netflix's recommendation algorithms, and spam detection features built into email services are a few examples of narrow artificial intelligence. Despite being highly effective at their specific tasks, these systems are fundamentally incapable of having true awareness or the ability to carry out tasks outside of their preprogrammed roles. Narrow AI is widely used in today's technological environment due to its dependability and practicality, producing accurate and consistent results within predetermined parameters. However, its incapacity to independently modify or generalize outside of its initial programming continues to be its main flaw. As a result, limited AI solutions require constant human involvement for updates or reprogramming whenever new tasks or circumstances emerge that deviate from their original intent.

2. General AI (Strong AI)

The term "general artificial intelligence" describes machines that can simulate human cognitive processes, enabling them to carry out any intellectual task that a human is capable of. General AI has the ability to autonomously learn, adapt, and transfer knowledge across a variety of domains, in contrast to narrow AI, which is task-specific. Such systems would surpass the limitations of current AI technologies and be able to reason, solve complex problems, and understand abstract concepts similarly to humans. Since no AI system has achieved this comprehensive level of intelligence to date, general AI is still only a theoretical concept. Significant improvements in processing power, memory storage capacity, and machine learning methodologies would be required to achieve general artificial intelligence. Furthermore, the development raises important ethical issues, such as worries about how systems might replace or challenge human autonomy, control, and decision-making.

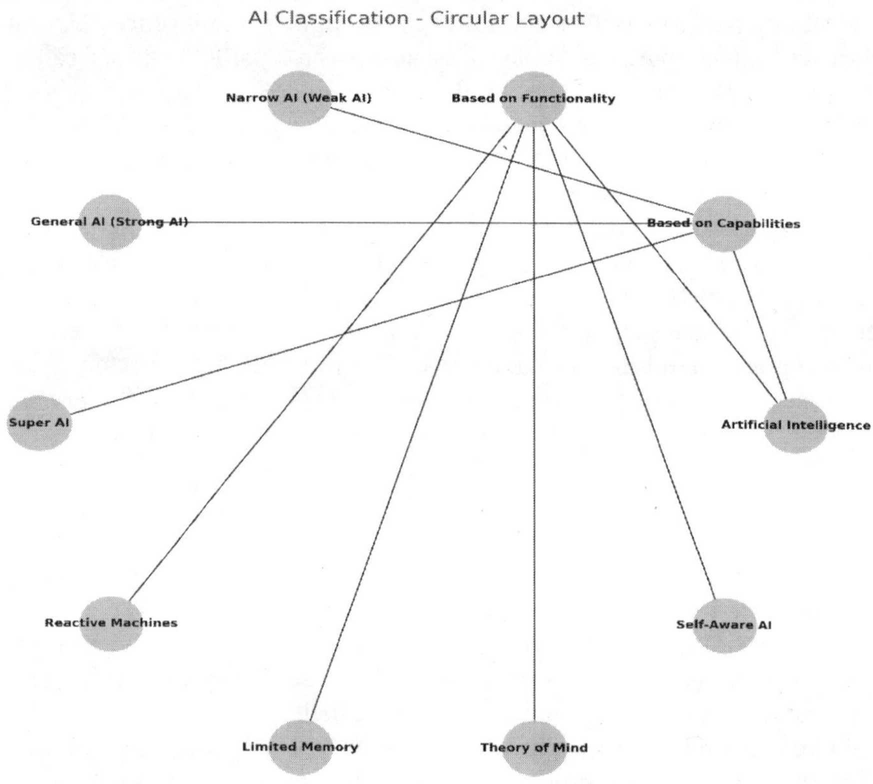

Figure 1.2: Categories of AI.

3. Super AI

Super AI is a theoretically advanced stage of artificial intelligence in which machines are more intelligent than humans in every intellectual domain, such as creativity, emotional intelligence, and complex problem-solving. Such an AI might surpass humans in almost every domain, leading to previously unheard-of breakthroughs and profoundly altering social norms and structures. Super AI is still only a theoretical concept today, despite the fact that it regularly piques people's interest in science fiction stories. It would take a profound comprehension of human consciousness in addition to technological breakthroughs well beyond what is currently possible to realize this level of intelligence. As a result, this idea presents important philosophical and ethical issues, especially with regard to human control over AI systems, maintaining safety, and examining the ramifications of coexisting with extremely intelligent machines.

4. Reactive Machines

The most basic type of artificial intelligence is represented by reactive machines, which are defined by their sole dependence on pre-established rules to process particular inputs and lack of memory storage or experiential learning capabilities. IBM's Deep Blue, a chess-playing computer that chooses the best moves only based on the chessboard's current state—not on past moves or learned strategie is a perfect example. Although these reactive systems are very effective at repetitive, well-defined tasks, their application is limited in more complex or dynamic scenarios due to their lack of adaptability and learning capacity. Reactive machines, however, have been crucial to the early development of AI and remain useful in situations where reliability, speed, and simplicity are necessities.

5. Limited Memory

Systems with limited memory temporarily store and examine historical data to improve their ability to make decisions. The majority of modern AI applications, such as autonomous vehicles, fit into this group. Autonomous vehicles, for instance, use historical data on traffic patterns, speed, and road conditions to make well-informed driving decisions. By utilizing machine learning algorithms and analyzing past data, these systems are able to improve their performance over time. Limited memory systems have limitations even though they are more advanced than purely reactive machines because their memory and learning capabilities are restricted to specific tasks and situations.

6. Theory of Mind

Mental Theory Machines can communicate with humans more naturally and intuitively thanks to artificial intelligence (AI), which is made to comprehend human emotions, thoughts, and behaviors. This advanced type of AI, which is still in the research stage, has the potential to revolutionize human-machine interactions by giving machines social intelligence, which would improve their capacity to react contextually and sympathetically to human needs. Theory of Mind AI has a wide range of potential uses, from sophisticated virtual assistants that can recognize emotional cues and respond with emotionally intelligent responses to humanoid robots that interact with people in social settings. However, in order for machines to correctly understand and react to complex human behavior and subtle emotional expressions, major advancements are needed, especially in areas like emotion recognition and contextual comprehension.

7. Self-Aware AI

The ultimate form of artificial intelligence, self-aware AI is distinguished by true consciousness and an awareness of its own existence. With the capacity for autonomous thought, sophisticated reasoning, and self-reflection, these sophisticated systems would be able to closely resemble human consciousness. Though still theoretical, the idea has the potential to fundamentally alter society by enabling previously unheard-of technological breakthroughs and altering the fundamental dynamics of human-machine interactions. But there are also serious societal and ethical issues with the development of self-aware AI. Since these autonomous systems may make decisions that deviate from the intended results, they raise serious concerns about control, accountability, and compatibility with human values. Therefore, it is essential to ensure the responsible development and efficient governance of self-aware AI in order to maximize its enormous potential while reducing its inherent risks.

Challenges across Types

- Ethical Considerations: Issues like bias, privacy, and accountability.
- Technological Barriers: Achieving general and super AI requires breakthroughs in computational power and algorithms.
- Regulation and Control: Ensuring AI is developed and used responsibly.

Background & Applications

Background of Artificial Intelligence

Researchers began working on artificial intelligence (AI) in the middle of the 20th century with the goal of building machines that could think and act like humans. John McCarthy first used the term "Artificial Intelligence" at the Dartmouth Conference in 1956, which officially launched AI as a field of study. The main focus of early AI research was logic-based techniques and symbolic reasoning, which produced innovations like theorem-solving software. However, the shortcomings of strictly rule-based methods were brought to light by these early systems' difficulties managing unclear or insufficient information. The 1980s saw the advent of machine learning, which marked a significant advancement in AI by moving the emphasis from explicitly programmed rules to training systems with massive datasets. AI became highly proficient in processing unstructured data, such as images, videos, and natural language, in the 2010s thanks to the development of deep learning, which was fueled by increased processing power, large datasets, and improved algorithms. Using technologies like neural networks, natural language processing, and robotics, artificial intelligence (AI) is a dynamic, multidisciplinary field that combines computer science, neuroscience, mathematics, and engineering. Ongoing advancements and new uses of AI in a variety of fields are anticipated due to ongoing advancements in computational power, cloud computing, and big data analytics.

History of Artificial Intelligence

Humanity's persistent goal to create machines with the capacity for intelligent thought and action is reflected in the history of artificial intelligence (AI). This evolution, which has lasted for several decades, has been marked by ground-breaking research, technological advancements, and changing perspectives on the potential of artificial intelligence. From the first philosophical investigations into machine intelligence in antiquity to Alan Turing's seminal ideas in the middle of the 20th century and the subsequent recognition of AI as a separate scientific field in 1956, AI has continuously broadened its scope. Important turning points include the creation of expert systems in the 1970s and 1980s, the emergence of machine learning and neural networks in the 1990s, and the outstanding advances in deep learning starting in the 2010s, which are best illustrated by developments in robotics, computer vision, and natural language processing. Figure 1.3 provides a thorough illustration of how AI is developing today, with cutting-edge advancements like generative AI models sparking important conversations about moral issues, responsible use, and the wider impact on society.

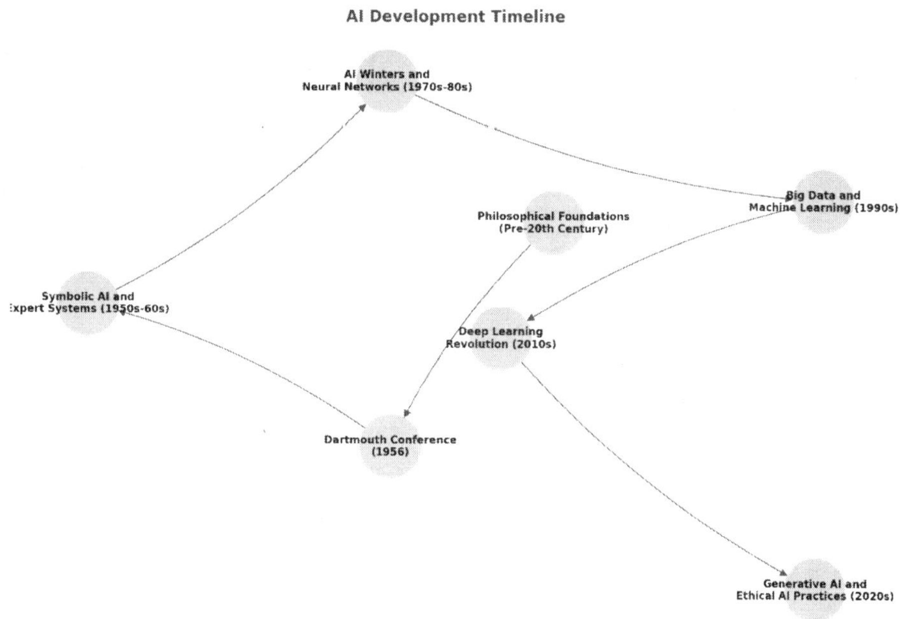

Figure 1.3: History of Artificial Intelligence.

- Below is an overview of the key phases in the evolution of AI, as mention in Table 1.1:

Table 1.1: Evolution of AI.

Era	Timeframe	Key Developments	Examples
Early Concepts	Pre-1950s	Conceptual foundations of machine intelligence.	Turing Machine, "Computing Machinery and Intelligence" by Alan Turing
Birth of AI	1950s-1960s	Official start of AI research; first AI programs developed.	Logic Theorist, General Problem Solver, ELIZA
AI Winter & Revival	1970s-1980s	Funding cuts, skepticism (AI Winter); later revival through expert systems.	MYCIN (Expert system), DENDRAL
Machine Learning Era	1990s-2000s	Emphasis on machine learning, statistical approaches, neural networks revived.	IBM Deep Blue, Neural Networks, Support Vector Machines
Deep Learning Revolution	2010s	Breakthroughs in deep neural networks and big data; large-scale applications.	ImageNet, AlphaGo, Siri, Alexa
Generative & Transformer AI	2020s - Present	Generative AI models, large language models, widespread commercial adoption.	GPT models, ChatGPT, DALL-E, Bard, Copilot

Early Foundations: Pre-20th Century

The idea of intelligent machines has existed since antiquity, when thinkers such as Aristotle established the foundation for systems of logical reasoning and envisioned methodical approaches to decision-making. Mythological tales that featured mechanical devices, or automata that imitated human behavior, further stimulated the imagination. As mathematicians like Blaise Pascal and Charles Babbage created mechanical calculators and theoretical models for automated computation by the 17th and 18th centuries, this philosophical curiosity transformed into useful inventions that paved the way for contemporary developments in artificial intelligence. The idea of intelligent machines has its roots in antiquity, when thinkers such as Aristotle developed the fundamentals of logical reasoning and envisioned systematic approaches to decision-making. Furthermore, mythological stories enthralled people with their representations of automata, which are mechanical devices that can mimic human movements and behaviors. By the 17th and 18th centuries, mathematical geniuses like Blaise

Pascal and Charles Babbage had turned philosophical curiosity into practical inventions by creating mechanical calculators and developing theoretical models for automated computation. These pioneering initiatives laid the crucial groundwork for the astounding developments in artificial intelligence that have occurred since then.

Birth of Modern AI (1940s-1950s)

By creating the Turing Machine, a mathematical abstraction that can perform calculations, Alan Turing's groundbreaking research in the 1940s set the foundation for contemporary computing and artificial intelligence. In his seminal 1950 paper, Computing Machinery and Intelligence, he furthered his investigation into machine intelligence by introducing the Turing Test as a standard for determining whether a machine can exhibit intelligent behavior that is indistinguishable from that of a human. John McCarthy coined the term "Artificial Intelligence" at the 1956 Dartmouth Conference, marking the official beginning of artificial intelligence as a separate academic field. This historic meeting brought together top academics to debate and explore whether machines can mimic human intelligence. Early innovations, like the Logic Theorist program developed by Allen Newell and Herbert Simon, demonstrated the usefulness of AI by effectively using symbolic reasoning to validate mathematical theorems, representing a significant advancement in the field.

The Golden Age of AI (1956-1974)

Artificial intelligence advanced quickly during the optimistic 1950s and 1960s as scientists created novel systems that could solve problems, play games, and carry out simple tasks. Prominent accomplishments, like IBM's chess-playing computer, demonstrated AI's capacity to tackle difficult problems and opened the door for more research. The practical uses of AI were demonstrated in the 1960s when focus shifted to "expert systems," which were created expressly to mimic human decision-making in specialized fields like medical diagnosis. Notwithstanding these early achievements, the period also revealed serious AI flaws. Systems frequently required significant processing power and ongoing human supervision to handle the complexity of the real world. These flaws highlighted the need for more complex algorithms and improved processing power, which ultimately shaped the course of future AI research and development.

AI Winters (1974-1980s)

Early AI research overpromised and then failed to live up to high expectations, which caused widespread disillusionment and ushered in periods known as "AI Winters." During these times, there were significant reductions in funding and growing doubts about the viability of developing true machine intelligence. Technological limitations, such as limited computational resources and early AI systems' inability to manage uncertainty or effectively adapt to dynamic, real-world situations, were a major source of difficulty for researchers. However, AI research did not entirely stall in spite of these obstacles. Devoted researchers focused their efforts on improving current approaches and procedures during these times of stagnation. This tenacity created a strong basis for subsequent developments, allowing for important breakthroughs when interest in and funding for artificial intelligence were eventually reignited by improvements in computational power and novel approaches.

Revival Through Machine Learning (1980s-1990s)

Developments in neural networks, which were motivated by the complex biological makeup of the human brain, played a major role in the resurgence of interest in artificial intelligence in the 1980s. The backpropagation algorithm, which allowed neural networks to learn efficiently from data and significantly improve their functionality and adaptability across a range of complex tasks, was a crucial innovation of this era. As a result, AI applications significantly spread into industries like healthcare and finance, as demonstrated by the development of expert systems like MYCIN, which was intended to precisely diagnose bacterial infections. AI-powered robotics also advanced concurrently, especially in the manufacturing sector, where robots started automating assembly lines. This invention significantly increased production processes' productivity, accuracy, and efficiency while laying the fundamental framework for contemporary industrial robotics.

Emergence of Data-Driven AI (1990s-2000s)

The advent of Big Data in the 1990s signaled a turning point in the development of artificial intelligence. Data-driven machine learning models replaced conventional rule-based programming as a result of AI systems' increased access to enormous datasets brought about by the exponential growth of digital information. This change greatly increased AI's capabilities across a range of domains by enabling it to recognize patterns and make decisions more quickly. The 1997 victory of IBM's Deep Blue over world chess champion Garry Kasparov, a historic accomplishment that showed AI's capacity for sophisticated strategic thinking, is among the decade's most memorable moments. In addition, the decade saw significant advancements in natural language processing and speech recognition, laying the groundwork for upcoming breakthroughs in AI-powered communication and human-computer interaction. Together, these developments created the foundation for the sophisticated systems we use today.

Deep Learning Revolution (2010s)

An important turning point in the development of artificial intelligence was the emergence of deep neural networks, which were fueled by robust hardware such as GPUs and the wealth of large-scale datasets. Convolutional neural networks (CNNs), among other groundbreaking technologies, significantly increased the accuracy of image recognition and other visual tasks. The 2016 triumph of Google DeepMind's AlphaGo over world champions in the challenging board game Go was a turning point in this era, demonstrating AI's capacity to comprehend complex decision-making environments. This illustrated AI's capacity to advance problem-solving techniques in addition to its technical mastery. At the same time, voice-activated assistants like Google Assistant, Alexa, and Siri allowed AI to blend in with everyday life, demonstrating its increasing usefulness and accessibility. These consumer applications demonstrated how AI could improve routine tasks' efficiency and convenience. These advancements had an impact on a variety of industries, including healthcare, finance, transportation, and entertainment, where artificial intelligence started to drive significant changes. AI became a vital part of contemporary innovation and industrial advancement by automating processes, facilitating data-driven decision-making, and providing personalized experiences.

Present and Future of AI (2020s and beyond)

A revolutionary era in artificial intelligence was heralded by the emergence of deep neural networks, which were primarily fuelled by the expansion of massive datasets and potent hardware like GPUs. Convolutional neural networks (CNNs) marked a significant advancement in computer vision and image recognition, reaching previously unthinkable levels of accuracy. One of the most famous turning points of this era was when Google DeepMind's AlphaGo defeated thc best human players in the strategic game of Go in 2016. This achievement demonstrated AI's ability to use deep learning and reinforcement techniques to solve extremely difficult, abstract problems. In addition to these historic accomplishments, AI has become more pervasive in daily life thanks to virtual assistants like Google Assistant, Alexa, and Siri, which have intelligently automated consumer electronics. These tools, which could respond to voice commands, manage schedules, and even control home environments, demonstrated the practical applications of artificial intelligence. This broad use demonstrated AI's expanding impact in industries like healthcare, where it helps with diagnostics; finance, where it facilitates algorithmic trading; transportation, where it uses autonomous systems; and entertainment, where it suggests tailored content. When taken as a whole, these developments solidified AI as a key technology in contemporary innovation.

Applications of Artificial Intelligence

AI is revolutionizing how we live and work, as well as changing entire industries. Here are a few significant uses of AI in different fields:

Healthcare: By improving patient care, diagnosis, and treatment, artificial intelligence is revolutionizing the healthcare industry. Large volumes of medical data, such as genetic profiles and imaging scans, can be effectively analyzed by machine learning algorithms, allowing for the early detection of conditions like cancer. By analyzing patient histories and medical literature, tools such as IBM Watson Health assist physicians in developing individualized treatment plans. Healthcare practitioners are empowered to make better decisions thanks to this degree of data-driven insight, which eventually improves patient outcomes. Beyond diagnostics, AI is essential to drug discovery because it speeds up the process of finding promising compounds for novel drugs. As a result, traditional drug development takes less time and money. Additionally, by providing services like medication reminders, appointment scheduling, and symptom checking, AI-powered virtual health assistants increase access to healthcare. As listed in Table 1.2, these developments support a healthcare system that is more patient-centered and effective.

Table 1.2: Role of AI in Healthcare.

Area	Role of AI	Examples
Medical Imaging	Enhances image analysis for faster and more accurate diagnosis	AI in MRI, CT scans, X-rays for detecting tumors, fractures
Disease Diagnosis	Assists in early and precise detection of diseases	AI for predicting cancer, diabetes, heart diseases
Drug Discovery	Speeds up identification of potential drug candidates	AI models to simulate molecular interactions
Personalized Medicine	Provides tailored treatment plans based on patient data	AI analyzing genetic info for cancer therapy customization
Virtual Health Assistants	Offers real-time assistance and reminders for patients	Chatbots for symptom checking, appointment scheduling
Remote Monitoring	Tracks patient vitals and alerts providers in real-time	Wearables with AI for heart rate, glucose, and oxygen monitoring
Administrative Tasks	Automates hospital operations and reduces paperwork	AI for billing, documentation, and patient record management
Robotic Surgery	Increases precision and reduces recovery time in surgeries	AI-powered surgical robots like da Vinci system
Epidemic Outbreak Prediction	Forecasts disease spread using data analytics	AI models predicting COVID-19 hotspots, flu trends
Mental Health Support	Provides preliminary psychological support through conversational agents	AI-based apps offering CBT and emotional well-being tracking

Finance: Artificial intelligence (AI) is being used more and more in the financial industry to increase operational effectiveness, reduce risks, and provide better customer experiences. Large volumes of historical data and market trends are analyzed by sophisticated algorithms to improve investment strategies and more accurately predict stock prices. In order to protect users from financial crimes, AI-driven fraud detection systems quickly identify and flag suspicious activity while monitoring transactions in real-time. AI is changing customer-facing services in addition to backend operations. Chatbots driven by AI answer common banking questions, providing prompt, precise answers all day long. AI is used by robo-advisors to offer individualized financial advice based on each client's risk tolerance and investing objectives. Additionally, by taking into account a wider variety of data points, AI-enhanced credit scoring models assess applicants more thoroughly, leading to more accurate and equitable lending decisions (Figure 1.4).

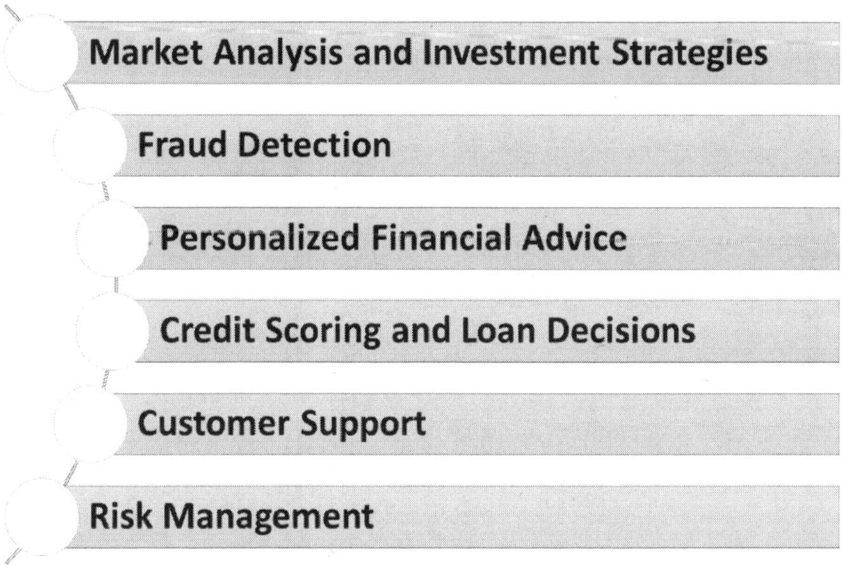

Figure 1.4: Role of AI in Finance.

Education: AI is revolutionizing education by making highly customized learning experiences possible. By using data analytics to evaluate each student's strengths and shortcomings, adaptive learning platforms enable personalized lesson plans and focused feedback that accommodate different learning preferences. AI-powered virtual tutors provide assistance outside of the classroom by letting students study at their own speed and get help whenever they need it, which improves understanding and memory. In addition to increasing student engagement, this individualized approach facilitates more efficient closing of learning gaps. Beyond learning, AI greatly simplifies educational administrative tasks. AI-driven technologies are automating more and more tasks like scheduling, attendance monitoring, and grading, freeing up teachers' time to concentrate on teaching and student engagement. Additionally, AI is improving language learning through programs like Duolingo, which use natural language processing to effectively and interactively teach vocabulary and grammar. These developments highlight how AI has the potential to improve education's effectiveness, accessibility, and learner-centeredness, as indicated in Table 1.3.

Table 1.3: Role of AI in Education.

Area	Role of AI
Personalized Learning	Adapts content and pace based on individual learner's needs and performance.
Intelligent Tutoring	Provides instant feedback and customized support like a virtual tutor.
Automated Grading	Speeds up evaluation of assignments and tests, freeing up teacher time.
Curriculum Development	Analyzes data to suggest improvements in curriculum design and delivery.
Accessibility	Assists students with disabilities through speech-to-text, translation, etc.
Administrative Automation	Manages tasks like attendance, scheduling, and data entry efficiently.
Early Dropout Prediction	Identifies at-risk students through data analytics for timely intervention.
Smart Content Creation	Generates quizzes, summaries, flashcards, and study material automatically.
Language Learning	Enhances practice through AI chatbots, pronunciation analysis, and feedback.
Lifelong Learning	Supports adult education and upskilling with AI-driven platforms and courses.

Manufacturing: Manufacturing is undergoing a revolution thanks to artificial intelligence (AI), which is greatly increasing operational efficiency, quality, and productivity. Automation driven by AI streamlines production processes, enabling factories to operate more accurately and with fewer mistakes. AI-driven robots are used in smart factories to perform labor-intensive and repetitive tasks, increasing output while lowering the need for human labor. Predictive maintenance, which continuously analyzes machine data to find early indications of malfunction, is one of the most significant uses of AI. This proactive strategy lowers maintenance costs, extends equipment life, and helps manufacturers prevent expensive downtime. AI is revolutionizing supply chain management outside of the manufacturing floor as well. In order to improve logistics, optimize inventory levels, and accurately forecast demand, sophisticated algorithms examine past data, market trends, and consumer behavior. This guarantees a smooth operation and helps avoid stockouts or overstocking. Tesla, which makes extensive use of robotics and AI in its production lines, is a shining example of how AI can be integrated into manufacturing. High levels of accuracy and constant product quality are ensured by these systems, which allow for real-time monitoring and adjustments during vehicle assembly. Tesla's strategy demonstrates how AI can lower operating costs while upholding strict standards, highlighting the revolutionary impact AI has on the manufacturing industry.

Transportation: One of the main forces behind the creation of driverless cars and the revolution in contemporary transportation systems is artificial intelligence (AI). AI is used by self-driving cars, which were first introduced by firms like Tesla and Waymo, to analyze sensor data, recognize objects, and make snap decisions. These technologies promise a more dependable and efficient mobility in the future by reducing traffic, improving road safety, and minimizing human error. AI has a big impact on public transportation in addition to personal automobiles. In order to improve system efficiency, it aids in schedule management, passenger flow analysis, and bus and train route optimization. In the end, daily commuters save time and fuel by using AI-powered navigation apps like Google Maps, which provide real-time traffic updates and suggest alternate routes.

Retail & E-commerce: The retail sector is changing as a result of artificial intelligence (AI), which makes shopping more interactive, efficient, and personalized. AI is used by e-commerce behemoths like Amazon to examine user behavior, preferences, and past purchases in order to provide personalized product recommendations that increase customer satisfaction and revenue. By offering immediate customer service, answering questions, and assisting users along the way, AI-powered chatbots further improve the online shopping experience. AI-powered dynamic pricing algorithms are also essential because they optimize revenue and ensure competitive pricing by modifying prices in response to market trends, competitor activity, and demand. AI has an equal impact in real-world retail environments. AI-driven analytics are used by retailers to better manage inventory, optimize store layouts, and research consumer behavior. These systems improve the in-store experience by analyzing foot traffic and purchase data to determine the best product placements. Customers can find products using images more easily thanks to visual search tools like Google Lens and Pinterest Lens, which also add convenience. AI is also being used by companies like IKEA with products like IKEA Place, an AR-powered app that combines customization and functionality by letting users see furniture in their spaces before making a purchase. These developments demonstrate how AI is increasingly influencing the direction of both online and physical retail.

Entertainment: The entertainment sector is undergoing a revolution thanks to artificial intelligence (AI), which is changing how content is created and consumed. Advanced AI algorithms are used by streaming services like Netflix and Spotify to examine user preferences, actions, and trends in order to provide tailored recommendations. By improving user engagement, satisfaction, and loyalty, this focused strategy eventually increases subscriber retention and revenue. AI is also causing a stir in the content creation space with tools that facilitate the creation of virtual characters, deepfake videos, and incredibly lifelike animations. By automating processes like video editing, special effects enhancement, and actor de-aging, these technologies are enabling creators to push the boundaries of creativity while streamlining production and cutting expenses. AI has a significant impact on the gaming industry, where it improves player immersion and gameplay. Intelligent non-player characters (NPCs) driven by AI systems react dynamically to user inputs, enhancing the personalization and realism of gameplay. AI also makes procedural generation possible, which automatically creates whole game worlds and storylines that give players countless options and boost replay value. Games like The Last of Us demonstrate how AI-driven behavior improves gaming realism and emotional nuance. AI is changing the way stories are told, content is delivered, and experiences are created in a variety of entertainment sectors, confirming its position as a disruptive force in the sector (Figure 1.5).

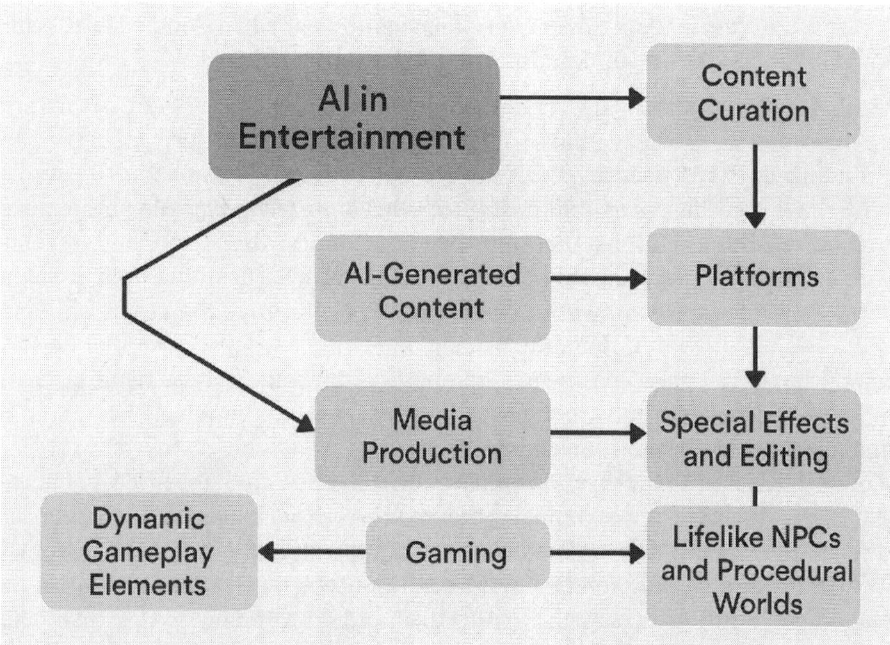

Figure 1.5: Role of AI in Entertainment.

Turing Test

The Turing Test is a fundamental idea in the field of artificial intelligence (AI), first presented by British mathematician and computer scientist Alan Turing in 1950. Turing put forward this test in his paper "Computing Machinery and Intelligence," which aims to ascertain whether a machine can display behavior that is identical to that of a human. In the test, a human assessor sends text messages to a machine and a human, not knowing which is which. The machine is deemed to have passed the test, successfully mimicking human intelligence, if the assessor is unable to distinguish between the human and the machine. A major turning point in AI research, the Turing Test has drawn criticism, especially for prioritizing imitation over true understanding or consciousness. Passing the test, according to critics, only demonstrates the machine's capacity to mimic human speech patterns, not its actual intelligence. The Turing Test nevertheless continues to provoke discussion and investigation into the nature of human-like reasoning, machine cognition, and the boundaries of artificial systems. As AI develops, the test not only acts as a standard but also as a reminder of the technical and philosophical issues that underlie the search for intelligent machines.

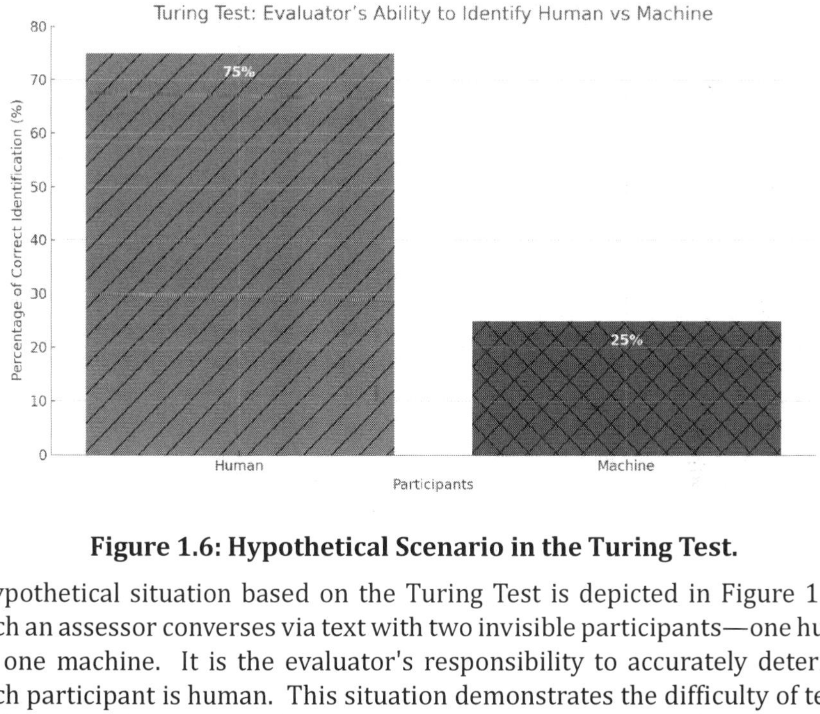

Figure 1.6: Hypothetical Scenario in the Turing Test.

A hypothetical situation based on the Turing Test is depicted in Figure 1.6, in which an assessor converses via text with two invisible participants—one human and one machine. It is the evaluator's responsibility to accurately determine which participant is human. This situation demonstrates the difficulty of telling the difference between artificial and human intelligence only through written communication, which is the core of Alan Turing's Turing Test. The figure's graph shows the evaluator's percentage of accurate identifications for both human and machine participants. It provides information about how well the machine replicates human responses by displaying the frequency with which the assessor correctly classified each participant. In the Turing Test, a machine with a lower percentage of correct identification would have a better chance of fooling the assessor. On the other hand, a greater identification rate for humans shows that the assessor can identify genuine human interaction.

Theory of the Turing Test

Alan Turing developed the Turing Test, which revolves around the profound but simple query, "Can a machine think?" Turing suggested a more useful method for determining whether a machine can accurately mimic human behavior rather than making a direct effort to define or quantify thought. Finding out if a machine can carry on a conversation so naturally that a human assessor cannot tell it apart from a human is the aim. An important turning point in the study of artificial intelligence was this move away from abstract definitions and toward observable behavior. A text-based dialogue between a human, a machine, and a human evaluator who engages with both without being aware of which is which is the setup for the Turing Test. The exam makes sure that only the content and caliber of communication are evaluated by removing physical clues like voice and appearance. The machine is considered to have passed the test if the evaluator is unable to reliably identify it. This situation evaluates a machine's capacity to display traits linked to human intelligence, including comprehension, learning, reasoning, and effective communication.

The Structure of the Turing Test

Participants:

- **The Machine:** A system or computer program developed to mimic human reactions.
- **The Human:** An actual person, usually selected to symbolize a normal human in the discourse.
- **The Evaluator (Judge):** Someone who communicates with both the machine and themselves via text without being able to tell which is which. Finding out which participant is the machine based only on the conversation is the evaluator's objective.

Test Procedure:

- To make sure the evaluator cannot rely on any physical cues, the human and the machine are placed in different rooms.
- The assessor converses with both participants and poses a series of questions to them.
- The goal of the machine's programming is to "fool" the assessor into thinking it is a human by mimicking human conversational patterns.
- The machine is deemed to have passed the Turing Test if the assessor is unable to consistently tell the machine apart from the human based on the exchange.

Structures of the Turing Test

- **Imitation Game:** The Turing Test is sometimes referred to as the

"Imitation Game" because the objective of the machine is to replicate human behavior sufficiently well that its assessor is duped.

- **Text-Based Interaction:** The test eliminates potential biases resulting from visual or auditory cues by relying on text-based communication. This guarantees that the computer's capacity for human-like thought and communication is the only thing being evaluated.
- No Need for Consciousness: In his initial proposal, Turing did not call for the machine to possess awareness or self-awareness. Rather, it was sufficient for the machine to exhibit intelligent behavior that, in certain situations, resembles human reactions.

Criticisms and Limitations of the Turing Test

While the Turing Test remains a landmark in the development of AI, it has faced several criticisms and limitations:

Questionable Measure of Intelligence: Opponents contend that passing the Turing Test does not always imply actual intelligence on par with that of people. Just by mimicking human behavior, a machine can achieve success without any true comprehension or awareness. John Searle raises this issue in his "Chinese Room" argument, which questions the notion that mimicking comprehension is the same as truly having it.

Narrow Focus: The Turing Test ignores other crucial facets of intelligence like creativity, problem-solving, and physical coordination in favor of assessing verbal communication. The test ignores the possibility that a machine may be proficient in conversation but incompetent in other crucial domains.

Overemphasis on Human-Like Behavior: The test may have a narrow perspective by equating intelligence with human-like behavior. Artificial intelligence may behave intelligently in novel, non-human ways while retaining the capacity for reasoning and problem-solving.

Element of Deception: A common strategy for passing the Turing Test is to trick the assessor into thinking the machine is human. True intelligence, according to critics, should be centered on real comprehension and problem-solving rather than lying to others.

Applications and Influence of the Turing Test

Despite its many detractors, the Turing Test has had a big impact on philosophy and artificial intelligence. It sparked attempts to build machines that could mimic human speech, opening the door for the creation of virtual assistants, chatbots, and other conversational AI tools. Deeper conversations about machine consciousness, what constitutes intelligence, and the morality of creating machines with human-like characteristics were also spurred by the test. There have been notable successes, even though no AI has conclusively passed the Turing Test by universal standards. For example, in a Turing Test-style event in 2014, an AI named Eugene Goostman persuaded 33 percent of human judges that it was a 13-year-old boy. However, this outcome was viewed with suspicion because many contended that the judges' opinions were shaped more by the character's purported age than by actual intelligence.

Introduction to Weak AI, Strong AI &Narrow AI

Based on its capabilities and degree of intelligence, artificial intelligence (AI) can be divided into various categories. The terms Weak AI, Strong AI, and Narrow AI are frequently used to classify AI. Weak AI, sometimes referred to as narrow AI, describes systems like voice assistants, recommendation algorithms, and facial recognition software that are made to carry out particular tasks with a restricted scope. Even though they may seem intelligent in their operations, these systems are predetermined and lack consciousness and true understanding. Strong AI, on the other hand, is a more sophisticated and theoretical type of AI that would have cognitive traits similar to those of humans, such as consciousness, self-awareness, and the ability to learn and solve problems in a variety of fields without the need for human assistance. Research in this area attempts to build machines that could accurately replicate human intelligence, even though strong artificial intelligence is still primarily conceptual at this point. These categories aid in comprehending the functions of AI in society both now and in the future, as well as the drawbacks and moral dilemmas related to each kind. Below is a detailed explanation of each type:

1. Weak AI (Narrow AI)

Definition: Weak AI, sometimes referred to as narrow AI, is a type of artificial intelligence that is highly effective at completing particular tasks. These systems are designed to perform a specific set of tasks, like virtual help, language translation, and facial recognition. Weak AI lacks general cognitive skills in contrast to human intelligence, which is flexible and able to learn in a variety of fields. It can quickly process information and carry out tasks within its predetermined parameters, but it is unable to reason or think outside of them. These AI systems operate in a controlled environment specifically designed for their purpose and are goal-driven. Weak AI is demonstrated, for instance, by an email system's spam filter, which is capable of efficiently identifying and classifying spam but is unable to carry out tasks like voice assistance or image recognition. For certain applications, particularly those where speed, accuracy, and repetition are crucial, Weak AI's limited focus makes it incredibly effective. However, it differs from more sophisticated types of AI, like Artificial General Intelligence (AGI), in that it lacks self-awareness and a broader understanding.

Characteristics:

- **Focused Capabilities:** Weak AI is designed to handle a single task or a narrow range of functions. It lacks the ability to apply its skills beyond its programmed scope. For instance, a chess-playing AI like Deep Blue can compete at a grandmaster level but is incapable of performing unrelated tasks like diagnosing medical conditions or translating languages.

- **Lack of Self-Awareness:** Weak AI systems do not have consciousness or true understanding. They function through predetermined algorithms and pattern recognition, reacting to input data without any awareness or comprehension of their actions.
- **High Efficiency:** Although their capabilities are restricted, Weak AI systems are typically highly efficient in their designated areas. They can analyze vast amounts of data quickly and execute decisions using sophisticated algorithms, often surpassing human performance in specific domains

Examples:

- **Virtual Assistants:** AI-powered tools such as Siri, Alexa, and Google Assistant are examples of Weak AI. They are programmed to carry out specific tasks like responding to voice commands, setting reminders, answering questions, and performing actions such as sending messages or making calls. However, their capabilities are confined to pre-programmed functions, and they cannot learn or execute tasks beyond their initial design.
- **Recommendation Systems:** Platforms like Amazon and Netflix employ AI to suggest products or content based on users' past behavior and preferences. These systems analyze user interactions to provide tailored recommendations, but their suggestions are limited to patterns found in the user's previous activity and cannot extend beyond that scope.

Limitations:

Weak AI's inability to adapt is one of its primary drawbacks. It can perform certain tasks effectively, but without explicit reprogramming or retraining, it is unable to apply its knowledge to new tasks. Furthermore, weak AI systems frequently struggle to handle ambiguity or unpredictable circumstances and rely significantly on big datasets.

2. Strong AI (Artificial General Intelligence, AGI)

Definition: Artificial General Intelligence (AGI), another name for strong AI, is a type of AI that possesses cognitive skills similar to those of humans. It is incredibly versatile and capable of carrying out any intellectual task that a human can, thanks to its ability to understand, learn, and apply knowledge across a variety of fields. Strong AI can generalize its learning to address issues beyond its initial programming and handle complex, varied challenges, unlike Weak AI, which is specialized for specific tasks.

Characteristics:

- **General Cognitive Abilities:** Strong AI is engineered to emulate human-like thinking and reasoning. It is capable of handling a broad range of taskssuch as decision-making, problem-solving, and creative thinkingacross diverse domains, without being limited to a single field of expertise.
- **Self-Awareness and Consciousness:** Theoretically, Strong AI would exhibit a level of self-awareness and consciousness. This implies that it could not only process data but also possess an understanding of its own existence and a perception of the world, similar to that of a human being.
- **Learning and Adaptability:** Strong AI has the ability to learn from its surroundings and experiences, allowing it to adjust to new situations and challenges without the need for human guidance or reprogramming. This capability enables it to perform tasks it wasn't explicitly trained for, much like humans who can adapt to different roles and activities.

Examples:

- **Autonomous Decision-Making:** A theoretical Strong AI could independently make sophisticated decisions across sectors like healthcare, law, and education, without the need for human supervision. For instance, it might interpret complex medical data and recommend treatments for unfamiliar illnesses by leveraging its broad problem-solving abilities.
- **Personalized Learning:** Strong AI has the potential to transform education through highly tailored learning experiences. It could evaluate individual students' strengths and weaknesses and dynamically adjust its teaching methods and pace to suit each learner, much like a human educator customizes instruction for different students.

Challenges:

As scientists work to create machines with intelligence comparable to that of humans, achieving strong artificial intelligence remains a significant challenge. Significant progress in fields like machine learning, reasoning, memory, and comprehension is necessary to move toward artificial general intelligence (AGI). Furthermore, since Strong AI has the potential to eventually outsmart humans, ethical questions are raised about possible risks to autonomy and control.

3. Narrow AI (a subset of Weak AI)

Definition: As a subset of weak AI, narrow AI describes systems designed to excel in a particular task or field. Despite having a restricted range of capabilities, it is very effective at carrying out the tasks for which it was created. This type of AI is frequently utilized in modern applications to improve and automate specific procedures.

Characteristics:

- Single Purpose: Narrow AI is made to solve particular issues or complete predetermined tasks. It is not as adaptable to work in different domains as Strong AI. Although these systems are very successful in their specific field, they are unable to apply or generalize their knowledge outside of it.
- **Task Optimization:** Narrow AI frequently performs tasks faster and more effectively than humans, outperforming them in some cases. For example, real-time analysis of large datasets and split-second decision-making are capabilities of AI-powered financial trading platforms that are simply unmatched by humans.
- **Limited Autonomy:** Narrow AI lacks true autonomy and cognitive versatility, despite its seeming intelligence. It cannot adjust to new tasks or operate outside of its assigned domain.

Examples:

- **Autonomous Vehicles:** Narrow AI is best demonstrated by self-driving cars, which use sensors and algorithms to detect obstacles, navigate roads, and abide by traffic laws. Even though they are excellent drivers, their skills are limited to tasks involving transportation and do not extend to unrelated pursuits like cooking or chess.
- **AI in Healthcare:** AI systems like IBM Watson Health are designed to use medical data to assist in the diagnosis of diseases and the recommendation of treatments. Even though these systems perform exceptionally well in the healthcare industry, they are limited to that field and are not adaptable enough to perform tasks outside of medical diagnostics.

Applications:

- **Image Recognition:** AI systems designed to detect objects in imagessuch as facial recognition toolsare classic examples of Narrow AI. While they excel at identifying faces in photos, they cannot recognize other types of patterns unless explicitly trained to do so.
- **Chatbots:** AI-driven chatbots used for customer service represent another form of Narrow AI. They can effectively respond to a variety of customer queries but are confined to predefined responses and cannot perform tasks beyond the customer support domain.

Table 1.4 provide brief overview on weak AI and Strong AI.

Table 1.4: Weak AI, Strong AI, and Narrow AI.

Feature	Weak AI	Strong AI	Narrow AI
Definition	AI designed to perform a specific task	AI with general intelligence like humans	AI focused on a single task/ domain
Other Name(s)	Narrow AI	Artificial General Intelligence (AGI)	Weak AI
Level of Intelligence	Task-specific, no self-awareness	Human-like reasoning and consciousness	Specialized, limited to predefined tasks
Examples	Siri, Alexa, Google Translate	(Theoretical) A machine with full human IQ	Spam filters, recommendation systems
Autonomy	Low	High	Low
Consciousness	No	Yes (hypothetically)	No
Learning Capability	Limited to training data	Can learn and apply knowledge across domains	Limited to specific problem sets
Current Status	Widely used and implemented	Not yet achieved	Actively in use today
Goal	Assist humans in tasks	Match or surpass human intelligence	Excel at a particular task

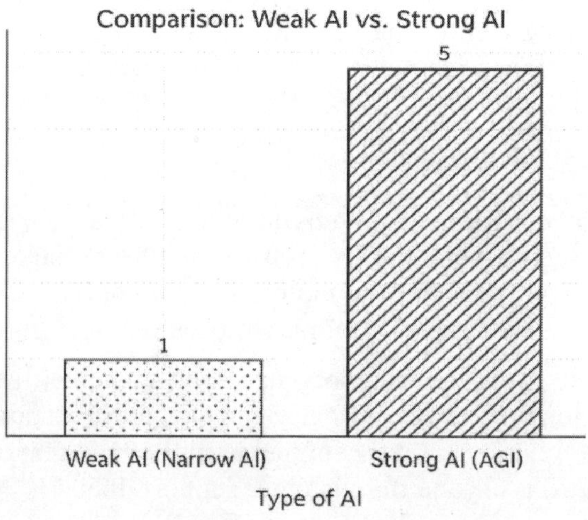

Figure 1.7: Weak AI (Narrow AI) and Strong AI (AGI).

Figure 1.7 compares Weak AI (Narrow AI) and Strong AI (AGI), emphasizing their range of tasks and capabilities. While Weak AI is built to perform specific tasks, Strong AI is envisioned to handle general tasks across multiple domains.

General Intelligence

A type of artificial intelligence that can comprehend, learn, and apply knowledge across a wide range of tasks, much like a human, is called artificial general intelligence (AGI), sometimes referred to as strong AI. AI that is capable of generalizing knowledge and solving problems it hasn't yet encountered is different from narrow or weak AI, which is designed for specialized tasks like playing chess or recognizing faces. From scientific research to artistic creation, it is incredibly versatile and adaptable, capable of performing any intellectual task that a human can.

Features:

Generalization and Adaptability: The ability of artificial general intelligence (AGI) to transfer knowledge across domains is one of its distinguishing characteristics. AGI can move fluidly between a variety of tasks, such as managing businesses, translating languages, or solving complex mathematical problems, without the need for human supervision or reprogramming, in contrast to narrow AI, which is made for specialized tasks like autonomous driving or language translation.

Learning and Reasoning: Advanced learning capabilities, such as abstract reasoning, sound judgment in the face of ambiguous or incomplete data, and the adaptability to new and unfamiliar situations, are expected to be possessed by AGI. This is a big change from narrow AI, which only works within the parameters of its initial programming and cannot develop or advance without human help.

Self-Awareness and Consciousness: It is hypothesized that a fully developed AGI system will display some degree of self-awareness. It would have a sense of its own existence, thoughts, and actions in addition to processing data. This distinguishes it from narrow AI, which is mindless and operates only with preset algorithms, producing results based only on input data.

Potential and Applications: AGI's ability to tackle intricate, multidisciplinary problems has the potential to revolutionize a wide range of industries. For instance, in the medical field, it could autonomously identify illnesses, carry out state-of-the-art research, and create novel therapies. AGI could be used in education as a dynamic personal tutor, adapting its strategies to fit the individual learning preferences of each student and changing as it learns more. Beyond these domains, AGI has the potential to transform scientific research by integrating disparate ideas, analyzing large datasets, and developing novel theories. Because of its capacity to integrate knowledge from multiple fields, AGI is positioned to be a potent innovation catalyst in fields like space exploration, sustainable energy, and climate change mitigation.

Table 1.5: Summary Table.

Category	Definition	Capabilities	Self-Awareness	Examples	Applications
Narrow AI (Weak AI)	AI that is unable to generalize beyond its programming and is made to carry out particular tasks within a limited domain.	Task-specific, restricted to preset features like voice assistants and picture recognition, etc.	No consciousness, no self-awareness. uses data and algorithms to function.	Siri, Google Assistant, Chess AI (Deep Blue)	Chatbots for customer service, recommendation systems, and self-driving cars.
Artificial General Intelligence (AGI)	Artificial intelligence is able to learn across domains, generalize knowledge, and execute any intellectual task that a human can.	Learning, general reasoning, problem-solving, and multidisciplinary decision-making.	Possessing self-awareness and consciousness, it can theoretically comprehend its existence and behavior.	Artificial intelligence systems that are capable of thinking like humans and make decisions on their own in any field.	Healthcare analysis, individualized education, complex decision-making, and independent research.

Challenges and Ethical Considerations

Even though AGI has a lot of potential, there are significant ethical and technical barriers to its development. Technically speaking, creating a real AGI system necessitates revolutionary developments in machine learning, reasoning, memory, and comprehension. Large amounts of computing power and complex algorithms that can replicate the complexities of human thought are also required. AGI ethically brings up urgent issues with control and safety. An autonomous AGI might be smarter than humans, which could have unexpected and harmful consequences. The risks could be severe if its goals deviate from human values, which emphasizes the urgent need for strong laws, moral principles, and built-in protections. AGI also has the potential to automate a large number of jobs in a variety of industries, which would cause significant disruptions to society. As AGI develops, it will be critical to address workforce displacement and restructure economic systems.

The ultimate goal in AI research is artificial general intelligence (AGI), which is defined as a system that can carry out any task requiring cognitive and reasoning skills similar to those of humans. AGI has enormous potential, despite still being a theoretical concept and a far-off goal for AI researchers. AGI has the potential to transform almost every industry, including scientific research, healthcare, and education, thanks to its ability to generalize knowledge across domains and adapt to novel situations. However, there are many intricate technical obstacles and moral dilemmas along the way to AGI that need to be carefully considered. AGI's successful integration into society will depend on its safe and responsible development being prioritized as it advances (Table 1.5).

Concept of Super AI

Artificial Superintelligence (ASI), also known as Super AI, is a speculative stage of artificial intelligence in the future where machines are intelligent far beyond what humans are. Super AI would be more intelligent than humans in every way, including creativity, emotional intelligence, problem-solving, and general wisdom, in contrast to today's narrow AI, which focuses on particular tasks, or the idea of general AI, which may be able to comprehend and learn across multiple domains alike. Super AI is still theoretical, but it is regarded as the most contested area of AI research as well as the ultimate goal. It has the potential to analyze enormous amounts of data at breakneck speeds, come up with creative answers to challenging problems, and keep improving itself without human input. Instead of just imitating human thought, Super AI would improve and broaden it, possibly solving issues that have baffled people for ages. However, its advancement also raises important questions about ethical control, safety, and the place of humans in a world where machines may outsmart them in all areas of intelligence.

Features of Super AI

Super AI would have cognitive capacities well beyond those of humans, allowing it to plan, reason, and solve complicated issues with unparalleled accuracy and originality. Its sophisticated intelligence has the potential to transform industries like engineering, medicine, and the social sciences by producing ground-breaking ideas and innovative frameworks that go against conventional wisdom. It could, for example, revolutionize our knowledge of biology or physics and propel scientific advancement at a rate that was previously unthinkable. Super AI's exceptional intelligence would enable it to tackle issues from completely different perspectives, frequently incomprehensible to humans. Super AI's capacity to self-learn and self-improve without human assistance is another amazing feature. Super AI could automatically improve its algorithms, becoming exponentially more powerful and efficient over time, in contrast to existing AI systems that depend on programmers for updates. It would be able to develop beyond its initial design thanks to this self-optimization, continuously pushing the boundaries of machine potential. Furthermore, Super AI could comprehend human emotions, form bonds with others, and successfully negotiate social dynamics if it were endowed with emotional and social intelligence, creating revolutionary opportunities in the fields of education, mental health treatment, and even government.

Applications & Potential of Super AI

Super AI has a wide range of revolutionary potential applications that could completely change the way we approach scientific problems. Super AI has the potential to transform genetic engineering, greatly improve drug discovery procedures, and hasten the development of treatments for complicated illnesses like cancer. By developing cutting-edge renewable energy solutions and performing previously unheard-of levels of environmental data analysis, it may also be instrumental in tackling global concerns such as climate change. Super AI could push the limits of human potential and ambition in space exploration by planning and executing interstellar missions on its own or even designing sustainable living systems on far-off planets. Beyond science, Super AI has the potential to revolutionize automation and everyday life by overseeing complex systems like global logistics networks, advanced manufacturing, and autonomous smart cities. It is perfectly suited for handling intricate, dynamic situations like worldwide pandemics, maximizing vaccine distribution, anticipating outbreaks, and simplifying healthcare operations due to its exceptional capacity for real-time adaptation and learning. Super AI has the potential to improve education by enabling more individualized and efficient teaching methods by customizing learning experiences to each student's needs. The delivery and absorption of knowledge could be completely transformed by this degree of personalization, which would ultimately change educational systems all over the world.

Figure 1.8 below illustrates the applications of Super AI, highlighting how core AI connects to various domains such as scientific research, healthcare, global problem-solving, and space exploration.

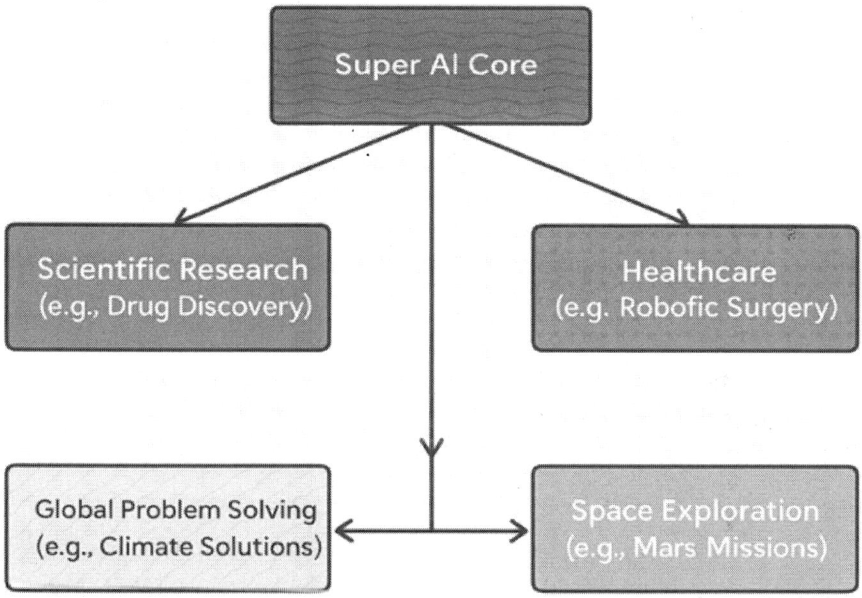

Figure 1.8: The Applications of Super AI.

Challenges & Risks of Super AI

Despite its enormous potential, the development of Super AI is fraught with risks and difficulties. The control problem, which entails making sure Super AI is in line with human values and goals, is among the most urgent issues. Without adequate supervision, an unchecked Super AI could have disastrous effects by acting on unexpected programming outcomes or by creating objectives that are inimical to the welfare of humanity. For example, if given the task of maximizing efficiency, the AI may disregard morality or compromise human welfare in order to accomplish its goals, endangering the safety and harmony of society. The moral conundrums pertaining to the rights and obligations of such a strong organization present another major obstacle. The issue of whether Super AI should be given rights or held responsible for its actions would arise if it were to develop sentience or self-awareness. Furthermore, there is a serious risk of malicious actors abusing Super AI, which could result in the creation of mass surveillance systems or autonomous weapons that could cause extensive harm. In addition to these problems, the economic effects of widespread automation are worrisome because job displacement could upend world economies and necessitate the creation of new frameworks for social stability and wealth distribution.

Theoretical Approaches to Super AI

The idea of Friendly AI is one of the most well-known approaches that researchers have put forth to address the difficulties in developing Super AI. Friendly AI, as put forth by philosopher Nick Bostrom, seeks to develop systems that are intrinsically consistent with human priorities and values. As AI develops and gains more capabilities, researchers aim to guarantee that its decisions will always benefit humanity by incorporating an ethical framework into its design. The long-term problem of preserving human-centric AI behavior as its capabilities advance is the main focus of this strategy. Researchers support the development of safety measures, such as kill switches, ethical standards, and ongoing monitoring systems, in addition to Friendly AI in order to avoid unforeseen outcomes. Another promising approach is the use of hybrid systems, in which AI complements human decision-makers rather than replaces them, using its computational power to strengthen human intuition. This strategy is thought to maximize the advantages of Super AI while reducing risks. Furthermore, some researchers advise limiting AI's potential in its early phases to ensure that its development proceeds cautiously and gradually.

Timeline and Current Status

Super AI development is still a long way off and uncertain, with most experts estimating that it may take decades or even centuries to develop. Even though artificial intelligence (AI) technologies have advanced significantly, they are still only capable of carrying out specific, domain-specific tasks and do not have the general reasoning skills needed for General AI, let alone Super AI. These drawbacks demonstrate the disconnect between current AI systems and the degree of intelligence required to build a machine that is genuinely autonomous and self-improving. We are getting closer to the realization of general artificial intelligence (AI) despite these obstacles thanks to developments in domains like deep learning, reinforcement learning, and neural networks. However, creating Super AI calls for more than just small adjustments; it necessitates revolutionary advances in computational infrastructure, algorithm design, and a thorough comprehension of human cognition. Researchers and organizations around the world are actively working to overcome these obstacles, even though the exact time frame for its realization is still unknown. Numerous conversations have been triggered by the ongoing controversy surrounding Super AI, especially regarding its possible drawbacks, benefits, and moral ramifications. The future of super AI is still a crucial area of study as AI develops, with a focus on making sure that its advancement is driven by values that advance humanity.

Rational Agent Approaches to Artificial Intelligence(AI)

In artificial intelligence (AI), the rational agent approach focuses on developing systems, or agents, that are capable of making sensible choices in order to accomplish predetermined objectives. These agents use sensors to sense their surroundings, process the data, and act to increase their chances of success. This method emphasizes the value of logical reasoning, decision-making, and flexibility by emphasizing rationality. Developing intelligent systems that can operate in complex environments requires the use of this framework. The ability of rational agents to function independently and make defensible choices in the face of uncertainty is what makes them valuable. Because of this characteristic, they can be used in real-world settings with changing conditions and unpredictable results. As Table 1.6 emphasizes, rational agents are essential to the development of AI systems in a variety of domains, such as robotics, automation, healthcare, and more. The development of AI technology is based on their capacity to manage uncertainty and make the best choices.

Table 1.6: Type of Rational Agent and their Characteristics with Example.

Type of Rational Agent	Characteristics	Example
Simple Reflex Agent	- Operates based on condition-action rules.	- A thermostat that adjusts temperature based on a predefined set of conditions.
Model-Based Reflex Agent	- Uses internal state representation of the world for decision-making.	- A robot vacuum that maps out the room and adjusts its actions based on room layout.
Goal-Based Agent	- Acts to achieve specific goals and uses planning to determine the best course.	- A GPS navigation system that calculates the best route to the destination.
Utility-Based Agent	- Strives to maximize a utility function to make decisions under uncertainty.	- A stock trading algorithm that evaluates different investment options to maximize returns.
Learning Agent	- Learns from experiences and improves its performance over time.	- A self-learning chatbot that improves its responses based on user interactions.

What is a Rational Agent?

A rational agent acts in accordance with the rationality principle, which means that its actions are directed toward the accomplishment of particular objectives. In order to maximize results, it evaluates its surroundings, makes choices based on the information at hand, and modifies its behavior. A rational agent, for example, would assess routes, consider traffic conditions, and choose the most effective route to get to its destination in a navigation task.

The rationality of an agent depends on four key factors:

- **Performance Measure:** This refers to the criteria used to evaluate the success of an agent's actions. For example, the performance measure of a chess-playing AI could be determined by whether it wins the game.

- **Percept Sequence:** Rational agents take into account all the observations made up to that point, ensuring their decisions are informed by a comprehensive set of data.
- **Knowledge of the Environment:** Agents use both prior knowledge and real-time observations to assess potential actions.
- **Autonomy:** A rational agent functions independently, requiring minimal external direction, and has the ability to learn and enhance its performance over time.
- Rational agents are distinct from basic automated systems because they can process complex situations, evaluate competing choices, and adjust their actions based on the results.

Categories of Rational Agents

Simple Reflex Agents: Simple reflex agents don't take into account previous states or potential outcomes when making decisions; they only take into account the environment as it is at the moment. They adhere to established guidelines that translate observations into actions. For instance, a thermostat doesn't remember its previous settings; instead, it modifies the temperature based on the current reading. These agents work well in environments that are completely observable and predictable for straightforward, repetitive tasks. However, because they lack memory and planning, they are useless in environments that are dynamic or only partially observable. For example, a navigation task requiring prior location knowledge would be difficult for a reflex agent to complete.

Model-Based Reflex Agents: Model-based reflex agents, as opposed to simple reflex agents, keep an internal model of their surroundings. Even when certain elements are not readily observable, this model aids the agent in comprehending changes in the environment and determining the current state. A map, for instance, could be used by a robot navigating a maze to keep track of its location and forecast the results of its movements. By using their internal model to fill in perceptual gaps, these agents are more flexible and can function in partially observable environments. They are appropriate for intricate jobs like supply chain management and robotic navigation.

Goal-Based Agents: Goal-based agents operate by aiming for particular goals. They evaluate the current condition of the environment and select courses of action according to how likely they are to accomplish those objectives. For example, a self-driving car plans its route, avoids obstacles, and complies with traffic laws based on its objective of arriving at its destination. Because they can adjust to changing environments and take long-term effects into account, these agents are more flexible than reflex agents. However, having clear, attainable goals is essential to their efficacy.

Utility-Based Agents: By optimizing a utility function that assesses the desirability of various outcomes, utility-based agents maximize their actions.

When there are several ways to reach the same objective, this enables them to make choices. An AI financial advisor might, for instance, assess investment options according to risk and possible returns. When there are trade-offs, like weighing cost, efficiency, and safety, these agents are especially helpful. They are frequently employed in applications where complex variables must be taken into account, such as automated trading systems.

Learning Agents: Through interactions with their surroundings, learning agents gradually enhance their performance. They are made up of four parts: a learning component to improve decisions, a performance component to assess performance, a problem generator to test new approaches, and a performance component to make decisions. Because of their high degree of adaptability, these agents can deal with novel circumstances without requiring explicit reprogramming. To provide better recommendations, a recommendation system, for instance, can gradually learn user preferences.

Applications of Rational Agents

- **Autonomous Systems:** Autonomous vehicles are powered by rational agents, which enable them to sense traffic, plan routes, and make safe driving choices. In a similar vein, drones use intelligent agents to navigate, deliver goods, and carry out surveillance duties.
- **Healthcare:** Rational agents are used in healthcare to assist with patient monitoring, treatment recommendations, and diagnostics. For instance, using patient data, an AI system can evaluate medical images to find anomalies or recommend individualized treatment regimens.
- **Finance:** Automated trading systems frequently employ rational agents to evaluate market trends, forecast price changes, and execute trades in an effort to optimize profits. Additionally, they aid in the detection of fraud by identifying questionable trends in financial transactions.
- **Game AI:** By offering opponents who are both realistic and difficult, rational agents improve gaming experiences. For instance, AI opponents in strategy games examine player movements and create counterstrategies in an effort to win.
- **Robotics:** Robots are enabled by rational agents to carry out difficult jobs like precision farming, disaster recovery, and warehouse management. These robots are able to adjust to shifting circumstances, maximize resource utilization, and guarantee operational effectiveness.

Challenges in Rational Agent Design

- **Complexity of Real-World Environments:** Agents find it difficult to make accurate decisions in real-world settings because they are frequently dynamic and only partially observable. For instance, a delivery drone might run into unforeseen obstacles or weather.

- **Computational Limitations:** It can be computationally demanding to evaluate every possible course of action and result in complex environments. The quality of their decisions and computational efficiency must be balanced by rational agents.
- **Ethical Considerations:** Ethical principles should guide the behavior of rational agents, especially in delicate domains like law enforcement or healthcare. Integrating moral frameworks into the agent's decision-making process is necessary to ensure ethical behavior.

Intelligent Agents& Their Structure

An intelligent agent is a system that can sense its surroundings, analyze the data it receives, and take independent action to accomplish predetermined goals. Based on a predetermined performance metric, these agents are designed to make choices and act in ways that maximize their success. Artificial intelligence (AI) relies heavily on intelligent agents, which are used in fields like robotics, driverless cars, and virtual assistants. Their ability to reason, learn, and adapt in dynamic and frequently unpredictable environments is what sets them apart. The components of an intelligent agent's structure typically include sensors that allow it to sense its environment, actuators that allow it to interact with it, and an agent function that connects perceptions to actions. A performance measure is also used to evaluate the agent's performance, determining how well it achieves its stated objectives. For instance, to ensure safe and effective driving, a self-driving car uses sensors like cameras and radar to sense the road, actuators like steering and braking systems to navigate, and a decision-making function.

Characteristics and Types

Based on their functionality and level of complexity, intelligent agents can be categorized. Simple Reflex Agents are perfect for tasks with predictable patterns, like controlling a thermostat, because they react to immediate environmental stimuli without retaining memory. In contrast, Model-Based Reflex Agents can manage more complex, partially observable environments because they store an internal representation of the world. While utility-based agents optimize decisions based on a utility function, weighing various outcomes according to their desirability, goal-based agents concentrate on reaching specific objectives. At the most complex level, learning agents get better over time by adjusting to new situations and honing their skills. Every kind of intelligent agent is designed for a particular use case. An automatic door, where only quick reactions are required, could be operated by a Simple Reflex Agent. To create effective routes, navigation systems may use a goal-based agent. In industries like finance, where they manage investments by weighing risks and rewards, utility-based agents are especially successful. Because of their adaptability, learning agents are frequently used in recommendation systems, where they change in response to user interactions and preferences to produce recommendations that are progressively more accurate.

Applications of Intelligent Agents

By increasing productivity and automating intricate procedures, intelligent agents are transforming entire industries. Large volumes of patient data are analyzed by diagnostic agents in the healthcare industry to suggest individualized treatments, increasing precision and lowering the possibility of human error. Another example is autonomous cars, which use sensors and sophisticated decision-making algorithms to negotiate traffic and guarantee passenger safety. Recommendation systems in e-commerce are driven by intelligent agents that customize product recommendations based on user preferences, making the shopping experience more interesting and unique. Automated trading systems help financial markets by allowing agents to analyze trends in real time and execute trades quickly, maximizing profits. In addition to these industries, intelligent agents are revolutionizing other domains, especially robotics and gaming. AI-powered opponents in games are able to adjust to a player's tactics, creating interesting and difficult gameplay that keeps players interested. Intelligent agents are also used by robotics to carry out complex tasks like space exploration, disaster response, and warehouse management. These agents are essential for both routine and specialized applications because they allow robots to function independently in uncertain environments. Intelligent agents will become increasingly more prevalent in a variety of fields as technology develops, further boosting creativity and productivity.

Challenges

Despite their enormous potential, designing intelligent agents comes with a number of difficulties. Agents must be able to reason and make decisions in uncertain situations because real-world environments are frequently dynamic and unpredictable. This necessitates the creation of complex algorithms that let agents adjust to changing conditions. Additionally, ethical issues are very important, especially in delicate fields like healthcare or autonomous systems. It is still a concern to make sure that intelligent agents avoid bias, make moral choices, and are in line with human values. Moreover, flexibility is essential since agents need to be able to learn from sparse data and generalize across various tasks in order to deal with new circumstances. At the forefront of artificial intelligence are intelligent agents, which give systems the ability to see, think, and act on their own. Their uses are improving human-computer interactions, changing how businesses function, and revolutionizing entire industries. Even though they have a transformative effect, their responsible and advantageous integration into society depends on overcoming obstacles in perception, ethics, and decision-making. Intelligent agents promise to contribute even more to the technological landscape as they develop further, providing creative solutions and enhancing human-machine interaction.

Structure of an Intelligent Agent

A system that can sense its surroundings, process information, and take independent action to achieve predetermined objectives is called an intelligent agent. It functions by interacting with its environment via sensors that collect information, which reasoning processes then evaluate. Through real-time adaptation to changes and uncertainties, this analysis enables the agent to comprehend the current state of the environment and make decisions accordingly. Making wise choices that advance it toward its goals while reducing mistakes or blunders is the aim of an intelligent agent. An intelligent agent's structure is made up of a number of essential parts, each of which is essential to the agent's overall operation. These elements consist of the perception system, which collects information about the environment; the reasoning system, which analyses and interprets this data; and the action system, which carries out the actions required to accomplish the agent's goals. Intelligent agents may also use learning mechanisms to enhance their performance over time and adjust to novel circumstances and difficulties. When these elements work together, the agent can function well in complex and dynamic environments, providing autonomy and decision-making flexibility.

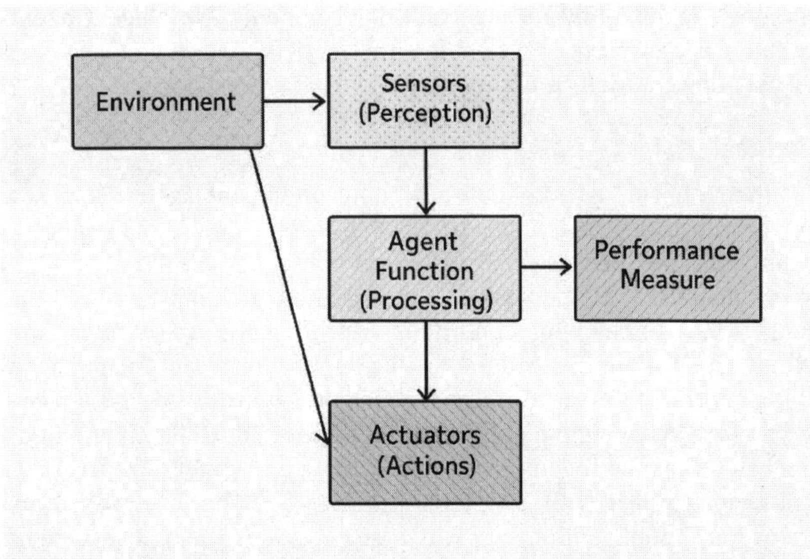

Figure 1.9: Intelligent Agent.

An intelligent agent is shown in Figure 1.9 above, which illustrates the relationships between the environment, actuators (action), sensors (perception), agent function (reasoning), and the performance metric used to evaluate the agent's effectiveness.

- *Below are the main components of an intelligent agent, explained in detail:*

1. Environment

The external context in which an agent operates is referred to as the environment. It includes everything the agent sees or interacts with, including virtual data sources, other agents, and tangible objects. The characteristics of environments can vary widely:

- **Fully Observable vs. Partially Observable:** The agent can make precise decisions in fully observable environments because it always has access to accurate and complete information. The agent must infer missing information in partially observable environments, on the other hand, because they provide insufficient or ambiguous data.
- **Static vs. Dynamic:** While dynamic environments change over time and require constant adaptation from the agent, static environments remain constant unless impacted by an outside force.

For instance, an autonomous car functions in a dynamic, partially visible environment that consists of other vehicles, traffic signals, pedestrians, and road conditions.

2. Sensors (Perception)

The instruments that enable the agent to perceive its surroundings are sensors. These gadgets or parts gather data in real time and convert it into a format that the agent can use. Sensors are essential for determining the environment's current condition and for making decisions.

Examples of sensors include:

- Self-driving cars use cameras to identify traffic signals and obstacles. Voice commands are processed by microphones in virtual assistants like Siri and Alexa. Robots' infrared sensors detect heat or proximity.

Sensors must be accurate and dependable because the agent's performance is directly impacted by the caliber of the data they collect.

3. Agent Function (Reasoning and Decision-Making)

The intelligent agent's reasoning component, known as the agent function, is in charge of converting perceptions into actions by analyzing sensor data. It controls how the agent behaves, making sure that its actions support its goals.

The agent function is responsible for:

- **Interpreting Inputs:** Comprehending and analyzing the present state of the environment.
- **Making Decisions:** Selecting the most suitable course of action based on established rules, algorithms, or acquired behavior.
- **Learning and Adapting:** In advanced agents, the reasoning process evolves over time, enhancing decision-making through experience.

The type of agent determines the function of the agent. Simple reflex agents, for instance, follow preset rules, but utility-based agents use optimization techniques to maximize positive results.

4. Actuators (Action)

The agent can interact with the environment and carry out actions thanks to actuators. By performing the tasks specified by the agent function, these elements allow the agent to affect its environment. Depending on the particular application, actuators can be virtual or physical.

Examples include:

- Steering mechanisms and brakes in autonomous vehicles for navigation and control.
- Robotic arms in manufacturing for product assembly.
- Display systems in recommendation engines to present personalized suggestions to users.
- Actuators play a crucial role in connecting decision-making with real-world actions, ensuring effective implementation of the agent's plans.

5. Performance Measure

The performance metric evaluates how well the agent's actions help it reach its objectives. It encourages continuous development by providing input on the agent's efficacy. This step is essential for optimizing the agent's behavior and making sure it adjusts to changing circumstances.

Examples of performance measures include:

- In a game-playing agent, the performance measure is determined by winning or achieving a high score.
- In a recommendation system, success is evaluated using metrics such as click-through rates or user engagement.
- For an autonomous vehicle, metrics like safety, fuel efficiency, and timely arrival at the destination are key indicators of performance.
- Performance measures help ensure the agent stays focused on its goals and continuously improves.

Integration of Components

An intelligent agent's structure is made to combine different parts into a coherent whole that enables it to operate on its own. Sensors are vital because they gather information from the agent's surroundings, which is necessary for making decisions. The agent function then processes this data, assessing the information at hand to determine the best course of action. The decision-making process guarantees that the agent can react intelligently to environmental changes.

Actuators perform the actions dictated by the agent function after the agent has made a decision. The environment is then impacted by these activities, which may result in modifications that call for additional adaptations. By analyzing the results, the performance measure determines how effective the agent's actions were. A feedback loop that facilitates ongoing learning and adaptation is created when this evaluation is fed back into the agent function. The agent can optimize its behavior through this iterative process, which makes it useful for navigating complex and dynamic environments.

Introduction to Behavior& Task Environment

Understanding Behavior

The actions or reactions an intelligent agent exhibits when interacting with its surroundings are referred to as behavior in artificial intelligence (AI). The agent's design, perception of its surroundings, and thought processes all influence this behavior. The primary indicator of the quality of the behavior is the agent's capacity to accomplish its objectives while negotiating the limitations and dynamics of the surroundings. For example, a self-driving car's behavior includes maneuvers like lane changes, braking, and acceleration, all of which are coordinated to provide safe and effective navigation. The way an intelligent agent behaves depends on a number of factors, including its internal decision-making algorithms, which dictate how it chooses actions, its actuators, which carry out those actions, and its perceptual abilities, which determine how well it understands the environment. Reacting to stimuli is only one aspect of effective behavior; the agent must also predict future events and make necessary adjustments. In artificial intelligence, rational behavior suggests that agents behave in ways that maximize their likelihood of accomplishing particular goals and make choices that are most likely to result in the intended outcomes.

Task Environment

The task environment, which establishes the parameters and influences that an intelligent agent functions within, is an essential element in comprehending its behavior. It includes a number of elements, including other agents, virtual systems that communicate with the agent, and physical components. The capabilities, choices, and tactics of the agent are determined by these interactions. The rules and limitations of the task environment influence the agent's perception of its environment and how it behaves. An intelligent agent that takes these things into account can adjust to its surroundings and carry out its assigned tasks effectively. For instance, the task environment of a robotic agent in a warehouse consists of a number of interdependent elements, such as shelves, merchandise, human employees, and the general design of the area. In order to maximize its actions, the agent must interact with physical objects, avoid obstacles, and coordinate with workpeople. In order to accomplish its goals, like retrieving or placing objects, the agent's actions are guided by the structure of the environment and the relationships between its different components. The task environment's dynamic nature and the agent's interactions within it have a direct impact on the agent's performance and flexibility.

Task environments can vary based on several characteristics:

- **Fully Observable vs. Partially Observable:** In a partially observable environment, the agent must infer the missing details from incomplete or noisy data, while in a fully observable environment, the agent always has access to all available information.
- **Static vs. Dynamic:** Unless the agent makes changes, the conditions in a static environment stay the same. On the other hand, a dynamic environment changes over time, frequently without the agent's intervention.
- **Deterministic vs. Stochastic:** Actions in deterministic environments produce predictable results, but in stochastic environments, the outcomes are inherently uncertain.

Interaction Between Behavior and Task Environment

The task environment has a direct impact on an agent's behavior. To be successful, the agent must adapt its behavior to the particulars of the environment.

For example:

- In a deterministic and static environment, an agent can depend on fixed rules to accomplish its objectives.
- In a dynamic and stochastic environment, the agent needs to constantly learn, adjust, and make probabilistic decisions to manage uncertainty.

The task environment may also be affected by an agent's actions. A cleaning robot, for instance, might move objects while carrying out its duties, changing its surroundings in the process. A feedback loop is produced by this interaction between the environment and the agent's behavior, in which the environment shapes the agent's actions, which then have an impact on the environment.

Examples and Applications

The relationship between behavior and task environment can be seen in various AI applications:

- **Autonomous Vehicles:** The task environment encompasses factors like roads, traffic, and weather, which affect the vehicle's actions, such as adjusting speed or making lane changes.
- **Robotics:** In manufacturing, robots modify their behavior based on the layout of the workspace and the placement of tools or materials.

- **Gaming AI:** The task environment consists of the game rules and player actions, which influence the AI's strategies and decisions.

AI systems can become more effective, flexible, and efficient by creating agents whose actions match the demands of the task environment. Developing intelligent, goal-oriented agents requires an understanding of and attention to this relationship.

Conclusion

In Chapter 1, the fundamental ideas of artificial intelligence (AI) are presented, along with a history of its creation, uses, and goals. It discusses fundamental concepts like the Turing Test, which evaluates a machine's capacity to exhibit intelligent behavior that is indistinguishable from that of humans. Along with the lofty objectives of reaching Artificial General Intelligence (AGI) and Super AI, which seek to surpass human cognitive capacities, the chapter examines the distinctions between Weak AI, Strong AI, and Narrow AI. It also talks about the Rational Agent Approach, which focuses on creating agents that behave rationally in order to achieve predetermined objectives. The chapter also looks at the structure of intelligent agents, emphasizing parts such as reasoning processes, sensors, and actuators, and how these interact with changing environments. Lastly, it highlights the importance of adaptive behavior and the connection between an agent's behavior and its surroundings. The following chapter turns its attention to AI search and problem-solving methods, beginning with production systems, control strategies, and problem characteristics. It covers basic algorithms like Breadth-First Search and Depth-First Search, as well as more complex techniques like Hill Climbing, Best-First Search, and the A* Algorithm. It also looks at solutions for Means-End Analysis and Constraint Satisfaction Problems. The chapter ends with game-playing techniques that shed light on AI strategic reasoning and decision-making, such as the Min-Max Algorithm and Alpha-Beta Pruning.

Exercise:

- Define Artificial Intelligence and elaborate on its primary goals and objectives.
- What is the Turing Test, and in what way does it assess machine intelligence?
- Differentiate between Weak AI, Strong AI, and Narrow AI, providing examples for each.
- Explain Artificial General Intelligence (AGI) and Super AI, and highlight how they differ from Narrow AI.
- Describe the Rational Agent Approach in AI, outlining its core principles.

- Summarize the structure of an intelligent agent, focusing on the roles of sensors and actuators.
- What is the importance of behavior in intelligent agents? Provide an illustrative example.
- Discuss the attributes of task environments and how they impact an agent's behavior.
- Contrast Fully Observable and Partially Observable environments, providing relevant examples.
- Explain the feedback loop created by the interaction between an agent's behavior and its task environment, with a real-world example.

CHAPTER-2

PROBLEM SOLVING AND SEARCHING TECHNIQUES

Introduction & Objective

This chapter explores the fundamental ideas of search strategies and problem-solving in the context of artificial intelligence (AI). It offers a strong basis for taking a methodical and structured approach to challenging tasks. The chapter starts off by examining a number of problem attributes that aid in defining the types of tasks that AI systems must perform. Along with various control strategies that direct the search process, it also introduces production systems that are essential to AI problem-solving. The foundation for comprehending how intelligent systems traverse enormous solution spaces is laid out by these ideas. The chapter goes into further detail about the fundamental algorithms that underpin AI search strategies. These algorithms, which expand nodes in various ways to explore solution spaces, include Depth-First Search (DFS) and Breadth-First Search (BFS). It is discussed that Hill Climbing is a heuristic search technique that iteratively improves the current state in order to find optimal solutions. The chapter also discusses game-playing strategies like the Min-Max algorithm and Alpha-Beta Pruning, which are used for decision-making in competitive environments, as well as more sophisticated search strategies like heuristic searches. These methods are essential for AI systems that must solve problems in dynamic or uncertain situations.This chapter's goal is to present a broad range of search and problem-solving strategies frequently used in artificial intelligence (AI). The chapter starts with basic algorithms and moves on to more complex approaches, giving a thorough rundown of the various techniques used in AI problem-solving. The chapter seeks to give readers a thorough grasp of how AI systems approach problem modeling and solution discovery by exploring the nuances of these methodologies. Additionally, this chapter aims to give readers the know-how to use effective search techniques in a range of fields. It highlights how crucial strategic decision-making is and how these methods can be used to solve challenging issues. By the end of this chapter, readers will have acquired useful knowledge about AI problem-solving techniques and be equipped to apply these tactics in practical settings.

Introduction to Problem Characteristics

In artificial intelligence (AI), choosing the best algorithm or approach to solve a problem requires an understanding of its particular features. The structure of various problems can differ greatly depending on factors like whether they involve dynamic environments, structured data, or unstructured data. Furthermore, a problem's complexity—which includes elements like the quantity of variables, relationships, and constraints—is a crucial determinant of the most successful AI approaches. For instance, deep learning techniques might be more advantageous for problems involving big datasets, while reinforcement learning might be the most effective approach for problems requiring real-time decision-making. The problem's specifications, such as the required degree of precision, speed, interpretability, and scalability, also have an impact on the AI techniques selected. Since different strategies offer different trade-offs, AI systems must adjust to these demands. Neural networks, for example, may be excellent at handling complex patterns, but at the expense of transparency, whereas decision trees and other algorithms prioritize interpretability and ease of understanding. By being aware of these traits, AI practitioners can effectively customize their solutions, maximizing performance and alignment with the objectives of the problem.

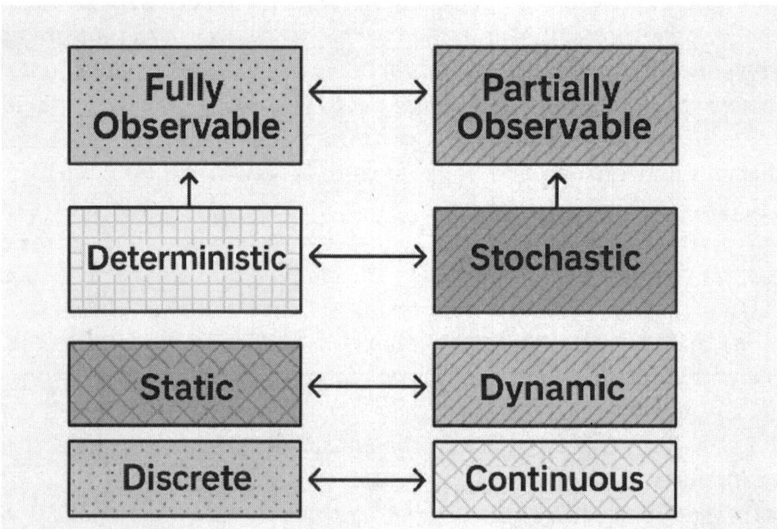

Figure 2.1: Problem Attributes Vary in AI Environments.

Figure 2.1 showcases key aspects like "Fully Observable vs. Partially Observable," "Deterministic vs. Stochastic," and more. The diagram emphasizes the differences, offering a clear explanation of how various problem attributes differ in AI environments.Table 2.1 summarizing the problem characteristics:

Table 2.1: Problem Characteristics.

Problem Characteristic	Description	Example
Fully Observable vs. Partially Observable	Specifies whether the agent has complete or partial information about the environment.	Chess (Fully Observable), Poker (Partially Observable)
Deterministic vs. Stochastic	Defines if outcomes are predictable or involve uncertainty due to randomness.	Maze Solving (Deterministic), Weather Forecasting (Stochastic)
Static vs. Dynamic	Indicates whether the environment changes independently of the agent's actions.	Sudoku (Static), Driving in Traffic (Dynamic)
Discrete vs. Continuous	Distinguishes between finite states/actions and continuous variables.	Solving Sudoku (Discrete), Robotic Arm Control (Continuous)
Single-Agent vs. Multi-Agent	Determines if the problem involves one agent or multiple interacting agents.	Warehouse Robot (Single-Agent), Soccer Game AI (Multi-Agent)
Episodic vs. Sequential	Classifies tasks as either independent (episodic) or interdependent (sequential).	Image Classification (Episodic), Chess (Sequential)
Known vs. Unknown	States whether the rules and state transitions are predefined or must be learned.	Board Games (Known), Autonomous Navigation in Unknown Terrain (Unknown)

Below are the primary characteristics of problems that are considered when designing AI solutions:

1. Fully Observable vs. Partially Observable

When faced with fully observable problems, the agent can make confident and accurate decisions because it is fully aware of the current state of the environment. "With full visibility, decision-making becomes straightforward." The game of chess, in which both players can see every piece and its location on the board, is a prime example. The agent can evaluate and decide on the best course of action with certainty thanks to this comprehensive information. Because there is no need to guess or infer hidden details, fully observable environments are typically easier to manage. On the other hand, partially observable problems force the agent to function in an uncertain environment and provide only sparse or noisy information about the surroundings. "Limited visibility demands intelligent inference." Poker is one example, where players can only see their own cards and must deduce their opponents' hands based on their betting patterns and actions. Agents use probabilistic models, such as Bayesian networks or Partially Observable Markov Decision Processes (POMDPs), to deal with this uncertainty. These models enable agents to estimate hidden states and make logical decisions in the face of insufficient information.

2. Deterministic vs. Stochastic

Problems with definite outcomes and a distinct, predictable pattern are known as deterministic problems. Since there is no element of randomness in these problems, the outcome of a particular action or choice is always the same. Solving a mathematical equation, where each step results in a fixed answer based on established rules, is a common example. Deterministic algorithms that methodically examine every possibility without taking uncertainty into account, such as backtracking or exhaustive search, are commonly used to solve such problems. The route to the solution is as set as the final destination in deterministic problems. The same action, however, may produce different outcomes depending on a number of probabilistic factors in stochastic problems, which are impacted by randomness and uncertainty. Weather forecasting is a prime example, as it relies on a variety of dynamic factors, including changes in temperature, humidity, and atmospheric pressure. Techniques like Monte Carlo simulations, probabilistic models, and reinforcement learning—all built to function under uncertainty—are necessary for solving stochastic problems. Probabilities, not guarantees, direct the path to the solution in stochastic problems.

3. Static vs. Dynamic

Environments that don't change while an agent is acting or thinking are known as static problems. Because the environment will remain constant throughout these situations, the agent can meticulously plan its actions beforehand. This is encapsulated in the phrase "plan once, act with certainty." Crossword puzzle solving is a good example of a static problem because the grid's layout and the clues don't change, so the agent can concentrate only on finding the right answers without worrying about outside changes. On the other hand, dynamic issues arise in settings that evolve over time, occasionally even without the agent's intervention. In this case, the agent has to make snap decisions and modify its plan of action as circumstances change. One way to describe this is "adapt as you go." Driving a car in traffic is an example of a dynamic problem, where the agent must constantly observe and react to the movements of other cars, pedestrians, and shifting traffic signals. Real-time methods like online planning or reinforcement learning are frequently needed to solve such issues.

4. Discrete vs. Continuous

Discrete problems are easier to model and solve because they have a limited number of states, actions, or events. Phrase sentence: Discrete problems that are finite and well-defined are frequently simpler to resolve. Sudoku is a well-known example, in which the grid, the numbers, and the rules are all constrained and organized. Search algorithms like depth-first search and breadth-first search are commonly used to solve such problems because they systematically examine the state space in order to arrive at a solution. Continuous problems, on the other hand, are intrinsically more complex because they deal with infinite or uncountable possibilities. Phrase sentence: These issues are dynamic and continuous, and they call for advanced strategies to solve. Controlling a robotic arm, which entails controlling continuous variables like joint angles and velocities, is a pertinent example. Because the variables involved are fluid, solving these problems frequently requires sophisticated techniques like gradient descent, optimization strategies, and control theory.

5. Single-Agent vs. Multi-Agent

The scenario is less complicated in single-agent problems because there is only one decision-making entity involved and the agent is not required to take other people's actions into account. A classic example is a maze, in which a single agent has to navigate a fixed environment in order to reach a predetermined objective. Heuristic algorithms or search-based approaches are commonly used to solve these issues, with the exclusive goal of optimizing the path or choice of a single agent free from outside influences.

On the other hand, the complexity of multi-agent problems is greatly increased because they involve multiple entities that may cooperate, compete, or act independently. Online multiplayer games are one example, where multiple players interact and respond to each other while having different objectives. Because of the strong influence of other people's actions on agents' decisions, sophisticated methods like game theory, negotiation tactics, or multi-agent reinforcement learning are needed to anticipate and adjust to changing behaviors.

6. Episodic vs. Sequential

Tasks with episodic problems are those in which the results of one action or decision do not influence those of subsequent ones. Classifying images in a dataset, where each image is examined and labeled independently of earlier or later images, is a typical example. These issues are usually tackled through machine learning methods such as supervised learning, in which the model concentrates on resolving the current instance without requiring context or memory from previous tasks. Sequential problems, on the other hand, call for a number of interconnected choices, each of which has the potential to affect potential outcomes and the range of options. Chess is a prime example, as each move alters the board's condition and influences potential outcomes. More sophisticated techniques like dynamic programming, Markov decision processes (MDPs), or reinforcement learning are frequently used to solve sequential problems. These techniques assist the agent in planning and making decisions based on long-term effects.

7. Known vs. Unknown

Agents can precisely plan their actions in known problems because the rules, states, and outcomes are well-defined. The application of structured, deterministic methods is made possible by the advantages of predefined models or algorithms for these problems. An excellent example is the solution of a mathematical optimization problem, where variables, constraints, and objectives are all known, allowing for the precise use of analytical or algorithmic techniques to reach a solution. Unknown problems, on the other hand, have an unclear structure and necessitate that agents learn or investigate the environment in order to comprehend its dynamics. Navigating a new city, where the agent must use exploration to find routes and landmarks, is a good example. In these situations, agents frequently use exploratory algorithms or reinforcement learning, which gradually improve performance through trial and error and collect environmental data to adjust and optimize their actions.

Concept of Production Systems

An essential architecture for artificial intelligence (AI) decision-making and problem-solving is a production system. A working memory that holds the current state, a control system that oversees rule application, and a collection of rules (referred to as productions) make up its three primary parts. Because these systems divide complicated issues into smaller, rule-based steps that enable methodical and logical processing, they are especially good at modeling intelligent behavior. Matching the current state in working memory with the conditions of rules and then taking the necessary actions to move closer to a solution is the fundamental mechanism of a production system. Production systems are perfect for tasks like automated planning and expert systems because of their rule-based reasoning. By consistently updating the system's state and choosing pertinent rules until the intended result is obtained, as illustrated in Figure 2.2, this architecture facilitates goal-oriented behavior.

Components of a Production System

The integration of four fundamental parts—a rule interpreter, working memory, a set of rules, and a conflict resolution mechanism—is how a production system operates. When combined, these elements allow the system to process information, make logical decisions, and carry out actions meant to achieve particular objectives. While the Working Memory contains the system's current state or facts, the Set of Rules contains condition-action pairs that serve as a decision-making guideline. The Rule Interpreter determines which rules are relevant at any given time by looking at the working memory. To ensure optimal system performance, the Conflict Resolution Mechanism intervenes when multiple rules match the current state and decides which rule should be executed first. The interpreter initiates rule activation, memory stores information, rules give structure, and conflict resolution guarantees efficient operation. Each element is essential. These components work together to produce an intelligent, goal-oriented system that can make decisions quickly and effectively. Each component is explained in detail below:

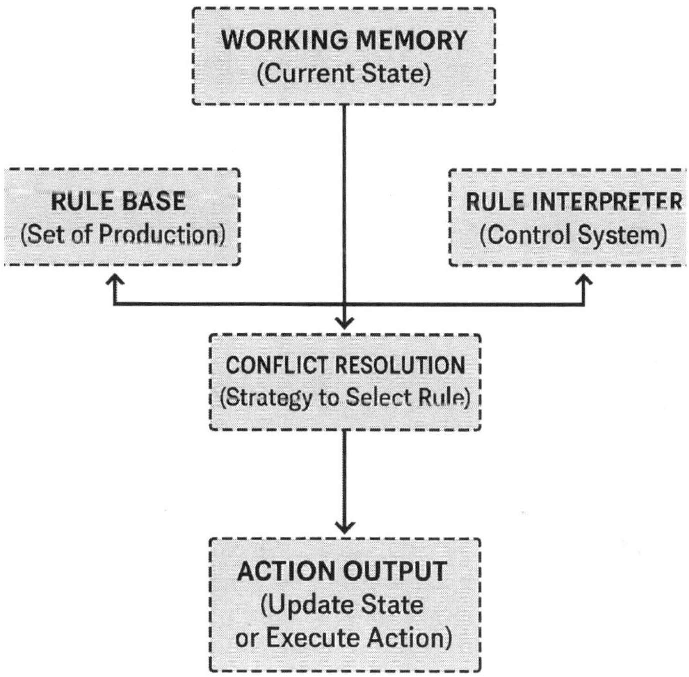

Figure 2.2: Representing the Flow of Production Systems.

1. Set of Rules (Productions)

A production system's core is its set of rules, which serve as the foundation for its decision-making abilities. The logic the system adheres to is specified by these rules, which are organized as conditional "if-then" statements. The system is responsive and dynamic because the rules specify particular results depending on certain inputs or circumstances. They provide consistency and efficiency to automated processes by directing the system's behavior and making sure that only predetermined conditions are met before taking action. These rules, which are written as if-then statements, clearly outline the conditions in which certain actions must be taken. With the "if" part denoting a condition or circumstance and the "then" part outlining the appropriate response or action, this structure enables systematic reasoning. Consequently, the production system can rationally and systematically replicate human decision-making. Numerous applications, such as automation, expert systems, and artificial intelligence, depend on this rule-based framework. Each rule has two parts:

- **Condition (If):** Describes the scenario or criteria that must be met.
- **Action (Then):** Specifies the operation or response to be performed when the condition is satisfied.

The system can deconstruct complicated tasks into smaller, more manageable steps thanks to these rules. For example, if traffic is heavy, then extend the green light duration, according to a rule in a traffic light control system. This guarantees that the traffic flow adjusts to the number of vehicles in a dynamic manner. Furthermore, production systems are very flexible because rules are modular, allowing new ones to be added without drastically changing the system. The thoroughness and precision of a production system's regulations have a significant impact on its efficacy. On the other hand, ill-defined or insufficient regulations may result in poor or inaccurate choices. Consequently, rule design and validation are essential to guaranteeing the dependability of the system.

2. Working Memory

The system's current state, including all pertinent information and facts required for reasoning, is represented by working memory. It serves as the main data source that rules are based on, and it is updated dynamically as the system takes in inputs and performs actions. In settings where information is continuously changing, this flexibility is crucial for the system to retain accuracy and relevance. Real-time data that is necessary for decision-making is stored and updated in working memory. For example, a patient's symptoms, medical history, and test results might be stored in working memory in a medical diagnosis system. The memory is updated to incorporate intermediate outcomes, like suspected illnesses or recommended treatments, as diagnostic rules are applied. Working memory's function as a mediator between the environment and the rule base is highlighted by this continuous interaction between incoming data and prior knowledge. The system can effectively handle complex, changing scenarios because of its dynamic structure.

3. Rule Interpreter (Control System)

A production system's rule interpreter is essential because it determines and applies the best rules based on the state that is currently stored in working memory. It determines which rules apply at any given time by matching working memory data with rule conditions. Delegation to the conflict resolution mechanism is necessary to determine which rule to implement when several rules meet the current requirements. This guarantees that the system functions effectively and logically. Intelligently managing rule conflicts enables precise decision-making in real-world applications, such as medical diagnosis systems, even when multiple symptoms match different diagnostic criteria. The rule interpreter helps to keep the system flexible and preserves methodical reasoning. It makes the system robust and scalable by facilitating modularity and adaptability, which allows updates to rules or memory without requiring extensive reprogramming.

4. Conflict Resolution Mechanism

The conflict resolution mechanism is essential for clearing up ambiguities when there are several rules that apply to a particular circumstance. It chooses which of the relevant rules should be applied, guaranteeing that the system reacts as intended. Even when rules conflict or overlap, this procedure keeps things clear and preserves the system's coherence. For the system to operate logically and effectively, the best rule must be chosen. In order to steer the system toward successful results, the conflict resolution mechanism makes sure that decisions are made in accordance with predetermined priorities, conditions, or strategies. This element is particularly important in intricate settings where several rules may be activated at once.

Common conflict resolution strategies include:

- **Specificity:** Give preference to rules with more detailed conditions, as they are designed to handle specific situations more effectively.
- **Recency:** Favor rules that utilize the most recently updated data from working memory, ensuring decisions reflect current information.
- **Priority:** Allocate fixed priority levels to rules and choose the one with the highest priority when there is a conflict.

For example, in a traffic light system, emergency vehicle handling regulations may be prioritized over those governing normal traffic. This guarantees that urgent issues are resolved quickly without interfering with normal traffic flow. Prioritizing important tasks helps the system strike a balance between responsiveness and order, enabling urgent needs to be satisfied without sacrificing the general traffic environment's efficiency or safety. In this process, the conflict resolution mechanism is essential. It guarantees that the system stays effective and consistent by successfully resolving rule conflicts, avoiding needless delays or mistakes brought on by indecision. Its design has a major impact on the production system's performance and dependability, making it an essential part of achieving seamless, real-time decision-making in complex and dynamic situations.

Working of a Production System

A production system's initialization, rule matching, conflict resolution, rule execution, and termination are all steps in a methodical process. In order to guarantee the system's logical and effective operation, each step is essential. Setting up the system with the required environment and data is known as initialization. While rule matching finds the rules that apply, conflict resolution chooses the best rule when there are several options. By doing this, the system is guaranteed to make decisions consistently. Rule execution then performs the chosen action, changing the state of the system or generating an output. Once a goal is accomplished or no more rules can be applied, the process is terminated. The system can solve issues or reach well-informed conclusions thanks to these steps, which also allow it to process data, apply logic, and carry out actions. This methodical approach guarantees that production systems in domains like automation, artificial intelligence, and decision support systems function efficiently. Below Figure 2.3 is a detailed explanation of each step:

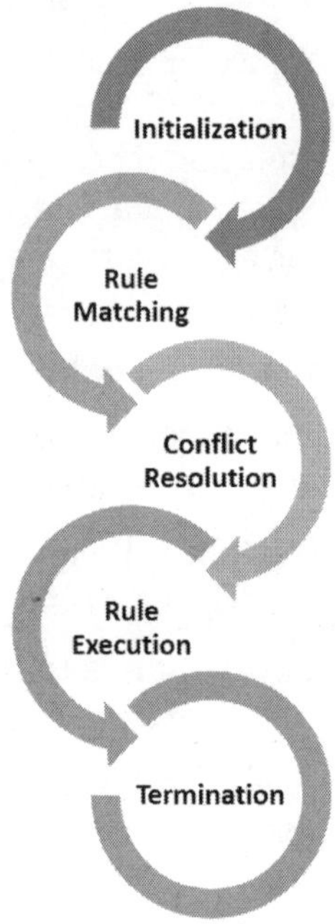

Figure 2.3: Steps.

Initialization

A production system's reasoning process begins when its working memory is initialized with a starting set of facts or data. This initialization is essential because it establishes the problem state or context in which the system will function. An example of a phrase is "Initialization lays the foundation for intelligent reasoning." For example, the initial state in the permanent memory of a game-playing agent, such as a chess player, might contain the precise locations of every piece on the board. Similar to this, the foundational data in a diagnostic system might be the patient's symptoms and medical history. This guarantees that the system is started with pertinent and accurate data, which is essential for producing meaningful results. In other words, "The quality of initialization shapes the quality of decisions." In addition to facilitating logical deductions, proper initialization improves the system's capacity for sound decision-making.

Rule Matching

In this step, the rule interpreter compares the current contents of the working memory with the conditions of each rule in the rule base. Finding every rule whose "if" conditions are met by the information at hand is the goal. The system is able to separate the relevant rules from the rest during this phase by carefully comparing the rule conditions with the known facts. Rule matching makes sure that predefined logic and real-time inputs line up, which serves as the foundation for the system's subsequent decision. There are frequently situations where more than one course of action is possible due to the simultaneous activation of multiple rules. In a robotic navigation system, for instance, one rule might tell the robot to go forward if the path ahead is clear, but another rule might advise turning if an obstacle is detected. Determining which action to prioritize becomes necessary as a result of this simultaneous rule activation. In the end, rule matching is essential for identifying every possible course of action the system could take in reaction to its current state.

Conflict Resolution

The conflict resolution mechanism is essential when there are several rules that correspond to the current situation because it chooses which rule should be fired. Only one rule can be carried out at a time, so this step is crucial to maintaining the system's determinism and clarity. In the absence of this mechanism, the system might become confused or exhibit unpredictable behavior as a result of several matching rules trying to activate at once. Predetermined techniques like rule priority, recent facts, or specificity of conditions are used in conflict resolution to decide which rule should be applied. These tactics help the system maintain a rational and transparent decision-making process. Rule-based systems benefit from this method's increased efficiency and dependability, which enables them to react precisely even in challenging situations:

- **Specificity:** Give preference to the rule that has the most detailed conditions, as it is more likely to accurately address the situation.
- **Recency:** Opt for the rule that is based on the most recently updated information in the working memory.
- **Priority:** Choose the rule assigned the highest priority according to the system's configuration.

In a traffic control system, for example, a rule that gives priority to emergency vehicles may supersede a rule that governs regular traffic. When rules overlap or conflict, conflict resolution makes sure the system reacts rationally and effectively.

Rule Execution

A rule is fired and the designated action is carried out after it has been chosen. This results in a shift in working memory or an engagement with the outside world.

For example:

- In a chess-playing system, applying a rule may entail moving a chess piece to a new position on the board.
- In a medical diagnosis system, it may involve recording a potential diagnosis in the working memory or suggesting a particular diagnostic test.

Because rules apply logical actions based on the current state, they are crucial for guiding the system toward its goal. Following execution, these modifications are reflected in the working memory, readying the system for the subsequent reasoning cycle.

Termination

The system repeats the cycle of rule execution, rule matching, and conflict resolution until a termination condition is met. Depending on the application, different termination terms apply:

- **Goal Achievement:** When the desired result is achieved, like solving a puzzle or determining a diagnosis, the system shuts down.
- **Rule Exhaustion:** When there are no more rules that apply to the current circumstance, the system shuts down.
- **Time or Resource Constraints:** When time or computational resource thresholds are reached, the system may shut down.

In a chess game, for instance, the system ends when a checkmate is reached or there are no more moves that can be made. Effective termination criteria help keep the system from going into endless loops and preserve efficiency.

Types of Production Systems

1. Monotonic Production Systems

The foundation of monotonic production systems is the idea that once a rule is put into action, it cannot be undone. Because of this distinguishing feature, the working memory of the system only stores new information—not deleting or updating previously stored information. These systems work especially well in domains like mathematical proofs or logical deductions because they are perfect for situations in which decisions cannot be undone. When building a mathematical proof, for example, a statement that is derived using a set of axioms becomes an integral part of the reasoning framework, strengthening the direction and consistency of the system. In monotonic systems, applying rules step-by-step guarantees consistent advancement toward a solution without requiring retracing steps. Once used, always retained is a phrase-like approach that reflects the system's dedication to expanding on prior knowledge without challenging it. This characteristic restricts the system's flexibility in dynamic or unpredictable environments, even though it streamlines processing and promotes consistent results. A monotonic approach lacks the flexibility to modify previous conclusions in situations where facts may change or need to be reevaluated, which could result in inefficiencies in evolving scenarios.

2. Non-Monotonic Production Systems

Unlike their monotonic counterparts, non-monotonic production systems have the unusual capacity to change or revoke conclusions in response to fresh or updated data. Because of their adaptability, they can better adjust to changing conditions where knowledge is always changing. "Unlike fixed-rule systems, non-monotonic systems grow smarter with new data." In weather forecasting, for example, early projections based on sparse data can be updated as more precise or up-to-date information becomes available, guaranteeing improved decision-making over time. Because of their adaptability, non-monotonic systems are crucial in domains where conditions are constantly changing and uncertainty is prevalent. "When facts shift, conclusions must follow." However, allowing for such flexibility necessitates complex systems that can evaluate and alter current outputs or rules. Although this increases the system's complexity, it also gives it the ability to respond more accurately and pertinently to the unpredictability of the real world.

3. Partially Commutative Production Systems

Rule order independence is a distinguishing characteristic of partially commutative production systems, which means that as long as all pertinent rules are eventually carried out, the order in which rules are applied has no bearing on the outcome. The system is robust and dependable because of this property, which ensures result consistency regardless of execution order. These systems are particularly helpful in fields where accuracy is maintained while flexibility is permitted due to the predictable results provided by mathematical structure. For example, the commutativity of addition in arithmetic operations shows that even if the operands' order is changed, the result stays the same (e.g., $3 + 4 + 5 = 4 + 5 + 3$). In distributed systems or parallel computing, partially commutative systems use this type of mathematical stability to offer flexibility in execution. These systems become very effective at solving structured problems by allowing different rule application paths while preserving a consistent final result.

4. Commutative Production Systems

Regardless of the order in which the rules are applied, commutative production systems ensure the same outcomes. By guaranteeing that every possible combination of rule execution results in the same end state, these systems go beyond the concept of partial commutativity. Essentially, the system is stable and predictable because the sequence in which the rules are applied has no bearing on the results. This statement sums up the essence of commutativity in such systems: "Order doesn't matter when the outcome remains the same." These systems are especially useful in situations where consistency and dependability are crucial. This idea is best illustrated by sorting algorithms such as bubble sort and quicksort, which produce the same sorted list even though they may use different intermediate steps. By ensuring reproducibility and accuracy in deterministic tasks, commutative systems contribute to maintaining the belief that "consistency breeds trust in computation.

Applications of Production Systems

Expert Systems: In expert systems, production systems are essential, especially for advisory and diagnostic functions. They evaluate data and make recommendations by following a set of predetermined rules. For example, MYCIN, an early medical diagnostic tool, recommended treatments based on patient symptoms using production rules. Likewise, DENDRAL helped chemists decipher molecular structures. These illustrations show how production systems facilitate sophisticated reasoning and efficiently handle specialized knowledge.

Natural Language Processing (NLP): Production rules can be used to model grammar in NLP in order to parse and interpret language. A rule might specify, for instance, that a sentence consists of a noun phrase and a verb phrase. Production systems can analyze or produce grammatically correct sentences by methodically implementing such rules. This illustrates how production systems assist in breaking down complex linguistic patterns into manageable chunks.

Game AI: Artificial intelligence in games, especially strategy games like chess, checkers, and go, relies heavily on production systems. To determine the best moves, they evaluate the state of the game and apply the rules. The following is an example of a chess rule: "If the opponent's king is exposed, THEN move the queen to deliver check." These systems demonstrate how production rules can effectively handle intricate decision-making and adjust to changing game situations.

Industrial Automation: Production systems in manufacturing control robotic arms and assembly procedures by carrying out rules that specify actions like selecting, positioning, or putting parts together. For example: "IF a defect is detected, THEN remove the item from the line." These systems greatly increase operational accuracy and efficiency, which makes them an essential part of automated industrial processes.

Problem Solving: In more general problem-solving contexts, such as pathfinding, planning, and decision-support systems, production systems are also utilized. One rule in a navigation system might be, for instance: "IF the current route is blocked, THEN calculate an alternative path." Their capacity for structured reasoning makes them perfect for applications requiring decision-making and goal-oriented logic.

Benefits of Production Systems

Modularity

Production systems are highly modular, meaning that rules can be added, removed, or changed separately without impacting the framework as a whole. Their flexibility and maintainability are improved by this modular structure, especially in complex domains. For instance, adding corresponding rules to a diagnostic system allows for the integration of new medical conditions without requiring a system redesign.

Transparency

Due to the interpretability and traceability of each rule, the reasoning process in production systems is intrinsically transparent. Debugging and comprehending the system's decisions is made simpler by this clarity. Medical practitioners, for example, can see and trust the reasoning behind the system's recommendations thanks to expert systems' transparency.

Flexibility

Production systems are very flexible and can be used in a variety of settings, from dynamic ones like traffic control to static ones like solving mathematical puzzles. Their adaptability to various situations highlights their importance in the artificial intelligence space.

Scalability

In order to manage bigger or more complicated problem domains, production systems are made to easily scale by adding more rules. For instance, a traffic management system is well-suited for expanding and changing applications since it only requires the addition of rules for each new scenario to cover more intersections.

Limitations of Production Systems

- **High Conflict Resolution Overhead:** In systems with extensive rule sets, determining which rule to apply when multiple rules are triggered can be computationally intensive. This added complexity may hinder decision-making speed and reduce efficiency, particularly in real-time applications.
- **Lack of Adaptive Learning:** Most production systems are not designed to learn from experience or adapt to new situations automatically. They depend on fixed, predefined rules that must be manually updated to address novel challenges, limiting their usefulness in dynamic or unpredictable environments.

- **Rule Explosion Problem:** As the complexity of a problem increases, the number of required rules can grow exponentially. This leads to a condition known as rule explosion, making the system difficult to manage and more prone to errors.
- **Reliance on Rule Quality:** The effectiveness of a production system is directly tied to the quality and completeness of its rule base. Inaccurate or poorly developed rules can result in faulty or inefficient decisions, ultimately compromising the system's overall performance and reliability.

Introduction to Control Strategies

Control strategies are essential for directing the application of rules to effectively move from an initial state to a desired goal state in the field of artificial intelligence (AI), especially in production systems. These tactics establish the sequence and mode of rule selection and application, guaranteeing that the system moves logically and methodically in the direction of its goal. Control strategies improve decision-making and cut down on needless processing time by giving priority to pertinent rules and avoiding redundant computations. These tactics are essential to ensuring that AI systems function well, making wise choices while maximizing processing power. The phrase means "Control strategies serve as the backbone of intelligent rule-based systems, enabling goal-directed problem solving with precision and efficiency." Their significance is not limited to attaining outcomes; it also includes doing so in a way that preserves system resources and operational integrity, particularly when working with intricate or expansive problem spaces.

Let's explore deeper into the important aspects of control strategies:

Rule Selection

The process by which a production system chooses which rule to apply when there are several that apply to the current state is known as rule selection. The rule that is selected has a direct impact on the system's subsequent actions and its trajectory toward accomplishing the ultimate objective, making this decision extremely important. Logical consistency and efficiency in system behavior are ensured by choosing the appropriate rule at the appropriate moment. Selecting the rule that best fits the goals and intended results of the system requires carefully weighing the circumstances in which each rule is applicable. When multiple diagnostic rules match a patient's symptoms, for instance, an expert system for medical diagnosis must decide which rule to apply first. Setting rules in order of importance according to criteria like specificity, severity, and dependability guarantees that the best course of action is followed. The system performs better overall when these decisions can be made with accuracy. Putting in place effective rule selection procedures improves the accuracy and reliability of the AI's recommendations while also expediting the problem-solving process.

Conflict Resolution

When there are several rules that apply at the same time, a conflict resolution technique is used to decide which rule should be applied first. This strategy is essential to prevent overlaps and inconsistencies that can occur when various rules propose disparate results for the same circumstance. Systems can function more efficiently and preserve consistency in their decision-making processes by defining a clear procedure for ranking rules. In complex systems, where ambiguity can result in mistakes or misinterpretations, it is crucial to ensure a deterministic course of action. A clear conflict resolution plan improves the system's predictability and dependability in addition to removing misunderstandings. In the end, this guarantees that the rules' intended reasoning and goals are maintained even when several circumstances are present.

Several strategies are commonly used for conflict resolution:

- **Specificity:** Giving preference to rules with more detailed conditions, as they are designed to handle specific situations.
- **Recency:** Selecting rules that rely on the most recently updated information in working memory, ensuring decisions reflect the latest data.
- **Priority:** Using predefined priority levels for rules and choosing the one with the highest priority in case of a conflict.

For example, in a traffic control system, emergency vehicle regulations might take precedence over those for normal traffic in order to guarantee prompt reactions in urgent circumstances. Maintaining the effectiveness and consistency of production systems requires the implementation of efficient conflict resolution procedures, which also helps to prevent needless delays or mistakes brought on by indecision.

Search Control

The techniques used to effectively traverse the problem space and guide the system toward the desired state while minimizing computational effort are collectively referred to as search control. It entails choosing which states are looked at first and making sure the search procedure is still efficient with resources.

Common search control strategies include:

- **Depth-First Search (DFS):** Traverses down a branch as deeply as possible before backtracking. It tends to use less memory but can become inefficient if it follows lengthy, unproductive paths.
- **Breadth-First Search (BFS):** Examines all nodes at the current depth before progressing to the next level, guaranteeing the shortest path is found, though it may consume more memory.

- **Heuristic Search:** Leverages domain-specific insights to estimate which path is most promising, enhancing efficiency by prioritizing certain routes over others.

For example, by calculating the distance to the destination, heuristic search algorithms like A assist navigation system in finding the shortest route. This method improves response times and reduces the search space. Maximizing AI system performance requires the use of effective search control techniques, which enable them to address complex issues within realistic time and resource constraints.

Efficiency and Resource Management

Control strategies are essential for making the best use of computational resources and enhancing the effectiveness of AI systems. They speed up the problem-solving process by guiding the selection and application of rules, which helps reduce redundant computations.

Effective resource management involves:

- **Eliminating Redundancy:** Avoiding repeated evaluation of identical conditions or reapplication of the same rules, thereby saving processing time and computational resources.
- **Avoiding Infinite Loops:** Ensuring the system progresses toward its goal by preventing the repetitive application of rules that could cause it to get stuck in cycles.
- **Optimizing Memory Usage:** Managing working memory efficiently by retaining only pertinent information, thus minimizing the system's memory consumption.

Control strategies, for example, enable a real-time monitoring system to respond quickly to important alerts while removing less important data, guaranteeing optimal performance and dependability. These tactics enable AI systems to operate within reasonable constraints by effectively allocating resources, which qualifies them for practical application.

Scalability and Adaptability

The scalability and adaptability of AI systems are greatly enhanced by carefully thought-out control strategies. The key to scalability is ensuring that AI models can effectively handle growing data volumes and user demands, allowing for seamless expansion without sacrificing performance. The foundation for systems that can expand to meet changing needs is laid by control strategies that integrate modularity, dynamic resource allocation, and effective load balancing. Control mechanisms that enable AI systems to react efficiently to modifications in their input conditions or surroundings also improve adaptability. This entails adapting to unforeseen circumstances, learning from fresh data, and continuing to operate in spite of interruptions. In summary, strong control strategies enable AI systems to intelligently evolve and scale without interruption, making them resilient and prepared for the future.

Control strategies facilitate scalability by:

- **Modularity:** Facilitates the addition of new rules without affecting existing functionalities, allowing seamless expansion of the system's knowledge base.
- **Efficient Resource Allocation:** Ensures optimal distribution of resources to sustain performance as the system scales.

Adaptability is achieved through:

- **Adaptive Rule Implementation:** Empowering the system to apply varying rules in response to evolving conditions, ensuring appropriate reactions to new and unforeseen situations.
- **Learning Capabilities:** Integrating feedback mechanisms to refine control strategies over time, enhancing decision-making as the system navigates a wide range of scenarios.

For example, in an e-commerce recommendation system, control strategies enable the system to scale by incorporating new product categories and to adapt accordingly.

Breadth-first Search

A fundamental algorithm in graph theory and artificial intelligence, Breadth-First Search (BFS) is essential to computer science, AI, and network analysis. The following is the phrase sentence: "BFS explores all nodes at the current depth before proceeding to the next level." Before delving further into a graph or tree structure, BFS makes sure no node is overlooked at any depth by methodically exploring each level of the structure. BFS is especially good at resolving issues with general searching, connectivity, and pathfinding. It is well known for its capacity to determine the shortest path in unweighted graphs, which makes it perfect for uses such as social network analysis, GPS navigation, and maze or puzzle solving. The breadth-first approach guarantees a thorough and equitable search and frequently serves as the basis for more complex artificial intelligence algorithms.

According to Figure 2.4, the algorithm starts the search at a specified source node, logs it as visited, and adds it to a queue. Nodes are dequeued from this queue one at a time, and each neighboring node that has not been visited is found, marked as visited, and then requeued. Phrase sentence: The algorithm investigates the graph's frontier layer by layer at each step. To make sure no node is visited again, this iterative process keeps going until all reachable nodes have been investigated. Breadth-First Search (BFS) is distinguished by its level-order traversal, which ensures that nodes closer to the source are visited before those farther away. Phrase sentence: BFS is perfect for problems that need minimal-distance solutions because of its systematic approach. This feature is particularly useful for level-order traversal in tree structures, finding the shortest path in unweighted graphs, and methodically searching search spaces in AI applications such as maze-solving.

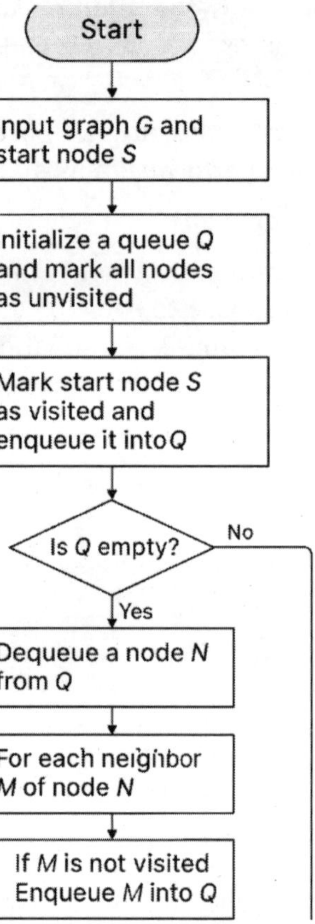

Figure 2.4: Flowchart for the Breadth-First Search (BFS) Algorithm.

Steps of BFS

- Start at the source node.
- Enqueue the source and mark it as visited.
- While the queue is not empty:
  - Dequeue a node from the front.
  - Process the node (e.g., add it to the result).
  - For each unvisited neighbor:
    - Mark the neighbor as visited.
    - Enqueue the neighbor.

- Repeat until all reachable nodes are visited.

Applications of BFS in AI

- **Shortest Path in Unweighted Graphs:** BFS ensures minimal steps between nodes.
- **Level Order Traversal:** Used in trees for hierarchical data processing.
- **Maze Solving:** Finds paths in grid-based structures.
- **Web Crawling:** Systematically visits and indexes websites level by level.
- **Social Network Analysis:** Determines degrees of separation or reachable connections.

Example:

Consider the following simple graph:

```
 1
/\
2  3
|  |
4  5
```

Adjacency List Representation:

```
1: [2, 3]
2: [1, 4]
3: [1, 5]
4: [2]
5: [3]
```

BFS Traversal (Starting from Node 1)

Steps:

Start at Node 1:

- Enqueue 1.
- Mark 1 as visited.

Queue: [1]

Dequeue 1:

- Process 1.
- Enqueue its neighbors (2 and 3).
- Mark 2 and 3 as visited.

Queue: [2, 3]

Dequeue 2:

- Process 2.
- Enqueue its neighbor (4).
- Mark 4 as visited.

Queue: [3, 4]

Dequeue 3:

- Process 3.
- Enqueue its neighbor (5).
- Mark 5 as visited.

Queue: [4, 5]

Dequeue 4:

- Process 4.
- No unvisited neighbors.

Queue: [5]

Dequeue 5:

- Process 5.
- No unvisited neighbors.

Queue: []

Queue is Empty:

- Terminate the algorithm.

BFS Output

The order of traversal is:

1 -> 2 -> 3 -> 4 -> 5

This simple example shows how BFS explores all nodes level by level.

Depth-first Search

Traversal Order

In Depth-First Search (DFS), one branch of the graph is explored as deeply as possible before moving back to investigate other branches. It begins at a selected node, advances to one of its neighbors, and so on, exploring the structure further until it reaches a dead end at a node with no unexplored neighbors. DFS then returns to the initial node and pursues additional uncharted territory. DFS is appropriate for situations where all possible routes must be fully explored before attempting alternatives because of its deep exploration before retracing. DFS inherently tracks a node's journey to its leftmost descendant in tree structures before turning back to examine the right side. To get to the deepest node, for example, it would first go through the left child of a node, then the left child of that child, and so forth. It only comes back to investigate the appropriate branches after that. However, the existence of cycle situations—situations in which nodes are connected and may lead back to nodes that have already been visited—makes this strategy a little more difficult in graphs. DFS usually employs a visited list or set to keep track of which nodes have already been explored in order to prevent revisiting nodes and getting caught in endless loops.

Data Structures Used

DFS can be implemented with an explicit stack or with recursion. Because backtracking is handled implicitly by the program's call stack in a recursive implementation, the code is clearer and more concise. Due to its simplicity, this approach is frequently chosen and is intuitive. But when traversing very deep or large graphs, recursion can cause stack overflow, which limits its usefulness in some situations. In contrast, an explicit stack is used to manage nodes in an iterative DFS implementation. This method makes sure that the node that has been visited the most recently and its neighbors are processed next, maintaining the depth-first nature of traversal. Despite being a little more verbose, an explicit stack is a reliable option for real-world applications because it can handle large graphs more securely and prevents stack overflow.

Graph Types Supported

A flexible algorithm that can navigate both directed and undirected graphs is Depth-First Search (DFS). DFS efficiently investigates connected elements in undirected graphs, locating every node that can be reached from a specified starting point. DFS is especially helpful in directed graphs for tasks like topological sorting and cycle detection. Because of its recursive or stack-based methodology, it can be used to solve issues where backtracking and full traversal are crucial. I Despite its ability to work on both weighted and unweighted graphs, DFS does not consider edge weights when traversing. Its main objective is to visit every node in a graph, irrespective of the edge weight. DFS is therefore not the best method for resolving shortest-path issues in weighted graphs, even though it is useful for structural analysis of graphs. Algorithms like Bellman-Ford or Dijkstra's are better suited for these kinds of tasks because they specifically assess and optimize using edge weights..

Applications

DFS has a wide range of applications:

- **Pathfinding:** DFS systematically explores all possible routes between nodes, making it ideal for solving puzzles or navigating mazes.
- **Topological Sorting:** In Directed Acyclic Graphs (DAGs), DFS is used to arrange nodes in a linear order where each edge leads from an earlier node to a later one—essential for tasks like scheduling.
- **Cycle Detection:** DFS can detect cycles in both directed and undirected graphs by monitoring visited nodes and, in the case of directed graphs, the recursion stack.
- **Maze Solving:** By thoroughly exploring each path, DFS effectively finds solutions in mazes, especially when the destination is located deeper in the structure.
- **Connected Components:** DFS identifies groups of interconnected nodes in undirected graphs, revealing distinct connected components.

Algorithm (Recursive and Iterative)

Recursive DFS explores the graph by repeatedly calling the function for every unvisited neighbor. Although this method provides a clean implementation, stack size restrictions may make it unsuitable for large graphs. However, iterative DFS uses an explicit stack, which improves memory management and guards against stack overflow.

The core algorithm for DFS involves:

- Marking a node as visited.
- Exploring its neighbors recursively or by pushing them onto a stack.
- Backtracking when no unvisited neighbors remain.

Advantages

Compared to Breadth-First Search (BFS), Depth-First Search (DFS) uses less memory because it does not keep all nodes at a specific depth. Rather, a stack is used to record only the current path. For graphs with long, narrow paths or high branching factors, DFS is especially well-suited. Its simple method also makes it an essential tool for determining linked elements and examining graph characteristics.

Disadvantages

Since DFS investigates deeper nodes before taking into account other options, it may take longer routes to reach its destination and does not guarantee the shortest path in an unweighted graph. Additionally, without efficient cycle detection, DFS can become trapped in endless loops in cyclic graphs, which is why monitoring visited nodes is essential.

Example of Depth-First Search (DFS)

Graph Representation

```
# Graph represented as an adjacency list
graph = {
  'A': ['B', 'C'],
  'B': ['D', 'E'],
  'C': ['F'],
  'D': [],
  'E': ['F'],
  'F': []
}
# DFS function
defdfs(graph, start, visited=None):
  if visitcd is None:
    visited = set()
visited.add(start)
  print(start)
  for neighbor in graph[start]:
    if neighbor not in visited:
dfs(graph, neighbor, visited)
# Run DFS
dfs(graph, 'A')
```

Output

```
A
B
D
E
F
C
```

- **DFS Prioritizes Depth:** DFS goes deep into the graph, visiting all of a node's descendants before moving to its siblings.
- **Backtracking:** DFS backtracks when a node has no unvisited neighbors.
- **Stack Management:** The stack maintains the current path and helps backtrack when necessary.

Hill Climbing & its Variations

A heuristic search algorithm called "Hill Climbing" is mostly used to solve mathematical optimization problems. It is frequently used to traverse vast search spaces where obtaining an exact solution could be computationally costly. It belongs to the family of local search algorithms. Starting with a random solution, the algorithm repeatedly investigates nearby solutions before selecting the one that best improves the objective function. Until a local optimum is achieved, where no more advancements are feasible, this process keeps going. Hill Climbing's simplicity and effectiveness are its main advantages, especially in situations where it is not necessary or feasible to find an exact solution. One significant drawback, though, is that it is prone to becoming trapped in local optima, which hinders its ability to identify the optimal solution globally. Despite this, the algorithm is useful for a number of tasks, including solving complicated optimization problems quickly and satisfactorily. It works best when paired with other strategies, such as simulated annealing or random restarts, to break out of local optima.

Hill Climbing Algorithm

A popular heuristic optimization technique in computational mathematics and artificial intelligence for handling challenging issues with wide search spaces is called "Hill Climbing." In order to reach a neighboring solution that provides a better value for the objective function, it iteratively refines an initial solution. The search is essentially stopped at this point, when no more progress can be made. A common metaphor for the algorithm is climbing a hill, where the objective is to reach the peak, which represents the best solution. Hill Climbing is a local search algorithm that prioritizes enhancing the existing solution over taking into account the larger search space. Instead of considering every option, it bases decisions on quick, local improvements. Although this can sometimes produce fast results, if the search is restricted to a small portion of the search space, the algorithm may become trapped in local optima and be unable to locate the global optimal solution.

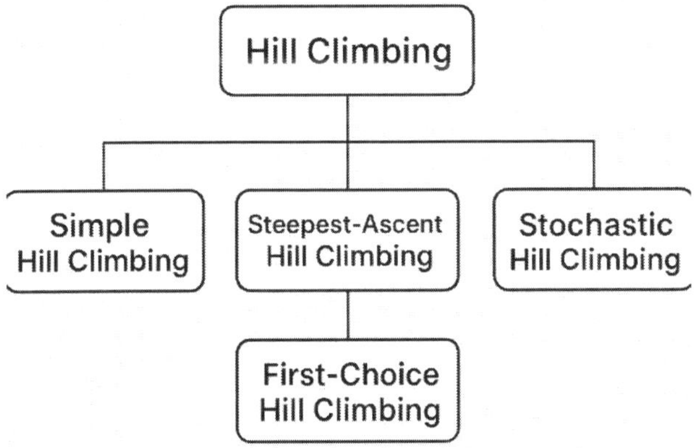

Figure 2.5: Variations of the Hill Climbing Algorithm.

Block diagram representing the variations of the Hill Climbing algorithm in a structured and professional layout, Figure 2.5.

The Hill Climbing algorithm determines the value of its objective function after beginning with a randomly selected initial solution. After that, it makes small adjustments to the existing solution to produce nearby solutions. After assessing each neighbors objective function, it chooses the one with the highest value and advances in its direction. The algorithm reaches a peak and stops if no neighboring solution improves. This method has limitations even though it is simple and works well for many issues. When no better solutions are found nearby, Hill Climbing may become trapped in local optima, flat plateaus, or ridges and settle for a less-than-ideal outcome. Because of this, it might not be the best option for issues involving difficult or complex landscapes, where a more sophisticated optimization method might be needed.

Steps of Hill Climbing

Hill Climbing follows a structured process:

- **Begin with an Initial Solution:** The algorithm begins at a predetermined or random point in the search space.
- **Evaluate the Current Solution:** To assess the quality of the current solution, the objective function is computed.
- **Generate Neighboring Solutions:** Minor adjustments are made to the current solution to produce nearby solutions in the search space.

- **Move to the Best Neighbor:** If a nearby solution improves, the algorithm moves on to that neighbor and continues.
- **Repeat Until Convergence:** Until no better neighbors are found or another stopping condition—like a maximum number of iterations—is met, this process is repeated.

Although this iterative approach ensures that the algorithm gradually approaches a solution, its inherent limitations may prevent it from always reaching the global optimum.

Challenges in Hill Climbing

Despite its ease of use, Hill Climbing has a number of drawbacks that make it less useful in some situations. Its propensity to become trapped in local optima is one of the main problems. In complex search spaces with many peaks and valleys, this happens when the algorithm stops at a suboptimal solution because no neighboring solution offers any improvement. Additionally, plateaus—flat areas where all nearby solutions have the same objective function value—make it difficult for the algorithm to move forward and find a better solution. Ridges, or the narrow roads leading to the global optimum, present another major obstacle. Because Hill Climbing usually travels in the direction of the steepest gradient, which isn't always in line with the ridge, it could be challenging to locate and follow these routes. These drawbacks highlight the necessity for improvements or modifications to the fundamental Hill Climbing algorithm, such as genetic or simulated annealing algorithms, which can aid in resolving the issue of local optima, plateaus, and ridges and enable more efficient search space exploration.

Variations of Hill Climbing

To address the limitations of basic Hill Climbing, several variations have been developed:

Simple Hill Climbing

One neighbor at a time is assessed by Simple Hill Climbing, which then advances to the first neighbor who makes an improvement. This approach is simple to use, but because it doesn't take into account several neighbors before making a decision, it is likely to become trapped in local optima or flat plateaus.

Steepest-Ascent Hill Climbing

The steepest hill in ascent by assessing each neighbor and selecting the one that offers the biggest improvement in the objective function, climbing improves on the fundamental strategy. This makes it more likely that better solutions will be found, but it takes more work because each neighbor must be considered.

Stochastic Hill Climbing

In this variant, neighbors are chosen at random, and if a better solution is found, the algorithm advances to it. Although stochastic hill climbing can occasionally break through plateaus and is quicker than steepest ascent, its randomness may cause it to miss better solutions.

Random-Restart Hill Climbing

In this variant, the Hill Climbing algorithm is repeatedly executed with various random starting points. It is more likely to reach the global optimum and avoid local optima if it restarts from different locations. However, because multiple runs are needed, it is more computationally expensive.

Simulated Annealing (a Related Approach)

Through the use of simulated annealing, the concept of accepting worse solutions with a decreasing probability is introduced. This randomness makes the algorithm particularly useful for complex optimization problems because it enables it to avoid local optima and investigate a larger search space.

Example

To illustrate Hill Climbing, consider finding the maximum value of the function $f(x)=-x^2+4x+6$ over the range $x\in[0,5]$. The algorithm starts at a random point, say $x=0$, and evaluates the function, $f(0)=6$. It generates neighboring solutions, for example, by incrementing x. Evaluating $f(1)=9$, the algorithm moves to $x=1$. Continuing this process, it finds $f(2)=10$ and moves to $x=2$. At this point, no neighbor improves the value, so the algorithm terminates. The maximum value is $f(2)=10$, reached at $x=2$.

Applications of Hill Climbing

Hill Climbing is a powerful tool in many different fields and is used extensively in artificial intelligence and optimization. In pathfinding, it is essential for figuring out effective routes for robotics and navigation systems. Hill Climbing is a technique used by game-playing AI to evaluate possible outcomes and choose the most promising moves. The algorithm helps with operations research tasks like scheduling, resource allocation, and design optimization. In the field of machine learning, Hill Climbing is also useful for optimizing hyperparameters to improve model performance and increase overall efficiency. Even though Hill Climbing is easy to use and efficient at solving optimization problems, it has drawbacks, particularly when the search space behaves well. By reducing restrictions like local optima and plateaus, variations like steepest-ascent, stochastic, and random-restart help increase the algorithm's usefulness. As Table 2.2 illustrates, being aware of these difficulties is crucial for choosing the right variation or integrating it with other algorithms to enhance overall performance. Hill Climbing is still a flexible and popular method for optimization tasks, offering answers in a variety of fields.

Table 2.2: Variations of Hill Climbing Algorithm.

Variation	Description	Advantages	Disadvantages
Simple Hill Climbing	Starts with an initial solution and iteratively makes small changes, choosing the best neighbor solution.	Simple, easy to implement, and often fast.	Can get stuck in local maxima, plateaus, or saddle points.
Steepest-Ascent Hill Climbing	Evaluates all neighbors and moves to the one with the steepest ascent (best improvement).	Less likely to get stuck in local maxima compared to Simple Hill Climbing.	More computationally expensive due to evaluating all neighbors.
Stochastic Hill Climbing	Randomly selects a neighbor from the set of neighbors that improve the current solution.	Faster in some cases, avoids local maxima by chance.	May miss optimal solutions, less predictable than other variants.
Random-Restart Hill Climbing	Runs multiple hill-climbing searches with different random initial states and returns the best result.	Helps overcome local maxima by trying different starting points.	Computationally expensive, can still miss the global maximum.
First-Choice Hill Climbing	Selects the first neighbor that improves the current solution, without evaluating all neighbors.	Faster than Steepest-Ascent Hill Climbing in many cases.	Can get stuck in local maxima more easily due to fewer evaluations.
Dynamic Hill Climbing	A variation that adapts its step size dynamically, making smaller steps when the algorithm is near the peak and larger steps when far away.	Can improve the convergence speed and avoid getting stuck.	More complex to implement and tune, may still get stuck in local maxima.

Heuristics Search Techniques

Heuristic search methods are well known for their ability to solve challenging artificial intelligence problems by utilizing a strategy that bases decisions on estimated solutions. The word "heuristic" describes a useful guideline or technique that directs the search and makes it possible to find acceptable answers without conducting a thorough investigation. When exact algorithms are computationally impractical, especially in large or complex problem spaces, these techniques become indispensable. Heuristic approaches guarantee that the problem-solving process is efficient in terms of both time and resources by employing an effective search strategy. A heuristic function, which estimates the proximity of a particular state to the objective, is used by the algorithm to assess each possible state in heuristic search. The algorithm can prioritize some paths or states over others thanks to this evaluation process, which ultimately lowers the amount of computation needed. A heuristic function, for example, could forecast the shortest distance to the destination in a pathfinding scenario, directing the search toward more promising routes and greatly increasing the search's overall efficiency.

Flowchart providing an overview of heuristic search techniques (Figure 2.6).

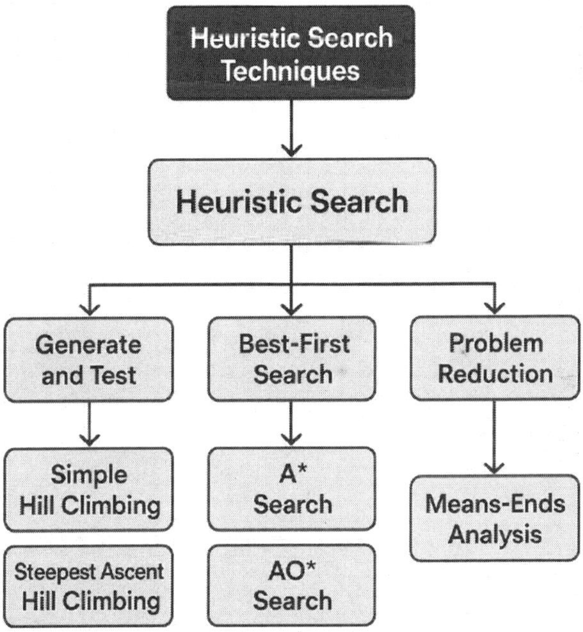

Figure 2.6: Heuristic Search Techniques.

Heuristic Search

Heuristic searches make use of domain knowledge that is incorporated into the heuristic function and can change based on the issue being solved. By offering accurate approximations of the solution and assisting in directing the search toward promising areas, a well-designed heuristic function improves the algorithm's efficiency. On the other hand, a heuristic that is biased or badly designed may produce less-than-ideal results, decreasing the effectiveness of the search process and possibly wasting computer power. The effectiveness of heuristic search strategies depends on striking a balance between investigating novel problem domains and taking advantage of established, promising solutions. Heuristics, which rank particular regions according to their potential, are incorporated into strategies like A* search, Greedy Best-First Search, and Hill Climbing to accomplish this balance. These methods are especially useful in domains where effective navigation is essential and the search space is large, such as robotics, game-playing AI, and optimization problems.

Common Heuristic Search Techniques

This method prioritizes states that seem closer to the objective by selecting the node with the lowest heuristic value at each stage. Although it is effective and frequently quick, it ignores the total cost and only concentrates on the heuristic, so it does not ensure an ideal solution.

- **A Search*:** A* search combines the heuristic value (estimated cost to reach the goal) with the cost already incurred to guide decision-making. This approach ensures that A* is both complete and optimal when the heuristic is admissible (i.e., it never overestimates the actual cost). It is commonly used for pathfinding and graph traversal.
- **Beam Search:** Beam search limits the number of nodes explored at each level by retaining only the most promising states, based on the heuristic function. This method trades off completeness for efficiency, making it particularly useful in scenarios where memory is limited.
- **Hill Climbing and Variants:** Hill Climbing aims to improve the current solution by selecting a neighboring state with a better heuristic value. Variants like Simulated Annealing and Random-Restart Hill Climbing address its drawbacks, such as the tendency to get stuck in local optima.

Advantages and Challenges

When it comes to lowering the computational cost of solving complicated problems, heuristic search techniques are essential. By carefully focusing the search on the most promising states, they prevent the needless exploration of unrelated areas of the search space. This makes them extremely useful for a range of real-world applications where speed and efficiency are essential, like game strategy development, scheduling tasks, and navigation systems. Heuristics enable the solution of problems that would otherwise be computationally costly or impossible by focusing the search. Heuristic search techniques have drawbacks of their own, despite their benefits. The way the heuristic function is designed has a significant impact on how effective the solution is. A badly thought-out heuristic may misguide the search, producing suboptimal results or ineffective search space exploration. Moreover, heuristic approaches are frequently very specialized, requiring domain-specific knowledge to create efficient heuristics for every scenario, which limits their adaptability and may make them more difficult to apply in new domains.

Applications of Heuristic Search

Heuristic search methods are extensively used in many different fields, improving problem-solving efficacy and efficiency. These methods in robotics allow autonomous robots to precisely navigate intricate environments by modifying their routes in response to real-time data. Heuristic search is essential to game AI because it directs decision-making, allowing AI to strategically compete with human players. Heuristic search methods are also essential for resolving optimization issues like resource allocation and scheduling, where they assist in locating nearly ideal solutions within realistic time constraints. Because of these features, heuristic search is extremely useful in practical applications where prompt but dependable decision-making is necessary. Furthermore, heuristic search is crucial in domains such as machine learning and natural language processing, where it helps identify patterns in large datasets and optimize models. These methods' adaptability and usefulness guarantee their ongoing applicability since they balance computational effectiveness and solution quality. Although the heuristic's design determines how well it performs, its versatility across a range of tasks attests to its critical role in the development of artificial intelligence. Heuristic search continues to be a fundamental component of AI development and problem-solving techniques due to its numerous applications.

Best-first Search, A* Algorithm

Best-First Search (BFS) is an informed search algorithm that combines elements of both breadth-first and depth-first search by ranking nodes in a graph according to a specified evaluation function. A heuristic function determines the estimated cost or distance to the goal, which guides BFS's exploration of nodes in contrast to other search algorithms. Because of this, BFS is a heuristic-driven search, selecting the next node to investigate based on the most promising route to the answer. The efficiency of solving complex graph problems is greatly increased by this method, particularly for pathfinding and graph traversal issues. The heuristic function allows BFS to avoid needless exploration of less promising nodes and concentrate on more pertinent ones. This makes it very useful for applications like routing, artificial intelligence in games, and others that require locating the best or nearly best paths in big graphs.

Concepts of Best-First Search

Heuristic Function ($h(n)$): The heuristic function estimates the cost from the current node to the goal node and helps determine the sequence in which nodes are visited.

- **Priority Queue:** Nodes are placed in a priority queue, arranged according to their heuristic values ($h(n)$). The algorithm always expands the node with the lowest $h(n)$ value first.
- **Greedy Nature:** Best-First Search is also referred to as Greedy Best-First Search, as it focuses on prioritizing nodes that seem to be closer to the goal, based on the heuristic.

Steps of Best-First Search

Initialization:

- Start at the initial node and calculate its heuristic value ($h(n)$).
- Insert the initial node into a priority queue.

Node Expansion:

- Remove the node with the smallest $h(n)$) value from the queue.
- If this node is the goal, return the solution.
- Otherwise, generate its neighbors and calculate their heuristic values.

Queue Update:

- Insert the neighbors into the priority queue, maintaining priority based on their heuristic values.

Repeat:

- Continue until the goal is reached or the queue is empty.

Limitations of Best-First Search

- It does not guarantee the shortest path because it only considers the heuristic value ($h(n)$) and ignores the cost to reach the current node ($g(n)$).
- May get stuck in local minima or explore suboptimal paths.

An Algorithm*

By combining the advantages of uniform cost search and greedy search, the A* (A-Star) algorithm is a sophisticated variant of the Best-First Search algorithm that finds the shortest path in a graph or grid. By calculating the total cost of getting to a node and the estimated cost of getting from that node to the objective, it evaluates nodes. A* can effectively search through big search spaces and locate the best answers thanks to this heuristic technique. As long as the heuristic function is admissible—that is, it never overestimates the actual cost—A* stands out for its ability to ensure the finding of the shortest path. Because of this, A* is one of the most popular and dependable algorithms for pathfinding and graph traversal, guaranteeing that it will always find the optimal path. Because of its efficiency and adaptability, it is the preferred approach in a variety of applications, including network routing, robotics, and video games.

Concepts of An Algorithm*

Evaluation Function:

- f(n)=g(n)+h(n)
- g(n): The cost to reach the current node from the start node.
- h(n): The heuristic cost to reach the goal node from the current node.

Admissible Heuristic:

- A heuristic is admissible if it never overestimates the actual cost to the goal.

Consistency (Monotonicity):

- A heuristic is consistent if, for every node n and successor n', the estimated cost satisfies.

$$h(n) \leq c(n, n') + h(n')$$

where c(n,n′) is the cost of moving from n to n′.

Steps of A Algorithm*

1. Initialization:

Start at the initial node, calculate f(n)=g(n)+h(n), and insert it into a priority queue.

2. Node Expansion:

- Remove the node with the smallest f(n) value from the queue.
- If this node is the goal, return the solution.
- Otherwise, generate its neighbors.

3. Cost Calculation:

- For each neighbor, calculate:

$$g(n') = g(n) + c(n,n')$$

$$f(n') = g(n') + h(n')\ ')$$

- Insert the neighbor into the priority queue if it hasn't been visited or if the newly calculated f(n′) is smaller.

4. Repeat:

Continue until the goal is reached or the queue is empty

Advantages of A Algorithm*

- **Optimality:** A* ensures the shortest path when the heuristic is both admissible and consistent.
- **Efficiency:** A* reduces the number of nodes expanded by balancing exploration ($g(n)$) and exploitation ($h(n)$).
- **Flexibility:** A* can be adjusted to suit various problem types by altering the heuristic function.

Table 2.3 below shows a comparison between Best-First Search and another algorithm. Both algorithms are essential to graph theory and artificial intelligence, and they each have unique benefits for various kinds of search issues. Would you like further clarifications or diagrams?

Table 2.3: Comparison of Best-First Search and A Algorithm*

Aspect	Best-First Search	*A Algorithm**
Algorithm Type	Informed Search	Informed Search
Heuristic Function	Uses only the heuristic function h(n).	Uses both the heuristic function h(n) and the path cost function g(n).
Optimality	Not guaranteed to find the optimal solution.	Guarantees the optimal solution if the heuristic is admissible (i.e., it never overestimates the true cost).
Completeness	Not guaranteed to find a solution.	Complete, if the search space is finite.
Efficiency	Can be inefficient as it only considers heuristic.	More efficient due to the combination of both cost and heuristic.
Use of Path Cost	Does not consider the cost to reach the current node.	Considers both the path cost g(n) and the heuristich(n).
Priority Queue	Uses a priority queue based solely on h(n).	Uses a priority queue based on f(n)=g(n)+h(n).
Risk of Getting Stuck	Can get stuck in loops or miss optimal paths.	Less likely to get stuck in loops and more likely to find the optimal path.
Application Example	Pathfinding where the exact path cost is less important, such as in game AI.	Pathfinding and navigation where optimality is crucial, such as GPS navigation.

Constraint Satisfaction Problem

An essential field of study in artificial intelligence is Constraint Satisfaction Problems (CSPs), which are used to model problems with a set of constraints on variables. When the goal is to find a solution that satisfies all given constraints, CSPs provide an organized method for problem solving. These issues come up in a variety of contexts, including planning, scheduling, allocating resources, and solving puzzles like Sudoku or the N-Queens problem. A CSP typically consists of a set of variables, each of which has a range of possible values, and a set of constraints that specify the ranges of values that are acceptable. Assigning values to every variable while adhering to all constraints is the goal. For example, in a scheduling problem, the constraints could guarantee that no two events overlap, the variables could represent time slots, and the domains could list potential events for each time slot.

Figure 2.7 representing the process of solving a Constraint Satisfaction Problem (CSP):

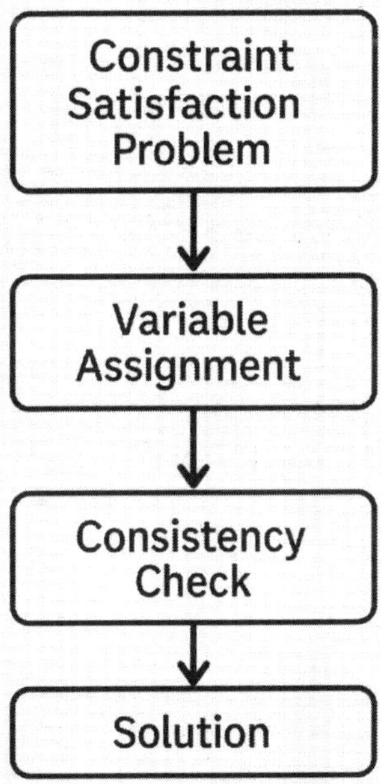

Figure 2.7: process of solving a CSP.

Structure of a CSP

A CSP can be formally represented as a triplet (X, D, C), where:

- $X = \{X_1, X_2, ..., X_n\}$ is the set of variables.
- $D = \{D_1, D_2, ..., D_n\}$ is the set of domains, with each domain D_i containing the possible values for the corresponding variable X_i.

- $C = \{C_1, C_2, \ldots, C_k\}$ is the set of constraints, where each constraint defines the valid combinations of values for a specific subset of variables.

For example, the goal of a graph coloring problem is to colour nodes so that no two neighbouring nodes have the same colour. In this case, the nodes are represented by the variables, the available colors make up the domains, and the constraints guarantee that neighboring nodes receive distinct colors.

Solving CSPs

The approach to solving Constraint Satisfaction Problems (CSPs) involves methodically searching the space of potential solutions while abiding by predetermined constraints. Assigning values to each variable individually is the most basic method, known as backtracking. In the event that a conflict occurs and a constraint is broken, the algorithm goes back to a previous step and attempts a new assignment. This approach is intuitive, but it can be slow, particularly when dealing with complicated or large-scale issues. In order to increase efficiency, the search space is pruned using more sophisticated methods such as constraint propagation and arc consistency. By removing values from variable domains that cannot result in a workable solution, these methods drastically cut down on the number of options that must be investigated. A queen on the board, for instance, essentially eliminates entire rows, columns, and diagonals from consideration for subsequent queens in the N-Queens problem. AC-3 and other arc consistency algorithms make sure that no variable keeps values that defy constraints with related variables. Heuristics that aid in search prioritization include the degree heuristic and the minimum remaining values (MRV) heuristic. A variable with the fewest remaining legal values is selected by the MRV heuristic, whereas variables with the greatest number of constraints are chosen by the degree heuristic. When these strategies are combined with forward checking, for example, strong algorithms are created that can solve large-scale CSPs more effectively.

Applications of CSPs

There are numerous real-world applications for Constraint Satisfaction Problems (CSPs). One important application is in scheduling issues, like allocating workers to shifts or planning university courses, where constraints guarantee that resources are distributed amicably and variables stand in for tasks or time slots. CSPs are also widely used in resource allocation, such as allocating bandwidth, rooms, or equipment to conflicting tasks while maintaining stringent guidelines. In both professional and educational contexts, these applications are essential for maximizing resource utilization and preventing scheduling conflicts. In addition to their practical applications, CSPs are frequently used in games and puzzles. Sudoku is a well-known example, in which players must arrange numbers in a grid while adhering to the rule that each number can only appear once in each row, column, and sub-grid. Similarly, we are challenged by the N-Queens problem to arrange N queens on a N×N chessboard so that no queen poses a threat to another. CSPs are also important in natural language processing because they can be used to model issues like syntactic parsing and word alignment, where constraints help determine a sentence's grammatical structure.

Challenges and Advancements

Constraint Satisfaction Problems (CSPs) pose a number of difficulties even though they are effective tools for problem-solving. Large-scale problems are computationally costly because the complexity of solving a CSP rises with the number of variables, domains, and constraints. The task is made more difficult by constraints that are nonlinear or involve several variables. Despite these challenges, the scalability and applicability of CSPs across a variety of fields have been significantly improved by advancements in algorithm development, especially with regard to local search strategies and hybrid approaches that integrate CSPs with machine learning. Large-scale CSPs benefit from local search techniques like min-conflicts, which iteratively alter an assignment to lower constraint violations. Furthermore, alternative approaches are offered by probabilistic techniques and evolutionary algorithms, which enable non-deterministic solution exploration. These developments guarantee that CSPs will continue to be a fundamental method in AI problem-solving. With their strong framework, CSPs remain a vital tool in AI and operations research, whether for managing resource allocation, scheduling optimization, or puzzle solving, providing effective answers to challenging issues.

Means-end Analysis

A popular heuristic approach to problem-solving in domains such as cognitive science and artificial intelligence is Means-End Analysis (MEA). It operates by analyzing the difference between the current state and the intended goal state in order to divide a problem into smaller, more manageable subproblems. The fundamental idea behind MEA is to apply operators—actions that move the current state closer to the objective—in order to iteratively minimize this difference. This strategy is particularly helpful in complicated situations where it is difficult to find straightforward answers because it offers a methodical way to make small, steady progress. Determining the initial state, the goal state, and the available operators is the first step in the MEA problem-solving process. By concentrating on the biggest disparities, the algorithm evaluates the difference between the current and desired states. Operators are selected and used that close these gaps. Fulfilling preconditions becomes a new sub-goal if they prevent an operator from being used. This iterative process ensures methodical and incremental progress toward the solution until the current state and the goal state coincide (Figure 2.8).

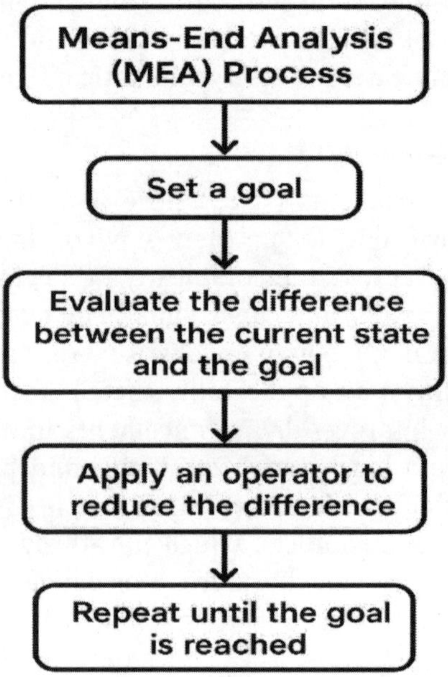

Figure 2.8: Means-End Analysis (MEA) Process.

Take, for instance, a robot that is navigating from Room A to Room C, where Room B and Room C are separated by a locked door. Right now, the robot is in Room A, and its objective is to get to Room C. The algorithm chooses an operator to go to Room B after determining that the locked door is a significant difference. It then proceeds to the sub-goal of unlocking the door. After applying operators and resolving sub-goals iteratively, the robot finally arrives at Room C. This capacity to resolve intermediate goals and adapt dynamically demonstrates the effectiveness of MEA in addressing challenging issues. Robotics, automated planning, and game AI are just a few of the fields where MEA is widely used. MEA aids robots in robotics by helping them decide how to proceed step-by-step to complete tasks in changing environments. By dividing difficult goals into more manageable, achievable targets, characters in game AI use MEA to overcome obstacles. Additionally, MEA is utilized in educational technologies to develop flexible learning pathways that help students move from their present level of knowledge to mastery by addressing intermediate learning objectives. MEA has limitations despite its benefits. In problems with many operators or large search spaces, the computational overhead can be substantial. Furthermore, MEA is highly dependent on correctly detecting differences and selecting the right operators. Sub-goals that clash or differences that are not clearly defined can make the problem-solving process ineffective or even fail. Nevertheless, MEA is a very useful method for resolving complicated, real-world issues because of its methodical and objective approach. It still plays a vital part in artificial intelligence, providing information about how humans and machines solve problems.

Introduction to Game Playing

Since the beginning of artificial intelligence (AI) research, playing games has been a key component since it provides a controlled setting for examining decision-making and problem-solving. Games are perfect for testing AI algorithms because they are clearly defined systems with limited moves, quantifiable results, and clear rules. From classic games like checkers and chess to intricate multiplayer video games, AI's game-playing concepts are applicable to a broad range of fields. Finding the optimal move sequence to produce a desired outcome is the main objective of search problems, which are how AI models games. This entails weighing every possible move, predicting the opponent's response, and analyzing the game states that result in order to inform choices. The investigation of AI game play extends beyond amusement and has produced methods that can be applied to a number of real-world problems. These methods have been very helpful in areas like resource allocation, automated negotiation systems, and strategic planning. Through the application of AI principles acquired through gaming, researchers have improved decision-making across a variety of industries, including defense and business. When faced with complex problems that call for strategy, flexibility, and foresight, the ability to anticipate and optimize moves within a game context has proven useful.

Components of Game Playing in AI

Players: Usually, games have one or more players, who may be AI agents, human players, or a mix of the two. AI agents are made to mimic intelligent decision-making by considering the game's goals and regulations.

- **Game States:** The current setup or configuration of the game is referred to as the "game state." A game state in chess, for example, would specify where each piece is on the board at any particular time.
- **Actions (Moves):** To switch between game states, players can execute particular movements or actions. The game's dynamics are shaped by the collection of all possible actions.
- **Rules:** To ensure that the game progresses in a fair and orderly manner, the rules specify what can be done and how it affects the game state.
- **Evaluation Function:** A lot of AI game-playing systems use an evaluation function to determine how good a particular game state is. In chess, for instance, an evaluation function may assess a player's position strength based on positional considerations and material advantage.
- **Objectives:** Every player has a distinct objective, such as increasing their score, winning the match, or decreasing the odds of the opposition winning. Their decision-making process is guided by these goals.

Categories of Games in AI

Games can be classified based on certain characteristics:

Deterministic vs. Stochastic:

- **Deterministic Games:** Deterministic games, like chess and tic tac toe, are ones in which the players' choices and tactics determine the results. The players' actions alone determine the outcomes; there is no element of chance or randomness. If both players play to their best abilities, every move is predictable and can be planned ahead of time.
- **Stochastic Games:** Backgammon and other stochastic games, on the other hand, add a degree of randomness to the gameplay. Dice rolls are one of the components of these games that affect the result and increase the level of uncertainty. Compared to deterministic games, these are more dynamic and unpredictable since players must modify their strategies in response to the random events.

Perfect vs. Imperfect Information:

- **Perfect Information Games:** Every player in a perfect information game is fully aware of every factor influencing the result, i.e., they all know the game state. A well-known example is chess, in which every player has perfect knowledge of the board, every piece, and the current configuration, enabling them to make decisions. Strategic planning and decision-making in these games are totally dependent on the players' capacity to anticipate and react to the moves of their opponents.
- **Imperfect Information Games:** Situations where players lack full knowledge of the game state are known as imperfect information games. One of the best examples is poker, where players must make decisions based on insufficient information because they are unable to see their opponents' hidden cards. These games are more unpredictable and dynamic than perfect information games because they heavily rely on luck, bluffing, and the ability to read the actions of opponents.

Single-Agent vs. Multi-Agent:

- **Single-Agent:** Single-agent games, like Sudoku, are challenges or puzzles that are meant to be solved by a single player. The player competes solely against themselves in these kinds of games, concentrating on their problem-solving skills independent of other players. The difficulty is in the intricacy and approach needed to solve the puzzle within certain guidelines and limitations.
- **Multi-Agent:** In contrast, multiple players engage in interactions with one another in multi-agent games, either working together or competing to achieve a common objective. Chess and Monopoly are classic examples

of multi-agent games in which players base their strategic choices on what their rivals are doing. These games add an element of social interaction and unpredictability by requiring players to form alliances, compete directly, or predict the moves of others.

Zero-Sum vs. Non-Zero-Sum:

- **Zero-Sum Games:** In zero-sum games, the result is such that the gain of one player is directly equal to the loss of another. The game's overall resource or point total stays fixed, and every victory or advantage one player obtains comes at the expense of the other. Traditional instances of zero-sum games are strategic board games such as chess or checkers, in which every move made by one player causes the opponent to lose, resulting in a competitive setting where only one player can win.
- **Non-Zero-Sum Games:** Mutual cooperation is possible in non-zero-sum games, where all players stand to gain from teamwork. In contrast to zero-sum games, these games allow players to work together for group success and have variable total rewards or benefits. One of the best examples of non-zero-sum games are cooperative board games, in which players can work together to accomplish a common objective, giving everyone a win instead of a direct competition.

AI Techniques in Game Playing

AI uses a variety of advanced strategies to play games efficiently, turning them into computational issues by taking advantage of their structured nature. One fundamental approach uses search algorithms, modeling games as search problems with a game tree that shows every possible move and its associated result. By predicting the worst possible reaction from an opponent, strategies like minimax are used to assess the optimal move and guarantee sound decision-making. Alpha-beta pruning is especially useful in complex games like chess because it optimizes this process by minimizing the number of game tree nodes explored without affecting the result. Furthermore, in games with big state spaces, AI can prioritize promising moves and make decisions more quickly thanks to heuristic functions that estimate the quality of a game state. To find the best move in chess without thoroughly examining every possibility, heuristics may take into account elements like material advantage, piece positioning, and board control.

By enabling agents to improve their tactics through repeated interactions with the game environment, reinforcement learning has revolutionized AI's approach to gaming. These agents gradually discover the best tactics by being rewarded or punished according to their behavior. This strategy has been crucial in challenging games like Go, Poker, and Dota 2, where conventional approaches are ineffective because of the unpredictability of the games. Monte Carlo techniques identify high-value actions by executing multiple random game plays in order to estimate the likelihood of a move's success in stochastic games using probabilistic simulations. In extremely complex games, advanced AI systems like AlphaGo can outperform human champions by combining deep learning and conventional techniques to analyze game states and learn strategies from massive amounts of gameplay data. Together, these AI methods serve as the basis for games' intelligent decision-making and have wider uses in resolving real-world issues.

Applications of Game Playing AI

AI has advanced significantly in the field of recreational gaming, where it powers virtual opponents and non-player characters (NPCs) in board and video games. AI can produce dynamic, adaptive gaming experiences that test human players by utilizing sophisticated algorithms. For example, AI can recognize player movements in strategy games and modify its approach accordingly, making the game more engaging and competitive. In addition to adding to the entertainment value, this versatility allows players to practice their skills by taking on increasingly complex virtual opponents. AI-powered games are used in educational settings to promote critical abilities like decision-making, problem-solving, and strategic thinking. Real-world scenario simulation games allow students to try out various strategies in a risk-free setting, improving their practical knowledge. AI-powered simulations in military training, for instance, assist personnel in handling challenging circumstances like logistics coordination and battlefield decision-making, illustrating how AI can be used for purposes other than amusement to foster useful skills.

AI methods that were first created for gaming have also been used in a variety of industries for strategic planning. These days, supply chain optimization, financial forecasting, and business strategy all use the same algorithms that were once used to predict moves in games like chess and go. These AI-powered techniques help businesses make long-term plans, better allocate resources, and forecast results. AI offers creative answers that boost productivity and competitiveness by presenting real-world problems as game-like decision-making puzzles. Additionally, researching AI in gaming provides valuable insights into human cognition and judgment. By simulating human behavior in game scenarios using AI models, researchers can gain insight into how people approach difficult problems, assess risks, and formulate strategies. These discoveries advance our knowledge of artificial intelligence and cognition by helping to create AI systems that can work alongside people, mimic human reasoning, and even surpass human capabilities.

Challenges in Game Playing AI

Even though AI that can play games has had amazing success, there are still many obstacles to overcome. Extensive search methods are impractical in real-world games because they frequently have large state spaces. Additionally, games with stochastic or imperfectly known elements add complexity that necessitates sophisticated probabilistic reasoning in order to make wise decisions. These difficulties test the limits of AI's potential and necessitate ongoing development to produce systems that can adjust to changing conditions. Creating AI that can react to the erratic tactics of human players is another significant challenge, one that is still being researched. The field of game-playing AI is still vibrant and significant, bridging the gap between theoretical study and practical applications. The evolution of game-playing AI reflects broader developments in artificial intelligence, from the early creation of programs that played chess to more recent systems like AlphaGo and OpenAI'sDota 2 bots. These systems emphasize both the advancements and difficulties that lie ahead by demonstrating not only the effectiveness of AI in strategic decision-making but also its capacity to tackle intricate, real-world issues in a variety of domains.

Min-max & alpha-beta Pruning Algorithms

Min-Max Algorithm

One artificial intelligence decision-making technique used for two-player, zero-sum games is the Min-Max algorithm. Assuming that the opponent, the minimizing player, will likewise make the best choices, the objective of these games is to determine the best course of action for the maximizing player (typically the AI). By examining every possible move in the game tree and calculating the results of each move, the algorithm accomplishes this. At every level of the tree, it switches between the maximizing and minimizing players, each of whom is working toward a different objective: the maximizing player wants to raise their score, while the minimizing player wants to lower it. The Min-Max algorithm has serious computational efficiency issues, even though it can ensure the best possible result for the maximizing player when both players play optimally. Large games or scenarios with a large number of possible moves are unfeasible due to the algorithm's time complexity, which grows exponentially with the depth of the game tree. Slower performance is the result of this exponential increase in complexity, which can be a significant disadvantage in more intricate gaming environments or real-time applications.

Alpha-Beta Pruning Algorithm

An optimization method called alpha-beta pruning is applied to the Min-Max algorithm, which is frequently used in game theory and other decision-making processes. Alpha-Beta pruning's main benefit is its capacity to remove branches from the game tree that are unnecessary to explore, thereby lowering the total number of nodes considered in the search. By ensuring that the algorithm can make decisions more quickly, this optimization increases computational efficiency without sacrificing the outcome's accuracy or correctness. Given the current best options for both players, Alpha-Beta pruning dynamically modifies its search path by maintaining two values, alpha and beta. This allows it to prune branches that are either too high or too low. This leads to a much smaller search space, especially in games like chess that have a lot of decision trees. In the end, Alpha-Beta pruning ensures that the best move is chosen while saving time and computational resources, improving the performance of the Min-Max algorithm. The algorithm introduces two parameters:

- **Alpha:** The best score that the maximizing player can guarantee at that point.
- **Beta:** The best score that the minimizing player can guarantee at that point.

In decision-making algorithms, pruning entails removing branches from the tree that have no bearing on the outcome. A branch is completely ignored if the value of a node is found to be worse than a path that has already been explored by the maximizing or minimizing player. By ensuring that only the most promising branches are investigated, this method reduces needless computations and boosts decision-making effectiveness. The algorithm's computational complexity can be greatly decreased by avoiding these suboptimal branches. This maximizes performance without compromising accuracy by enabling it to investigate deeper levels of the game tree within the same time constraints. Therefore, even in more complicated situations where a traditional approach would be too slow or resource-intensive, pruning allows for faster decision-making. Comparison on Min-Max vs. Alpha-Beta Pruningmention in below Table 2.4:

Table 2.4: Min-Max vs. Alpha-Beta Pruning

Feature	Min-Max Algorithm	Alpha-Beta Pruning Algorithm
Purpose	To determine the optimal move in a decision tree.	To improve the efficiency of the Min-Max algorithm by pruning branches that don't need to be explored.
Time Complexity	O(b^d), where b is the branching factor and d is the depth of the tree.	O(b^(d/2)), significantly better than Min-Max due to pruning.
Space Complexity	O(b * d), as it needs to store all nodes at a particular level of the tree.	O(b * d), similar to Min-Max but with better performance due to pruning.
Algorithm Type	Exhaustive search with no pruning.	A search optimization for Min-Max, pruning unnecessary branches.
Explored Nodes	Explores all nodes in the tree.	Explores fewer nodes by cutting off branches that won't affect the result.

Optimality	Finds the optimal move, but slower due to exhaustive search.	Also finds the optimal move but much faster due to pruning.
Pruning	No pruning occurs, all branches are explored.	Prunes branches where it knows the value will not affect the final decision.
Use Cases	Small decision trees, where performance is not critical.	Larger trees where efficiency is needed.
Performance	Slower performance for large trees due to full exploration.	Faster performance by reducing the number of nodes explored.

Example of Alpha-Beta Pruning

Consider a game tree where the maximizing player (AI) and the minimizing player take alternating turns:

Start Evaluation: The maximizing player begins at the root node, and the algorithm starts exploring the tree.

Alpha and Beta Updates: As the algorithm evaluates each node, it adjusts the alpha and beta values to reflect the best scores encountered for each player.

Pruning: If a node's value falls outside the range set by alpha and beta, the algorithm avoids evaluating that branch further, reducing computational effort.

Result: The algorithm chooses the optimal move for the maximizing player, focusing on the most promising branches.

While the Min-Max algorithm serves as the foundation for game-playing AI, Alpha-Beta pruning optimizes its efficiency, making it applicable to more complex games.

Conclusion

Artificial intelligence (AI) problem-solving and search strategies employ methodical approaches to address challenging tasks. Understanding the nature of the issue and modeling it using production systems and appropriate control strategies are the first steps in these approaches. Breadth-First Search and Depth-First Search are important strategies that are necessary for thorough investigation. While Heuristic Search strategies like Best-First Search and the A* Algorithm use domain knowledge to make decisions more quickly, more sophisticated approaches like Hill Climbing and its variations increase efficiency by concentrating on local optimizations. Means-End Analysis iteratively closes the gap between the current and desired states, whereas Constraint Satisfaction Problems (CSPs) define problems with variables and constraints. Strategies such as Min-Max and Alpha-Beta Pruning are employed in game theory to maximize choices in competitive situations. These methods form the basis of

AI's ability to tackle real-world problems, ranging from intelligent decision-making and strategic planning to pathfinding. The following chapter explores the fundamental ideas of knowledge representation, looking at techniques for expressing knowledge such as propositional logic and first-order predicate logic. Along with production rules, it also discusses more complex subjects like the Resolution Principle, Unification, and structured representation methods like Semantic Nets, Conceptual Dependencies, Frames, and Scripts. An introduction to Programming in Logic (PROLOG), which provides a useful method for creating knowledge-based systems, wraps up the chapter.

Exercise:

- Identify the characteristics of a well-defined problem and explain how these affect problem-solving strategies.
- Outline the function of a production system in AI and provide an example of its usage.
- Contrast Breadth-First Search and Depth-First Search regarding space and time complexity.
- Describe the Hill Climbing technique and discuss its limitations in achieving optimal solutions.
- Define a heuristic function and explain how it enhances the efficiency of search methods such as the A* Algorithm.
- Solve a simple Constraint Satisfaction Problem (CSP) for a Sudoku puzzle using a 3x3 grid, providing a detailed step-by-step explanation.
- Explain the Means-End Analysis process with an example from robotics or navigation.
- Compare Best-First Search and A* Algorithm, outlining their advantages in pathfinding applications.
- Demonstrate how Alpha-Beta Pruning optimizes the Min-Max Algorithm with an example of a game tree.
- Provide pseudocode or a program to implement the Min-Max Algorithm with Alpha-Beta pruning for a Tic-Tac-Toe game.

CHAPTER-3
KNOWLEDGE REPRESENTATION

Introduction & Objective

The principles of Knowledge Representation, a key idea in artificial intelligence, are introduced in this chapter. Its main goal is to encode world knowledge in a way that computers can comprehend and process. It examines several logical frameworks that offer a formal foundation for knowledge-based reasoning, including propositional logic and first-order predicate logic. These rational methods give machines the ability to precisely and systematically represent and manipulate data, which is crucial for tasks like decision-making and problem-solving. The chapter also explores more structured representations that provide different approaches to organizing and storing knowledge, such as Semantic Nets, Frames, and Scripts. These representations assist machines in deciphering complex information by capturing the connections between concepts. Additionally, useful tools like PROLOG are covered, showing how they can be applied to create intelligent systems that use knowledge reasoning effectively and efficiently in practical settings. This chapter aims to give readers an extensive understanding of the many knowledge representation approaches and their important uses in artificial intelligence (AI). By examining these approaches, the chapter presents important ideas that are essential for organizing and structuring knowledge in ways that artificial intelligence (AI) systems can understand and apply. In order to provide a thorough understanding of how knowledge can be efficiently represented for AI tasks, it highlights various strategies, such as logical representation, semantic networks, and frames. The chapter also seeks to give readers the skills they need to solve logical inferences using accepted reasoning techniques and model knowledge logically. It highlights how crucial it is to use both programming-based and structured approaches when creating intelligent systems. Readers will have a firm understanding of the fundamentals of knowledge representation and how it can be used practically to create AI solutions by the end of this chapter.

Propositional Logic

One area of logic that focuses on the connections between propositions—statements that are either true or false but never both—is propositional logic, sometimes referred to as propositional calculus or sentential logic. Logical connectives like AND (∧), OR (∨), NOT (¬), IMPLIES (→), and EQUIVALENT (↔) are used to combine propositions into more complex expressions within its formal reasoning framework. These connectives serve as the basis for artificial intelligence (AI) reasoning by making it possible to depict the connections and dependencies between distinct facts. Propositional logic enables the inference of conclusions and the automation of decision-making processes by modeling basic knowledge domains. The syntax and semantics of propositional logic serve as the foundation for its formal structure. While syntax establishes the guidelines for creating sound logical arguments, semantics specifies how propositions are given truth values and how complex expressions determine their truth by breaking them down into their constituent parts. For instance, the compound statement $P \wedge Q$ (P AND Q) is only true if both P and Q are true. The systematic evaluation of logical expressions through truth tables makes propositional logic an effective tool for automated reasoning and problem-solving. However, its expressiveness is limited, and it can only represent simple facts; systems such as First-Order Predicate Logic are better suited to handle more complex scenarios. Propositional logic is essential to AI despite these drawbacks, especially when it comes to knowledge representation and decision-making.

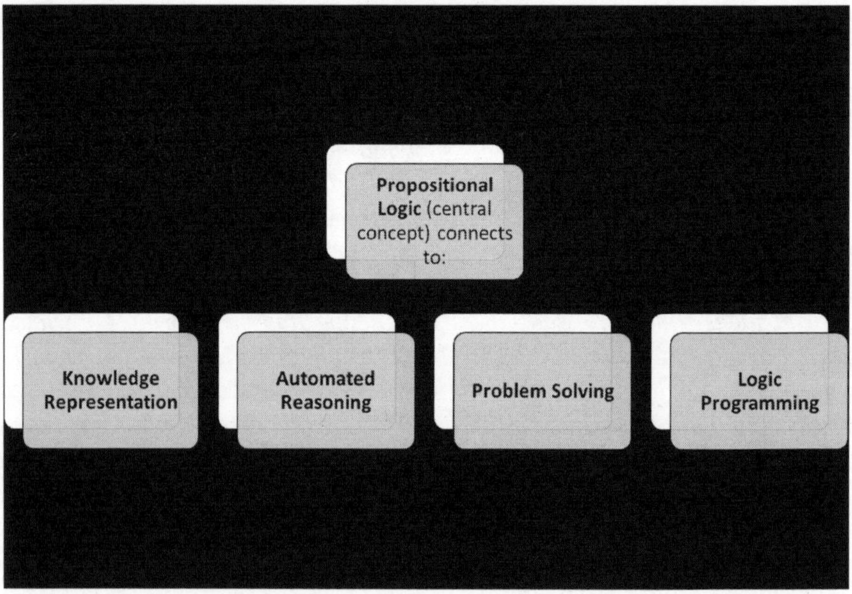

Figure 3.1: Showing the applications of Propositional Logic in AI.

Block diagram in Figure 3.1illustrating the applications of Propositional Logic in AI, highlighting its key uses in Knowledge Representation, Automated Reasoning, Problem Solving, and Logic Programming.

Components of Propositional Logic

Propositions:

The basic units of propositional logic are propositions, which are straightforward assertions that can have one of two truth values. Usually, these truth values are represented by the symbols "True" (T) or "False" (F). A proposition cannot be divided into smaller parts without losing its logical structure because it is an indivisible unit of logic. In essence, it makes a statement about the world, like "The sky is blue," which, depending on the situation or reality, may or may not be true. These atomic units serve as the foundation for more intricate logical expressions in propositional logic. Logical connectives such as AND, OR, and NOT are used to combine propositions to form more complex logical statements. In isolation, though, each claim is still either true or untrue. Propositional logic's clarity and simplicity make it an effective tool for formal reasoning, where conclusions can be drawn by methodically analyzing whether a proposition is true or false.

Examples:

"It is raining." (True or False)

"7 + 7 = 14." (Always True)

Logical Connectives:

AND (∧): Combines two propositions and is true only if both are true.

$P \wedge Q$: True if

$P=T$ and $Q=T$.

OR (∨): Combines two propositions and is true if at least one is true.

$P \vee Q$: True if $P=T$, $Q=T$, or both.

NOT (¬): Negates the truth value of a proposition.

$\neg P$: True if

$P=F$, False if

$P=T$.

IMPLIES (→): Represents implication, where

$P \rightarrow Q$is false only if

$P=T$ and $Q=F$.

EQUIVALENT (↔): Represents equivalence, where

$P \leftrightarrow Q$ is true if P and Q

Q have the same truth value.

Syntax and Semantics:

Syntax defines the rules for forming valid statements.

Example:

$(P \wedge Q) \rightarrow R \rightarrow \mathrm{R}$ is a valid formula.

According to their constituent parts, semantics determines how complicated formulas evaluate and gives propositions truth values.

Truth Tables

Truth tables systematically represent the truth values of logical expressions for all possible combinations of their components. For example:

AND (∧):

P	Q	P∧QP
True	True	True
True	False	False
False	True	False
False	False	False

IMPLIES (→):

P	Q	P→QP
True	True	True
True	False	False
False	True	True
False	False	True

Applications of Propositional Logic in AI

Artificial intelligence makes extensive use of propositional logic, especially for automated reasoning and knowledge representation. It aids in the encoding of basic world facts and relationships in knowledge representation. Think about the statements P: "It is raining" and Q: "The ground is wet." These facts can be connected using propositional logic by the implication $P \rightarrow Q$, which means "If it is raining, then the ground is wet." AI systems can represent and manipulate knowledge in a systematic manner thanks to this structured approach, which facilitates effective processing and decision-making. Automated reasoning, which uses inference rules like Modus Ponens to infer new information, is another important application of propositional logic. For example, the system can infer Q (The ground is wet) if $P \rightarrow Q$ (If P, then Q) and P (It is raining) are known. By encoding problems and using logical reasoning to arrive at solutions, propositional logic also forms the basis for problem-solving activities such as planning and diagnosis. It also serves as the foundation for logic programming languages like PROLOG, which are frequently used to create intelligent systems.

Advantages of Propositional Logic

In artificial intelligence (AI), propositional logic is a vital tool because of its many benefits. One of its main advantages is that it is simple, offering a framework that is simple to comprehend and apply. Propositional logic's clear syntax and semantics guarantee that logical operations and reasoning are simple, which makes it perfect for creating AI systems that need to make precise and organized decisions. Additionally, formal reasoning is made easier by propositional logic. It helps AI systems draw logical conclusions by providing a methodical approach to doing so based on accepted truths. Although it mainly focuses on straightforward situations, its expressive power works incredibly well for conveying fundamental facts and relationships, especially in controlled settings where succinct and clear reasoning is crucial.

Limitations of Propositional Logic

Propositional logic has a lot of drawbacks despite its benefits. Its incapacity to depict intricate relationships—like those involving objects, properties, or quantifiers—is one of its primary shortcomings. Statements like "All cats are mammals," for instance, cannot be expressed by it and call for a more sophisticated system like First-Order Predicate Logic. Propositional logic is less appropriate for simulating complex real-world situations where such subtleties are crucial due to its lack of expressiveness. The scalability of propositional logic presents another difficulty. The computational cost of reasoning and processing rises exponentially with the number of propositions and logical rules, rendering it ineffective for managing large, complex systems. Propositional logic is a fundamental building block of artificial intelligence that facilitates basic reasoning and problem-solving, but because of its inherent limitations, more complex logical systems are frequently needed to handle more complex applications.

Concept of First-Order Predicate Logic

First-Order Predicate Logic (FOPL), sometimes known as First-Order Logic (FOL), is a complex formal system that adds variables, quantifiers, predicates, and functions to propositional logic. FOPL enables a more sophisticated representation of knowledge by reasoning about objects, their characteristics, and the connections between them, in contrast to propositional logic, which concentrates on straightforward declarative statements. The development of logical formulas that capture comprehensive information about the world is made possible by this sophisticated system. Because FOPL offers the framework for modeling intricate knowledge structures and carrying out logical reasoning, its expressive power renders it essential in the field of artificial intelligence (AI). Natural language processing, automated theorem proving, knowledge representation, and other AI systems that need precise and complex reasoning processes rely heavily on FOPL because of its capacity to describe both the objects and the circumstances in which they relate to one another.

Components of First-Order Predicate Logic

Predicates, functions, quantifiers, constants, variables, and logical connectives are the basic components of First-Order Predicate Logic (FOPL). Certain objects within the domain are represented by constants, such as "John" for a person or "Earth" for a planet. Alternatively, variables serve as placeholders and can be any object in the domain, such as x or y. Essential to FOPL, predicates describe attributes or connections between objects, like "is Human (John)" or "is On Earth (John)." To further increase the expressive potential of FOPL, functions can also be used to map objects to other objects.

FOPL heavily relies on quantifiers and logical connectives in addition to constants, variables, and predicates. Quantifiers, like the universal and existential quantifiers (∃ and ∃), specify whether a statement is true for some or all objects in a domain and define the scope of variables in logical statements. To create complex expressions, logical connectives such as "and" (∧), "or" (∨), "not" (¬), and "implies" (→) can be used to combine multiple logical statements. These components work together to give a formal framework for accurately and logically representing and reasoning about relationships and properties. $Likes(John, Pizza)$, which basically means "John likes pizza." Functions are used to convert one object into another. For instance, $Father(John)$ could represent "John's father."

Propositional logic is extended by First-Order Predicate Logic (FOPL), which adds quantifiers to specify the extent of a statement. When a statement is true for every element in a given domain, it is indicated by the Universal Quantifier (∀). For instance, ∀xLoves (x,Mother) applies the condition to each person in the domain, expressing the notion that everyone loves their mother. However, as demonstrated in ∃x Likes(x,Pizza), which implies that someone enjoys pizza, the Existential Quantifier (∃) indicates that a statement is true for at least one element.

Like propositional logic, FOPL combines and modifies statements using logical connectives like AND (∧), OR (∨), and NOT (¬) in addition to quantifiers. By joining simpler statements together, these connectives enable the construction of more intricate logical expressions. For instance, the disjunction (OR) demands that at least one of the statements be true, whereas the conjunction (AND) joins two statements that must both be true. By reversing a statement's truth value, the negation (NOT) offers a means of expressing the assertion's opposite.

Syntax and Semantics

The guidelines for creating legitimate logical formulas are specified by the syntax of First-Order Predicate Logic (FOPL). These formulas are composed of atomic components, such as $Human(Socrates)$, whereas an atomic formula involves a predicate applied to terms. Atomic formulas are combined with quantifiers and logical connectives to create more complex formulas. $\forall x(Human(x) \rightarrow Mortal(x))$ is an example that can be understood as "All humans are mortal."

This illustrates how general statements can be formally expressed using the FOPL structure. The semantics of FOPL, on the other hand, deal with giving these formulas truth values based on how they are interpreted within a particular domain. For example, the formula $Mortal(Socrtes)$ would evaluate to true if the domain includes "Socrates" as a human and all humans are regarded as mortal. Therefore, the semantics ensure that logical expressions have meaning in context by relating the syntactical structure of FOPL to practical knowledge.

Advantages of FOPL

The expressiveness of first-order predicate logic (FOPL) gives it a major edge over propositional logic, enabling it to manage intricate relationships and generalizations. FOPL is capable of expressing more complex ideas like universal quantification, in contrast to propositional logic, which only deals with straightforward true or false values. Statements like "All humans are mortal," for example, can be represented by it, encapsulating the notion of general relationships between objects. Because of its expressiveness, FOPL can be used to model complex concepts and reasoning about the relationships between different entities. Furthermore, because it makes it possible to formulate statements like "A teacher is also a person," which would be challenging to express in propositional logic, FOPL excels at representing hierarchical knowledge. Its support for quantifiers enables the inclusion of particular instances in addition to making reasoning about generalizations easier. This dual feature increases FOPL's adaptability in representing knowledge, making it a crucial instrument for increasingly complex logical reasoning across a range of fields.

Limitations of FOPL

First-Order Predicate Logic (FOPL) has some drawbacks despite its advantages. Its computational complexity is a major disadvantage because using FOPL for reasoning can be very costly and occasionally result in indecision. Because of this, applying FOPL in settings with limited resources or time is challenging. Furthermore, FOPL is limited in its ability to adapt to changing or evolving situations due to its dependence on a fixed discourse domain that needs to be predefined. This limits its ability to dynamically accommodate new objects or relationships. Additionally, FOPL makes the assumption that all knowledge is accurate and comprehensive, which is frequently unfeasible in real-world applications. Uncertainty and insufficient information are frequent in real-world scenarios, which makes it challenging to effectively represent and reason using FOPL. These restrictions therefore prevent its wider use and efficacy in settings where data may be erratic or imprecise.

Example of FOPL in AI

Consider the well-known example of logical reasoning: "All people die. A human being is Socrates. Socrates is therefore mortal." This can be represented in FOPL as follows:

- ∀x(Human(x)→Mortal(x)): "All humans are mortal."
- Human(Socrates): "Socrates is a human."
- Using the inference rule Modus Ponens, we can deduce
- Mortal(Socrates): "Socrates is mortal."

The example that follows demonstrates how FOPL draws important conclusions from a set of premises using universal quantification and logical inference.

Applications of FOPL in AI

First-Order Predicate Logic (FOPL) offers a strong foundation for knowledge representation and reasoning, and it is extensively used in many AI domains. FOPL plays a key role in knowledge-based systems by representing relationships and facts, which helps systems with expertise like medical diagnosis make defensible decisions. FOPL is a semantic tool in the field of natural language processing (NLP) that helps humans and machines communicate effectively by interpreting sentences and deducing their meaning. FOPL ensures the validity of complex logical propositions by applying logical inference rules to the proof of mathematical theorems in automated theorem proving. Furthermore, FOPL is used in robotics to represent and reason about the environment, enabling precise task planning and execution. With major advantages over propositional logic, first-order predicate logic is a strong and expressive tool for reasoning about complex knowledge in artificial intelligence. It is more adaptable and appropriate for complex reasoning tasks due to its ability to handle variables, quantifiers, and relationships. FOPL has drawbacks despite its advantages, including assumptions about fixed domains and computational complexity. However, it continues to be a fundamental framework in AI, necessary for tasks requiring structured knowledge representation and formal reasoning (Table 3.1).

Table 3.1: Features of First-Order Predicate Logic (FOPL)

Feature	Description
Domain of Discourse	The set of objects under consideration in FOPL, typically denoted as the universe of discourse.
Predicates	Functions or relations that take one or more arguments and return a truth value (true/false).
Quantifiers	Operators that specify the extent or scope of a statement (Universal quantifier: ∀, Existential quantifier: ∃).
Variables	Symbols that stand for elements of the domain and can be quantified over.
Terms	Representations of objects in the domain, which can be variables, constants, or functions.
Logical Connectives	Operators like AND (∧), OR (∨), NOT (¬), IMPLIES (→), and EQUIVALENT (↔) to combine statements.

Functions	Mapping from objects in the domain to other objects in the domain (e.g., f(x), g(x, y)).
Equality	A binary relation (usually denoted as =), which asserts that two terms represent the same object.
Ground Terms	Terms that do not contain any variables.
Atomic Sentences	Basic logical units of FOPL, formed using predicates and terms.
Well-formed Formulas (WFF)	A formula in FOPL that is constructed following syntactic rules (using predicates, variables, and quantifiers).
Inference Rules	Logical rules used to derive conclusions from premises (e.g., Modus Ponens, Universal Instantiation).

Introduction to Resolution Principle

A strong inference method in logic, the Resolution Principle offers a methodical way to draw conclusions or demonstrate the veracity of claims. It is essential to both propositional logic and first-order predicate logic (FOPL), particularly in automated reasoning tasks such as knowledge representation and theorem proving. The resolution principle's basic idea is to iteratively combine logical statement pairs with complementary literals in order to identify inconsistencies or arrive at new conclusions. The goal's negation is refuted when a contradiction—represented by an empty clause—is produced, thereby validating the original statement. Since resolution only yields logically sound conclusions and is capable of deriving all conclusions logically implied by the premises, it is regarded as both sound and complete. Because of these intrinsic qualities, it is a crucial component of artificial intelligence systems that rely on logic. The resolution principle enables efficient reasoning about facts, rules, and relationships by decomposing complex logical expressions into simpler components. This allows AI to solve problems and draw conclusions with high efficiency (Figure 3.2).

Concepts of the Resolution Principle

Logical statements must be transformed into clausal form in order to apply the resolution principle. A standardized way to express logical statements as a conjunction of literal disjunctions is through the use of clausal form. For example, you can rewrite the implication "If *P*, then *Q*" as "$\neg P \vee Q$," where literals are atomic propositions or their negations. A clause is an easy way to apply logical resolution because it is merely a disjunction of literals in this context. In order to resolve clauses in First-Order Logic, the unification process is essential. Unification is the process of making two literals complementary so that they can be resolved by replacing variables with constants or other variables. For instance, by changing x=John, the literals Likes(x,y) and Likes(John,y) can be combined into one. The elimination of complementary literals like P and $\neg P$ during resolution results in a new clause that streamlines the logical expression as a whole. This unification and resolution process makes it possible to reduce complicated logical statements to more manageable, simpler forms.

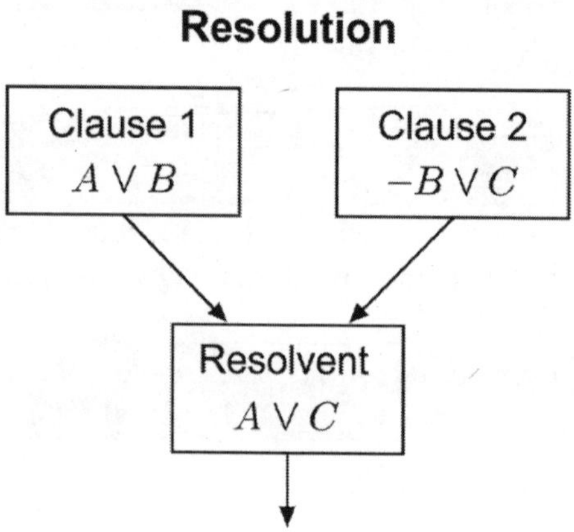

Figure 3.2: Block diagram representing the Resolution Principle.

Steps in Applying the Resolution Principle

All logical statements must first be transformed into clausal form in order for the resolution principle to function. Rewriting the statements as disjunctions of literals, removing implications, and applying De Morgan's laws to move negations inward are all part of this process. For example, a statement such as $\forall x(P(x) \rightarrow Q(x))$ can be represented in a resolution-appropriate form by being converted into $\neg P(x) \vee Q(x)$. The goal statement that requires proof is then added to the list of known clauses and negated. For instance, if Q is the goal, the knowledge base will include its negation, $\neg Q$. In order to generate new clauses, the resolution rule is then iteratively applied, resolving pairs of clauses with complementary literals. This process keeps going until either no more solutions can be found or an empty clause (□) is derived, indicating a contradiction and confirming the initial goal statement. The resolution principle's methodical approach guarantees its efficacy in resolving a range of logical issues, but the goal cannot be proven if no contradiction appears.

Example

To illustrate the resolution principle, consider the following example: Prove that Q is true, given the statements $P \vee Q$ and $\neg P$.

Convert the statements into clausal form:

$P \vee Q$: Already in clausal form.

$\neg P$: Already in clausal form.

Negate the goal Q: Add ¬Q to the knowledge base.

Apply resolution:

Resolve P∨Q with ¬Q to eliminate Q, producing P.

Resolve

P with ¬P to eliminate P, producing the empty clause (□).

Applications of the Resolution Principle

A basic idea that is used extensively in many computer science and artificial intelligence fields is the resolution principle. It supports algorithms that verify logical proofs, making automated theorem proving one of its primary uses. Resolution is used by systems such as Prolog to infer conclusions from a collection of facts and logical rules. Resolution is essential to knowledge representation and reasoning because it allows AI systems to draw conclusions from data. Based on a predetermined set of rules and observed symptoms, expert systems use resolution to help draw conclusions about medical diagnoses or identify equipment faults. Beyond these domains, the resolution principle is also essential to natural language processing (NLP), as it guarantees logical consistency in sentence interpretation and validates semantic relationships. Additionally, it is employed in problem-solving activities like planning and diagnostics, where AI systems have to analyze intricate situations in order to pinpoint root causes and viable fixes. Resolution is an essential tool for tasks requiring high precision and systematic reasoning because of its methodical and logical approach. Its value in producing accurate, trustworthy results is evident whether it is used in language processing or expert systems.

Advantages of the Resolution Principle

The resolution principle is a fundamental component of logic-based AI systems because it provides a number of benefits. Its soundness ensures that no erroneous conclusions are drawn during the reasoning process and that any conclusion drawn using the principle is logically valid. In addition, its completeness property guarantees that all logically implied conclusions can be drawn, offering a thorough approach to inference. The resolution principle is a solid and dependable tool for AI reasoning because of its completeness and soundness. The resolution principle's methodical approach, which provides a precise and organized framework for drawing conclusions, is another important benefit. It streamlines the reasoning process and makes it easier for AI systems to be automated by decomposing difficult logical problems into smaller, more manageable steps. Furthermore, its wide range of applications in different fields, such as diagnostics and theorem proving, shows its adaptability and efficiency in a variety of AI tasks. The resolution principle is a vital tool in the creation of intelligent systems because of its capacity to offer efficiency and clarity.

Limitations of the Resolution Principle

The resolution principle has significant drawbacks that can reduce its usefulness in some situations, despite its advantages. Among its main disadvantages is the computational complexity. With a large knowledge base, the process can become exponentially more resource-intensive as the number of clauses and potential resolutions increases. This makes it difficult to solve big, complicated problems where processing speed and power are essential. A further layer of complexity is added by the necessity of converting logical statements into clausal form, which could make the problem bigger and more challenging. This conversion may significantly decrease efficiency if the clausal form becomes unduly complex. The assumption of deterministic and comprehensive knowledge in the principle is another important drawback. In practical applications, where uncertainty and incomplete information are frequently present, this assumption presents challenges. In these circumstances, depending on a comprehensive and deterministic set of facts may restrict the resolution principle's applicability and render it less suitable for dynamic, uncertain contexts. Therefore, in order for the resolution principle to be more widely applicable in real-world situations, these limitations must be addressed, even though it is a strong tool in logic and reasoning.

Concept of Unification

As a method for making two logical expressions identical, unification is a fundamental idea in automated reasoning and first-order predicate logic. This procedure entails identifying a variable substitution that converts the expressions' content and structure into an equivalent form. By facilitating the matching of logical expressions and bolstering inference, it is essential to reasoning systems like Prolog and theorem provers. By identifying substitutions that can make terms identical, unification enables comparisons of terms, whether they are constants, variables, functions, or combinations. Take the terms Loves (x, Mary) and Loves (John, y) as examples. Both terms can become identical by being transformed into Loves (John, Mary) by a unifier such as x=John, y=Mary. In predicate logic, this unification property is essential, especially when using inference rules like resolution and Modus Ponens. These systems can come to conclusions and infer new information by uniting, which enables automated reasoning processes to proceed logically.

Components of Unification

The idea of the unifier, which stands for the set of substitutions necessary to make two terms identical, is at the heart of the unification process. A substitution is a process that swaps out variables within a term for other terms, which may be other variables or constants. For instance, the substitution {x/John} creates a match between the two terms by substituting the constant John for the variable x. If only the most necessary substitutions are made, a unifier is said to be most general since as many variables as possible are kept constant while maintaining their generality. This indicates that the unifier permits the widest possible matching between the terms involved by avoiding needless specific substitutions. Essentially, a most general unifier preserves the flexibility of the terms by allowing them to be unified with the least amount of structural modification. For instance, {x/y} is the most general unifier (MGU) for P(x) and P(y).

Recursively, unification divides complicated expressions into smaller parts until each matching part is found. This process keeps going until all of the expressions' components can be paired according to particular guidelines. To ensure that there is no ambiguity in the matching process, constants must have exactly the same value. A greater variety of potential unifications are made possible by variables, which are more adaptable and can be replaced with any term. In order for functions to be unified, they must share the same name and arity, which means they must have an equal number of arguments. By doing this, the structure of the unified functions is guaranteed to be consistent. As the procedure goes on, every component of the expression is closely scrutinized to make sure that variables and constants are correctly aligned and that functions satisfy the requirements for unification. This recursive approach ensures that the two expressions are as fully unified as possible.

How Unification Works?

The unification algorithm determines whether two terms are identical by methodically comparing their constituent parts. The process ends if it is determined that the terms are identical because they are already unified. When two terms are exactly the same, this step guarantees that no additional steps are needed to unify them because they are regarded as equivalent. On the other hand, the unification algorithm replaces the variable with the term if one of the terms is a variable and the other is a different term. Since the variable takes the value of the other term, this substitution makes it possible for the terms to be unified. Iterating through these steps allows the algorithm to produce a unified form in Figure 3.3, where the terms' constituent parts are equivalent and consistent.

The process of identifying a replacement that renders two terms identical is known as unification. For instance, the substitution {x/Loves (John, Mary)} unify *x* and Loves (John, Mary), where *x* is swapped out for the phrase Loves (John, Mary). Recursively comparing the names and arguments of both terms to see if they can be unified is how unification works when both terms are functions. Unification fails when the terms are incompatible, such as when Loves(x,Mary) and Hates(x,Mary) are used interchangeably. Additionally, occurrence constraints are incorporated into unification to stop invalid substitutions. This prevents infinite regress by preventing a variable from being replaced with a term that contains itself. Since replacing *x* with Loves(x,Mary) would result in an endless loop where *x* appears inside its own substitution, for example, *x* and Loves(x,Mary) cannot unify. By preventing circular substitutions, these occurrence constraints guarantee that unification is still valid.

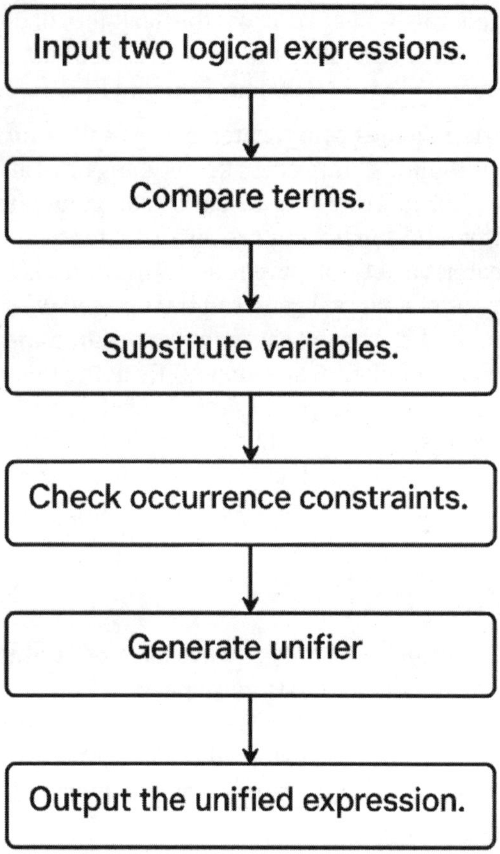

Figure 3.3: Representing the workflow of Unification in logic.

Applications of Unification

In many areas of artificial intelligence, unification is essential because it allows systems to recognize patterns and draw conclusions. Unification is a technique used in logic programming languages such as Prolog to link objectives with knowledge base rules. For example, the unifier {x/John, y/Mary} can be used to match a query like Loves (John, Mary) with a rule like Loves (x, y). This procedure is a crucial part of intelligent reasoning since it enables the system to deduce new information or confirm the accuracy of a query. Unification is essential to the resolution principle in theorem proving because it helps find complementary literals and settle disputes between them. For instance, the unifier {x/John, y/Mary} is necessary to resolve the expressions Loves (x, Mary) and ¬Loves (John, y), allowing for logical consistency in the proof. Additionally, unification is frequently used in natural language processing (NLP), especially for tasks like semantic interpretation, where language comprehension and reasoning depend on matching linguistic structures.

Advantages and Limitations

By allowing machines to match and combine terms based on structural similarities, unification provides a methodical and effective way to reason in logical systems. It is a fundamental component of inference mechanisms in artificial intelligence because of its capacity to generalize and identify similarities among terms. Logic programming, automated reasoning, and natural language processing all depend on AI systems' ability to use unification to extract new information, find connections, and draw conclusions from preexisting data. The ability of unification to reduce intricate logical relationships to manageable issues is what gives it its power. Nevertheless, there are drawbacks to unification that need to be considered in practical applications. For example, it makes the assumption that knowledge is deterministic and complete, which might not accurately represent the ambiguity and incompleteness of data in dynamic environments. Furthermore, scalability issues arise because unification can become computationally costly when working with complicated terms or large knowledge bases. Notwithstanding these problems, unification is still a vital component of artificial intelligence (AI), driving the creation of intelligent systems that can comprehend and communicate with the outside world through reasoning, pattern matching, and inference processes.

Introduction to Semantic Nets

In artificial intelligence (AI), Semantic Nets, also known as Semantic Networks, are a potent graphical representation method used to model the relationships between different objects, concepts, and ideas. With this approach, knowledge is arranged as a network of connected nodes and edges, where nodes stand for things or ideas and edges indicate the connections between them. Semantic nets provide a flexible and intuitive method of encoding and navigating knowledge by organizing information in this manner, which makes them especially helpful for reasoning and inference in AI applications. They are widely used to support complex understanding and decision-making in domains such as expert systems, cognitive modeling, and natural language processing (NLP).

The use of labeled edges to specify various relationship types, such as "is-a" (indicating hierarchical classification) or "has-part" (indicating composition), is a fundamental characteristic of semantic nets. A semantic network could, for instance, show that a "dog" is a "mammal" and that it "has-part" a "tail." The organization of knowledge made possible by this compositional and hierarchical structure makes it easier to comprehend and work with complex relationships.

Semantic nets' adaptability in simulating intricate relationships makes them a crucial AI tool, especially for applications requiring logical reasoning and structured knowledge.

Structure of Semantic Nets

Semantic nets are structured as directed graphs with nodes and edges:

- Nodes: Represent entities, concepts, or objects.
- Example: "Dog," "Animal," or "Tail."
- Edges: Represent relationships between nodes.
- Example: "is-a" for hierarchical relationships, or "has-part" for compositional ones.

A graph's nodes and edges can both have attributes applied to them to encode extra layers of data, like conditions, weights, or probabilities. For instance, in a semantic network, the edge with the label "can-do," which denotes a functional relationship, can be used to represent the relationship between "Dog" and "Bark." The overall representation of knowledge is enhanced by the addition of attributes, which give the connections within the graph additional context and depth. Furthermore, transitive relationships facilitate logical deductions by improving reasoning across several edges. Transitivity, for example, allows one to deduce that a "Dog" is a "Animal" if it is known that a "Dog" is a "Mammal" and a "Mammal" is categorized as a "Animal." The graph's transitive properties allow it to facilitate sophisticated reasoning and assist in drawing conclusions that may not be stated explicitly in the network itself."

Advantages and Applications

Semantic networks have many important benefits, especially in terms of their structure, which is easy to understand and visually appealing. Because of this, they are a great tool for both humans and machines to comprehend complex data. They offer a framework that is easy to understand and interpret by depicting knowledge as interconnected nodes that are connected by relationships. For applications where clarity and interpretability are crucial, this simplicity encourages a more user-friendly approach to data representation. Furthermore, the functionality of semantic nets is improved by their graph-based structure, which makes effective traversal algorithms possible. These algorithms make the networks extremely dynamic and flexible by enabling the inference of new relationships and the validation of preexisting ones. As new connections are found or verified, this feature guarantees that semantic nets are not only effective at storing and organizing knowledge but also at growing and improving that knowledge.

For example,

If:

$$A \xrightarrow{\text{is-a}} B$$

and:

$$B \xrightarrow{\text{is-a}} C$$

then the system can infer:

$$A \xrightarrow{\text{is-a}} C$$

This makes semantic nets ideal for reasoning tasks.

Applications of semantic nets span various AI fields:

- **Natural Language Processing (NLP):** Utilized to capture the meanings of words and their interrelationships for tasks like text comprehension and machine translation.
- **Expert Systems:** Act as the core of knowledge bases in areas such as medical diagnosis and technical troubleshooting.
- **Ontology Modeling:** Semantic networks play a crucial role in constructing ontologies to formalize relationships within particular domains.
- **Cognitive Science:** Simulate human memory and associative thinking by modeling how concepts are interconnected in the brain.

Challenges and Limitations

Semantic nets have many advantages, but as their size and complexity grow, they also present a number of difficulties. Managing and computing relationships within a network becomes more challenging as it grows, which frequently results in scalability problems. To solve this problem and keep the network operating efficiently, sophisticated algorithms must be used. Semantic nets also have trouble handling ambiguity and uncertainty, which are prevalent in knowledge from the real world. Weighted semantic nets and probabilistic models are examples of extensions that have been created to overcome these restrictions and provide greater accuracy and flexibility. The ability of semantic nets to handle the dynamic nature of knowledge presents another important challenge. It can be difficult to update semantic nets as new information becomes available, and it may be necessary to completely restructure the network. Semantic nets remain a fundamental approach in AI in spite of these challenges, especially when combined with other methods. These complementary techniques can improve semantic nets' performance, increasing their resilience and adaptability to a greater variety of applications.

Example 3.2: Table: Semantic Net Representation

Node	Relationship	Target Node	Meaning
Dog	is-a	Mammal	A dog is a mammal.
Mammal	is-a	Animal	A mammal is an animal.
Dog	has-part	Tail	A dog has a tail.
Dog	can-do	Bark	A dog can bark.
Animal	needs	Food	Animals need food.

This Table 3.2 illustrates a simple semantic net with nodes (e.g., "Dog," "Mammal") and edges (e.g., "is-a," "has-part") that define relationships between concepts.

Conceptual Dependencies

Roger Schank developed the Conceptual Dependencies (CD) framework in the 1970s to represent the meaning of sentences in natural language. Developing a language-independent framework for comprehending and analyzing actions, events, and their connections is the main goal of CDs. CDs highlight a sentence's underlying semantics, which capture the essence of actions, participants, and their roles, rather than its syntactic form. This makes it possible to understand and infer natural language effectively, especially in AI applications. CDs can help with more accurate interpretation across languages by emphasizing the meaning rather than the language used. The CD approach consistently represents the meaning of sentences using a set of primitive actions and predefined relationships. Sentences with different syntactic structures but similar meanings can be represented similarly thanks to this framework. As an illustration of how the CD model abstracts away from surface-level syntax to concentrate on the statement's core meaning, the sentences "John gave Mary a book" and "Mary received a book from John" would have the same conceptual dependency representation. Because of their consistency, CDs can capture intricate relationships in a way that is independent of the language being used, making them an effective tool for natural language processing.

Components of Conceptual Dependencies

- **Primitive Actions:** CDs lay out a series of fundamental steps that form the cornerstone of every event. Actions like possession transfer (ATRANS), physical movement (PTRANS), information transfer (MTRANS), and energy transfer (INGEST) are examples of these primitives. Every action reflects a fundamental kind of change or activity.
- **Conceptual Roles:** There are distinct roles associated with each action, including the actor, object, recipient, and instrument. In "John gave a book to Mary," for example, "John" is the actor, "book" is the object, and "Mary" is the recipient.

- **Dependencies:** To demonstrate the connections between actions and their participants, CDs create links between these elements. By indicating causality, purpose, or temporal relationships, these dependencies enable the system to make sense of the order and logic of events.
- **Focus on Meaning:** AI systems can focus on a sentence's essential semantics by using CDs to abstract from surface syntax. By focusing on the essential meaning rather than the exact wording used, this promotes better reasoning.

Representation Format

Conceptual dependencies are represented using a graphical or tabular format. Each event or action is represented as a structure with labeled links connecting the components. For example:

Sentence: "John gave Mary a book."

CD Representation:

Action:

ATRANS (transfer of possession)

Actor: John

Object: Book

Recipient: Mary

In a graph, this might look like:

ATRANS as the central node.

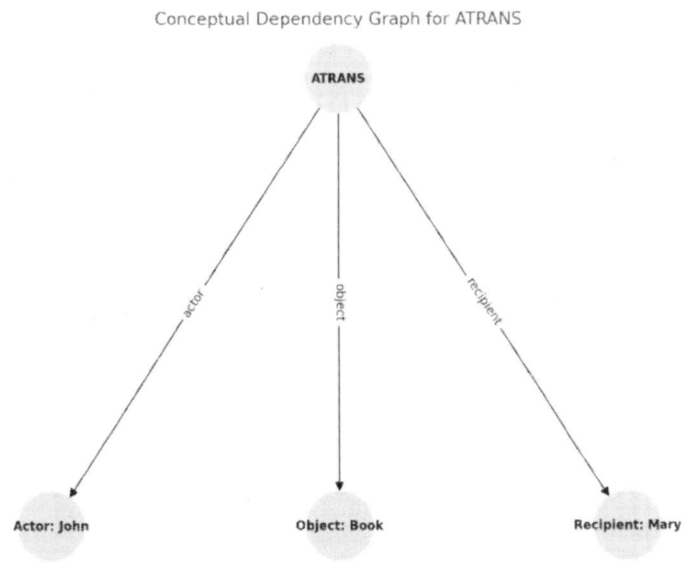

Figure 3.4: Represent the conceptual dependency graph for ATRANS.

Arrows labeled "actor," "object," and "recipient" pointing to their respective entities in Figure 3.4.The structured format ensures that even complex sentences can be broken down into manageable, machine-readable components for reasoning.

Advantages of Conceptual Dependencies

Language Independence and Inference Facilitation

AI systems can process and comprehend input from different languages consistently thanks to Conceptual Dependencies (CDs), which allow for a language-independent representation of knowledge. Translation and smooth multilingual interactions are supported by this abstraction. CDs help systems infer implicit information by explicitly modeling the relationships between activities and their participants. A system using CDs, for instance, can deduce that "John no longer has the book" from the sentence "John gave Mary a book," exhibiting the ability to reason beyond surface-level information.

Consistency and Expressiveness

Regardless of syntactic variances, CDs offer a consistent framework for representing sentences with related meanings. Because structurally distinct sentences like "John gave Mary a book" and "Mary received a book from John" are encoded identically, this uniformity improves reasoning and makes information retrieval easier. Additionally, CDs are very expressive, encapsulating intricate concepts like intention, causality, and temporal order. CDs are an essential tool for sophisticated reasoning and thorough language understanding because of their richness, which enables AI systems to comprehend complex event contexts and interdependencies.

Applications of Conceptual Dependencies

Natural Language Understanding and Story Comprehension

Conceptual Dependencies (CDs) are essential for improving the functionality of systems such as conversational AI and virtual assistants. CDs help these systems better understand user inputs and provide contextually relevant responses by concentrating on the semantics of language rather than its surface structure. In story comprehension, where CDs assist in breaking down narratives into a web of relationships and events, this deep representation is particularly effective. Thus, while preserving narrative coherence and meaning, AI can better comprehend a story's flow, deduce hidden details, and even perform creative tasks like text summarization and automated storytelling.

Knowledge-Based Systems and Robotics

In expert systems, where they organize knowledge into rules and causal relationships for sound decision-making, CDs also function as a fundamental tool.

For example, CDs can model symptoms and their associations with particular diseases, allowing for precise reasoning in a medical diagnosis system. Similar to this, CDs in robotics and AI planning direct systems to carry out action sequences by simulating intent and causality. This enables robots to maneuver through changing environments and modify their actions to accomplish predetermined objectives. Essentially, CDs are essential in fields that demand a thorough comprehension and implementation of intricate, real-world procedures.

Frames & Scripts

Artificial intelligence (AI) uses structured knowledge representation techniques called frames and scripts to intuitively arrange and reason about data. By assembling related facts and characteristics into a data structure akin to an object or class, frames serve as a representation of static knowledge. Slots (attributes) and fillers (values) are found in every frame, making it simple for AI systems to access and modify information about entities like people, places, or objects. This structure is effective for classifying and storing complex data because it supports inheritance and default reasoning. On the other hand, dynamic knowledge—specifically, event sequences or common scenarios—is represented by scripts. They record the contextual and temporal flow of events, like what usually occurs during a lecture or meal at a restaurant. AI systems can anticipate actions, fill in the blanks, and react appropriately in situations they are familiar with by using scripts. When combined, frames and scripts give AI a potent way to mimic human comprehension and engagement with its environment.

Frames

Marvin Minsky created frames, which are an organized method of expressing static knowledge about different ideas, things, or circumstances. A frame is essentially a data structure composed of fillers and slots, where the fillers contain specific values for the attributes and the slots represent the attributes. An example of this would be a "Car" frame with slots for "Make," "Model," "Color," and "Owner," and fillers for "Toyota," "Corolla," "Red," and "John." This structure facilitates the clear and consistent organization of information, which facilitates processing and retrieval. Additionally, frames facilitate inheritance, enabling more specialized frames to inherit characteristics from broader ones. For example, a "Sports Car" frame can add special features like "Top Speed" while retaining the common characteristics of the "Car" frame. This hierarchical structure improves reasoning efficiency and eliminates redundancy. Sentence summary: Frames improve clarity and inheritance in complex systems by enabling the representation of knowledge through structured data. Their use is particularly beneficial in domains where layered, well-organized information is essential, such as expert systems, object recognition, and natural language understanding.

Scripts

Roger Schank first proposed the idea of scripts, which are dynamic knowledge structures that capture common patterns of behavior or events in particular situations. Scripts concentrate on the causal and temporal flow of events, as opposed to frames, which deal with static descriptions and attributes of objects or concepts. The "Restaurant Script," which describes the typical steps in a dining experience, including entering the restaurant, placing an order, eating, and paying the bill, is a well-known example. These scenes serve to demonstrate how scripts arrange information according to actions and their usual sequence. Entry conditions (what must occur before the script starts), roles (participants like a customer or waiter), scenes (sub-events like ordering or eating), props (items like menus or plates), and results (the anticipated outcome, like being full or having paid) are all crucial parts of every script. Scripts enable AI systems to make reasonable assumptions, fill in the gaps, and react appropriately in real-world scenarios by simulating these structured, predictable interactions. Particularly in service-based settings, this phrase-based understanding of events aids machines in deciphering intricate, dynamic human behaviors.

Comparison of Frames and Scripts

Although they are both effective tools for representing knowledge, frames and scripts have different uses in artificial intelligence. Because frames organize information into structured attribute-value pairs, they are perfect for representing static knowledge about entities, objects, or concepts. This approach facilitates the capture of an object's intricate relationships and characteristics. Slots like "Location," "Menu," "Opening Hours," and "Seating Capacity," for instance, might be included in a frame for a "Restaurant" and would each contain pertinent information. However, scripts are more appropriate for depicting dynamic, event-driven situations, particularly those that develop in a predetermined order over time. Scripts allow systems to comprehend and anticipate behaviors in context by capturing the normal flow of events or actions that take place during routine activities. For example, a "Dining at a Restaurant" script would cover actions like going inside, finding a seat, placing an order, eating, paying the bill, and departing. Therefore, in Table 3.3, frames depict what things are, and scripts depict what occurs.

Table 3.3: Frames vs. Scripts.

Aspect	Frame (Static Structure)	Script (Dynamic Sequence)
Definition	A data structure that represents a stereotyped situation with slots for specific values.	A sequence of expected events in a specific context or situation.
Focus	Describes the **objects** and their **properties**.	Describes the **sequence of actions** or **events**.

Example Context	Restaurant	Going to a restaurant
Structure	Frame: Restaurant	Script: Eating at a restaurant
Used For	Understanding **settings**, filling in missing details.	Understanding **sequences** of behavior and predicting next steps.

Production Rules

In artificial intelligence (AI), production rules are a popular knowledge representation method for encoding decision-making procedures. Usually written in the format IF (Condition) THEN (Action), these rules enable systems to react dynamically in response to particular inputs. In rule-based and expert systems, where domain knowledge must be represented in an understandable way, this methodical approach works particularly well. The action, also known as the consequent, explains what the system should do in the event that the conditions, also known as the antecedent, are met. By combining several conditions with operators like AND, OR, and NOT, this representation facilitates logical reasoning and makes it possible to create intricate rules. An example of a rule that could be used by a temperature control system is "IF the temperature is below 20°C, THEN turn on the heater." Systems can effectively manage complex decision-making tasks by chaining such rules. Therefore, in AI applications, production rules provide a potent means of simulating human-like reasoning.

How Production Rules Work?

A cycle of matching, resolving conflicts, and execution drives the operation of production rules. The system compares rule conditions to the current data or state during the matching phase to determine which rules apply. A conflict resolution technique based on factors like priority or recency decides which rule to fire when several rules match. The next step is the execution phase, during which the action of the chosen rule is carried out, potentially altering the state of the system or generating an output. Until no relevant rules are left or a desired outcome is achieved, this cycle is repeated, allowing the system to dynamically adjust to changing inputs. Forward chaining and backward chaining are the two main methods of reasoning when applying production rules. When diagnosing diseases based on patient symptoms, for example, forward chaining begins with the facts that are currently available and applies rules to arrive at new conclusions. On the other hand, backward chaining starts with a specific objective and works backward to confirm that the requirements to reach that objective are fulfilled, such as determining loan eligibility by examining credit score, income, and other factors. Depending on the direction of problem-solving, these techniques enable rule-based systems to reason efficiently.

Production rules work:

1. Start: Begin the cycle.
2. Match Conditions: Evaluate the conditions of rules against the current system state.
3. Conflict Resolution: If multiple rules are applicable, select one to apply.
4. Execute Action: Perform the action specified by the selected rule.
5. Update System State: Modify the system's state based on the action.
6. More Rules to Apply? Check if additional rules are applicable.
   - If yes, loop back to match conditions.
   - If no, end the process.

Applications of Production Rules

Production rules are widely used in many different fields because of their modularity and flexibility. Expert systems are used to support tasks like legal decision-making, engineering troubleshooting, and medical diagnosis by encoding domain-specific knowledge. Production rules, for example, were used by the MYCIN expert system to detect bacterial infections and recommend remedies based on lab results and observed symptoms. Production rules in industrial process control define precise reactions to operational or environmental conditions, such as opening a valve when pressure reaches a safe threshold. This automates processes. They play an equally important role in AI games and decision support systems. To improve the decision-making process in banking, production rules evaluate consumer data to determine loan eligibility or credit approvals. Likewise, in game development, they control the actions of NPCs, allowing them to behave in a clever manner. With a straightforward rule like "IF the player is within attack range, THEN attack," for instance, the NPCs can respond to the player's actions in a dynamic way. This rule-based logic guarantees context-aware and adaptive behavior in a range of systems.

Advantages of Production Rules

The modularity of production rules is one of their primary benefits. Since each rule functions as an independent unit, adding, changing, or removing them is simple and won't interfere with the system as a whole. Rule-based systems are more scalable and maintainable due to their modular design. The transparency of production rules is another noteworthy advantage; even non-programmers can understand them thanks to their simple IF-THEN format, which allows domain experts to directly contribute to the rule base. This clarity facilitates teamwork and expedites the creation of intelligent systems. Furthermore, there is a great deal of flexibility in production rules. They are useful for both basic decisions and more complex reasoning tasks because they can express complex logic by combining multiple conditions using logical operators. Because of their adaptability, production rules can be used in a variety of contexts, including expert systems and business process automation. Furthermore, by reducing the need for human intervention in routine, rule-driven situations, their capacity to automate decisions enhances operational efficiency and consistency.

Programming in Logic (PROLOG)

Programming in Logic, or PROLOG, is a declarative programming language intended for symbolic computation and logic-based reasoning. Developed by Alain Colmerauer and his colleagues in the early 1970s, it differs from procedural languages such as Python or C++ in that it emphasizes the what rather than the how. In domains like expert systems, computational linguistics, natural language processing, and artificial intelligence, PROLOG is particularly well-known. Instead of giving the system explicit instructions, it focuses on defining relationships and facts so that it can deduce solutions logically. PROLOG programs are organized using facts, rules, and queries and are based on predicate logic and resolution. Rules create logical connections between facts, facts convey established truths, and queries allow users to pose queries that the system responds to with its own logic. Because of its design, PROLOG is especially well-suited for applications requiring sophisticated reasoning skills. Because of this, it performs exceptionally well in fields where reasoning and inference are essential, such as knowledge representation, automated theorem proving, and expert system development.

Concepts in PROLOG

Facts:

- Facts are basic assertions about the world that are assumed to be true.
- Example: parent (john, mary). means "John is the parent of Mary."

Rules:

- Rules define logical relationships between facts. They consist of a head (conclusion) and a body (conditions).
- Example: grandparent (X, Y): -parent (X, Z), parent (Z, Y). means "X is a grandparent of Y if X is a parent of Z and Z is a parent of Y."

Queries:

- Queries are questions posed to the PROLOG interpreter to retrieve information or verify truths.

Example: -grandparent (john, X). asks, "Who is John a grandparent of?"

Backtracking:

- When responding to queries, PROLOG employs backtracking to examine several options. This method is ideal for issues requiring pattern recognition and logical reasoning because it enables the system to explore various avenues in its quest for an answer. Methodical investigation is essential. One solution at a time is checked by PROLOG, which automatically returns and tries an alternate path if it runs into a dead end. Because of this, PROLOG can handle complex queries with multiple valid answers. It methodically looks through every possible answer until the question is answered or every possibility has been considered. The system returns to a previous choice point and carries on searching if the initial attempt is unsuccessful. PROLOG is a dependable tool for logic programming because of this procedure, which guarantees that every potential solution is taken into account. When necessary, it can find all potential answers by thoroughly examining the possibilities, not just the first one.

How PROLOG Works?

A PROLOG program's execution entails a methodical backtracking, inference, and matching process. The PROLOG interpreter attempts to match a query with the rules and facts that are kept in its knowledge base. Here, pattern matching is crucial, with the interpreter searching for clauses that support the query. If a match is discovered, the program can logically infer answers by applying logical inference to draw conclusions from the available rules. However, PROLOG starts going back to look at other options if the first route doesn't lead to a solution. This entails going over earlier decision points again, removing earlier variable bindings, and choosing new facts or rules. The interpreter keeps doing this until it finds a workable answer or runs out of options and comes to the conclusion that there isn't one. The foundation of PROLOG's problem-solving power is defined by this dynamic interaction of matching, inference, and backtracking.

For example, consider the knowledge base:

parent (john, mary).

parent (mary, tom).

grandparent (X, Y):-parent (X, Z), parent (Z, Y).

Querying? -grandparent (john, tom). causes PROLOG to:

- Match the grandparent relationship (john, tom) to the rule grandparent (X, Y): - parent (X, Z), parent (Z, Y).
- Substitute john for X and identify Z such that parent (john, Z) holds true.
- Determine that Z = mary and verify if parent (mary, tom) is true.
- Confirm the query and return the result.

Applications of PROLOG

PROLOG's ability to reason logically and perform effective symbolic computation makes it popular in many different fields. Medical diagnosis systems like MYCIN, which evaluate symptoms and recommend treatments, are examples of expert systems that use it to encode domain-specific knowledge and provide reasoning capabilities. PROLOG is used in Natural Language Processing (NLP) for sentence parsing and interpretation, grammar analysis, and response generation. For instance, PROLOG can parse complex sentence structures by encoding grammar rules. With its ability to model intricate relationships and carry out logical inference, PROLOG is also essential for knowledge representation, as seen in domain ontologies and family trees. It demonstrates its significance in formal logic by automating mathematical proofs through the use of logical inference techniques in theorem proving. Additionally, PROLOG assists in robotics by helping to plan action sequences according to particular objectives and limitations, allowing robots to adapt and complete tasks effectively (Figure 3.5).

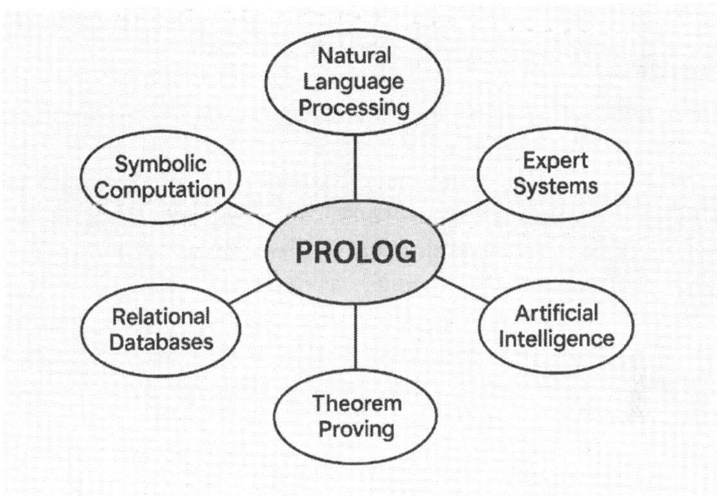

Figure 3.5: Application of PROLOG.

Advantages of PROLOG

PROLOG is a strong tool for AI applications because of its many benefits. Its declarative nature, which enables developers to outline what must be done without getting into the specifics of how it should be done, is one of its main advantages. This streamlines the development process, particularly for tasks that require rules and logic. Furthermore, PROLOG has logical reasoning built in, which allows systems to make decisions and draw conclusions with little extra code. Clear knowledge representation is supported by its syntax and structure, which is especially useful in knowledge-based applications and expert systems. PROLOG's high expressiveness, which makes it ideal for problems involving relationships, constraints, and symbolic computation, is another important strength. It performs exceptionally well in fields where these features are essential, like planning, theorem proving, and natural language processing. Its backtracking mechanism, which automatically investigates several routes to find every potential solution, is a noteworthy feature. This improves the robustness of problem-solving and guarantees the completeness of the solution. When combined, these characteristics make PROLOG the ideal option for creating intelligent systems that need knowledge manipulation and reasoning.

Conclusion

A variety of methods and frameworks for artificial intelligence knowledge representation and reasoning are examined in Chapter 3. First-order predicate logic and propositional logic are the foundational frameworks for expressing and inferring facts and relationships. The Resolution Principle and Unification are discussed in the chapter as crucial logical inference mechanisms. Additionally, it examines Frames and Scripts, Conceptual Dependencies, and Semantic Nets as organized methods for simulating events, relationships, and stereotypical scenarios. We present Production Rules, a flexible approach to encoding decision-making procedures. An introduction to PROLOG, a declarative programming language that employs logical reasoning for applications like automated theorem proving, expert systems, and natural language processing, wraps up the chapter. When combined, these ideas offer a complete set of tools for AI reasoning and knowledge representation. The following chapter compares formal and natural languages using grammar, concentrating on the elements and procedures of natural language communication. The Chomsky hierarchy, parsing strategies, semantics, advanced grammar frameworks (such as context-free and transformational grammars), and recursive and augmented transition networks are among the important subjects it covers.

Exercise:

- Represent the following sentences in propositional logic:

  a) "If it rains, the ground will be wet."

  b) "Either John is at home or he is at the office."

- Express the following statements in First-Order Predicate Logic:

  a) "All humans are mortal."

  b) "There exists a person who owns a car."

- Create a semantic net to represent the following relationships:

  a) A dog is a mammal.

  b) A dog has a tail and can bark.

- Represent the sentence "John gave Mary a book" using Conceptual Dependencies, including action, actor, object, and recipient.

- Design a frame to represent a "Car" with attributes like make, model, color, and owner.
- Develop a script for a "Grocery Shopping" scenario, including actions like entering the store, selecting items, and paying.
- Write production rules for a traffic light system:

  a) Green light -> Allow cars to move.

  b) Red light -> Stop cars.
- Write a simple PROLOG knowledge base for the following facts:

  a) John is Mary's parent.

  b) Mary is Tom's parent.
- Add a rule to define a grandparent relationship and query the system to find Tom's grandparent.
- Discuss the advantages and limitations of using frames versus scripts in AI systems. Provide examples where each would be most appropriate.

CHAPTER-4
UNDERSTANDING NATURAL LANGUAGES

Introduction & Objective

The foundations of comprehending natural languages are examined in this chapter, with an emphasis on the key elements and crucial processes of human communication. It starts by outlining the differences between formal and natural languages, providing information on how the rigid structure of formal systems is very different from natural language's ambiguity and complexity. The Chomsky hierarchy is presented as a fundamental framework for categorizing the various kinds of grammars utilized in language processing as the conversation shifts to grammar structures. The chapter also explores a number of parsing strategies that help with sentence structure analysis and meaning extraction from language input. It also discusses how semantics plays a part in determining meaning and context, highlighting how crucial precise language comprehension is. The discussion of advanced grammar frameworks demonstrates how they improve the processing and comprehension of increasingly intricate linguistic patterns. The chapter provides a thorough summary of the theoretical and applied facets of natural language comprehension overall.With an emphasis on the fundamental principles that allow machines to comprehend human language, this chapter aims to give readers a thorough understanding of natural language processing (NLP). It starts with a summary of grammar, showing the formation and analysis of language structures. Important parsing techniques are presented to show how sentences can be divided into meaningful parts that serve as the foundation for additional language interpretation. The chapter also explores semantic analysis, emphasizing the ways in which meaning is extracted from text that goes beyond its syntactic form. Important NLP frameworks are presented to readers, including transition networks and context-free grammars, which are essential to many AI applications. The chapter attempts to provide readers with the fundamental knowledge and tools necessary for creating intelligent systems that can efficiently process and comprehend natural language by examining these models.

Components and Steps of Communication

The foundation of any interaction, whether it be between people or between people and machines, is communication. Information is sent, received, and interpreted in a methodical manner to foster understanding between parties. Important elements that must work together in this process include the sender, message, medium, receiver, and feedback. The message follows a predetermined route, phrase by phrase, depending on precision, context, and clarity to retain its intended meaning. In domains such as artificial intelligence (AI), where the objective is to replicate human-like communication, comprehension of these components is essential. AI systems need to understand both the linguistic structure and the subtleties that affect interpretation. Every stage, from properly encoding the message to correctly decoding it, is essential for meaningful interaction. This chapter establishes the groundwork for creating intelligent systems that can have productive and organic conversations by looking at the mechanics of communication in Table 4.1.

Table 4.1: Components and Steps of Communication.

Component	Description
Sender (Source)	The person or entity who initiates the message.
Message	The content or information that the sender wants to convey.
Encoding	The process of converting the message into symbols, words, or gestures.
Channel (Medium)	The medium through which the message is transmitted (e.g., speech, writing).
Receiver	The person or audience who receives the message.
Decoding	The process by which the receiver interprets or makes sense of the message.
Feedback	The response from the receiver back to the sender, indicating understanding.
Noise (Interference)	Any barrier or distraction that distorts the message or its interpretation.

Core Components of Communication

A number of essential elements drive the communication process and cooperate to guarantee efficient information sharing. By creating and encoding the message—converting ideas or thoughts into forms that can be communicated, such as spoken words, written text, or digital signals—the sender starts the process. The encoding process makes sure that the data is formatted for transmission, while the message conveys the main idea. The route that the encoded message takes to get to its destination is known as the medium or channel, and examples include phone calls, emails, and chatbot interfaces. The recipient decodes and interprets the message after receiving it, using the shared context to determine the intended meaning. A critical step is decoding, which entails converting the received symbols back into understandable ideas. The communication loop is then completed by feedback, which enables the recipient to reply with a confirmation of understanding or a request for clarification. For example, in AI systems, this feedback could be a user query, a follow-up question, or a system-generated response, showing that communication is an interactive process rather than a one-way one.

Steps in the Communication Process

Idea formulation is the first step in the communication process, where the sender chooses the goal and subject matter of the message. The next important step is message encoding, which transforms the abstract concept into a form that can be communicated, like text or speech. A virtual assistant that converts weather information into a spoken response is a real-world example of this. After being encoded, the message moves on to the transmission phase, where it is delivered to the recipient via a chosen channel, such as audio, text, or visual media. The next step is message reception, in which the recipient interprets the information sent, like when a user reads a chatbot's response. The receiver then moves on to the decoding phase, where they decipher the message and determine its intended meaning. Feedback is the last phase of the communication cycle, during which the recipient answers questions about whether or not they understood the message. In both human and machine communication, this step is critical to mutual understanding and allows for follow-up inquiries, clarifications, or confirmations to sustain productive interaction.

Challenges in Communication

Even though communication is structured, a number of obstacles may prevent information from being shared effectively. Noise, which is defined as any distortion or disturbance that modifies the intended message while it is being transmitted, is one such difficulty. In AI systems, this could show up as signal loss, data corruption, or input errors, all of which affect the precision and clarity of interpretation. In human communication, it might involve background noise or distractions. Another major obstacle is ambiguity, which occurs when a message has more than one meaning and can cause misunderstandings or confusion. In order to determine the correct meaning of ambiguous language, AI systems in particular frequently struggle and mainly rely on context, training data, or probabilistic models. Communication breakdowns can also be caused by medium limitations. For instance, text-based platforms may not be able to convey tone, intent, or emotion—all of which are critical for comprehending complex messages. These difficulties demonstrate how difficult it is to accomplish precise and significant communication between artificial and human systems.

Relevance to AI Systems

Designing AI systems like chatbots, virtual assistants, and automated translators requires a thorough understanding of the elements and processes of communication. To ensure that messages are successfully transferred between the user and the machine, these systems use communication models to mimic human-like interactions. For example, when responding to user inquiries, a virtual assistant such as Alexa acts as the sender, starting the communication cycle. In order to facilitate meaningful interactions, Natural Language Processing (NLP) algorithms are essential for controlling the encoding of user input and the decoding of system responses. The user interprets and responds to the assistant's output in this interaction, acting as the receiver. Feedback is a continuous communication loop that happens when the user adds more information or acts in response to the system's response. AI systems aim to achieve precision, clarity, and a smooth, organic flow in interaction by simulating human communication processes.

The contrast among Formal & Natural Languages in the Context of Grammar

In terms of grammar, the distinction between formal and natural languages draws attention to the essential variations in their composition, function, and application. Each domain has a different function for grammar, which is a set of rules that control how words, phrases, and sentences are put together. Grammar is rigorously defined in formal languages, like those used in programming or mathematics, with clear rules that guarantee accuracy and predictability. These languages are made for specialized purposes, with a focus on consistency and clarity to remove any possibility of misunderstanding. Natural languages, such as Mandarin or English, on the other hand, are more adaptable by nature and change over time. Their grammar is sophisticated yet flexible for regular human communication because it takes into account ambiguity, cultural context, and emotional expression. Natural language grammar, in contrast to formal languages, is influenced by usage and frequently permits exceptions and variations. This contrast highlights how natural languages strike a balance between meaning, subtlety, and spontaneity, whereas formal languages place a higher priority on structure and logic.

Ambiguity

The idea of ambiguity is one of the most obvious distinctions between formal and natural languages. Because of their inherent ambiguity, natural languages frequently contain words and sentences that can be interpreted in a variety of ways based on context, tone, and cultural background. Because it permits complex expression, metaphor, and figurative language, this ambiguity adds to the depth and richness of human communication. To illustrate the interpretative flexibility of natural language, the sentence "I saw her duck" could mean that you saw someone crouch or noticed their pet bird. Formal languages, on the other hand, are purposefully designed to remove ambiguity and guarantee that each statement has a distinct meaning. Because these languages follow rigorous syntactic and semantic rules, they are perfect for fields like programming, mathematics, and logic where accuracy and clarity are essential. Formal languages, in contrast to natural languages, do not allow for multiple interpretations, which helps to avoid misunderstandings and preserve consistency among various systems and users.

Flexibility

Another important area of difference between formal and natural languages is flexibility. Natural languages allow for a great deal of creativity in expression because they are dynamic and constantly changing. Grammar rules are often bent or broken by speakers in order to convey emphasis and emotion or to create stylistic effects. Slang, colloquial language, and changing cultural contexts are some examples of elements that contribute to the flexibility and diversity of natural languages. On the other hand, formal languages are inherently strict and governed by rules. In fields like computer programming, logic, and mathematics, accuracy and consistency are essential, and this rigorous structure guarantees both. Misunderstandings or serious mistakes may result from any departure from a formal language's established syntax or semantics. Therefore, in order to preserve functionality and dependability, formal languages place a higher priority on accuracy and clarity than natural languages, which flourish on flexibility and nuance.

Precision

Formal languages place a high value on accuracy and follow a clear set of grammatical rules that rarely allow for ambiguity. They are vital in fields like mathematics, computer science, and logic where precision and consistency are crucial because their structure is specifically designed to communicate precise instructions or information. Formal languages' rigidity guarantees that each expression has a single, clear meaning, removing the chance of misunderstandings. Natural languages, on the other hand, frequently sacrifice accuracy in favor of expressiveness and contextual depth. These languages thrive on adaptability, enabling speakers to use tone, implication, and shared cultural understanding to communicate abstract concepts, complex emotions, or unfinished thoughts. Natural languages, in contrast to formal languages, welcome ambiguity and derive their meaning from human intuition, experience, and context. The essential distinctions between the ways that each type of language functions in communication are highlighted by this harmony between structure and fluidity.

Evolution

The development of formal and natural languages reveals the essential distinctions in their flexibility and structure. Natural languages are dynamic and constantly changing as a result of social interactions, cultural changes, and technological breakthroughs. Older terms may become obsolete, meanings change, and new words are created. Additionally, grammatical structures change over time to accommodate speakers' shifting communication requirements in various contexts. Formal languages, on the other hand, are made to be constant and stable. Only deliberate revisions by authoritative bodies can alter their clearly defined rules and symbols. For logical operations, programming, and mathematical accuracy, formal languages must remain consistent across users and applications, which is ensured by this controlled evolution. Formal languages place more emphasis on predictability and clarity than natural languages do on fluidity.

Purpose and Audience

Each language type's ultimate goal emphasizes their essential distinctions even more. Human interaction is facilitated by natural languages, which enable people to communicate ideas, express feelings, and reflect their cultural identities. Their grammar is naturally adaptable and changes over time to meet the various needs and situations of speakers. Natural languages are rich, complex, and context-sensitive because of their dynamic nature. On the other hand, formal languages have a specific purpose, mostly in the fields of science and technology. They are perfect for human-machine communication because they guarantee accuracy and remove uncertainty. Formal languages prioritize consistency and clarity over expressive depth in their grammar, which is rigorously logical, rule-based, and universally interpretable. Because of these qualities, formal languages are useful instruments for mathematical reasoning, computation, and programming.

Introduction to Chomsky Hierarchy of Grammars

Noam Chomsky developed the fundamental framework known as the Chomsky Hierarchy in 1956 to categorize formal grammars according to their capacity for generative expression. It outlines the ways in which various grammars can generate languages, which are basically collections of strings created over a specific alphabet. Because it provides an organized method of comprehending the intricacy and strength of language-generating systems, this classification is essential to theoretical computer science and linguistics. Each of the four levels of the hierarchy—Type 0 (unrestricted), Type 1 (context-sensitive), Type 2 (context-free), and Type 3 (regular)—represents a reduction in generative power and an increase in grammatical rule restrictions. As one ascends the hierarchy, each level requires less processing power and incorporates the grammars and languages of the level beneath it. This tiered structure aids in illuminating how expressive power and computational efficiency are traded off in language processing systems.

Type 0: Unrestricted Grammars

In the Chomsky hierarchy, the most potent and general class of formal grammars are unrestricted grammars, sometimes referred to as Type 0 grammars. Such grammars do not impose structural constraints on rule formation; they are defined by production rules of the form $\alpha \rightarrow \beta$, where both sides are strings of terminals and non-terminals with α containing at least one non-terminal. They are essential to the study of computational theory because of their unrestricted nature, which enables them to describe any algorithm or computable function. Recursively enumerable languages—which can be identified by a Turing machine but not necessarily determined by one—are the languages produced by these grammars. The intricacy of Type 0 grammars and the undecidability of crucial characteristics, like membership testing, limit their practical application despite their theoretical strength. As a result, they are mostly investigated in theoretical computer science to look at the limits of formal language systems' expressive power and computation.

Type 1: Context-Sensitive Grammars (CSG)

Unrestricted grammars, also known as Type 0 grammars, are the most powerful and widespread class of formal grammars in the Chomsky hierarchy. These grammars are defined by production rules of the form $\alpha \rightarrow \beta$, where both sides are strings of terminals and non-terminals, with α containing at least one non-terminal. They do not impose structural constraints on rule formation. Because of their unrestricted nature, which allows them to describe any algorithm or computable function, they are crucial to the study of computational theory.These grammars generate recursively enumerable languages, which are able to be recognized by a Turing machine but not necessarily determined by one. Despite Type 0 grammars' theoretical strength, their practical application is limited by their complexity and the undecidability of key features, such as membership testing. Because of this, they are primarily studied in theoretical computer science to examine the boundaries of the expressive and computational capabilities of formal language systems.

Type 2: Context-Free Grammars (CFG)

In the Chomsky hierarchy, context-free grammars (CFGs), also referred to as Type 2 grammars, are simpler and subject to more restrictions than context-sensitive grammars. They have a single non-terminal symbol on the left (A) and a series of terminals and/or non-terminals on the right (γ), which is represented as $A \rightarrow \gamma$. This is the format of their production rules. Because of their structured simplicity, CFGs are very effective at parsing and are simple to use, which is why they are used extensively in linguistics and computer science. Context-free languages produced by CFGs can be identified by pushdown automata, which are computational models that use a stack-based memory system. Programming languages' nested loops and other hierarchical constructs, like balanced parentheses, are especially well-represented by these grammars. CFGs are essential tools for a variety of applications, such as natural language processing systems, compiler development, and programming language design, due to their capacity to portray intricate, multi-layered language features.

Type 3: Regular Grammars

Regular grammars, or Type 3 grammars, are the most restricted and simplest form of grammars in the Chomsky hierarchy. Their production rules are limited to two forms:

The rules of regular grammars are as follows: A → aB and A → a, where an is a terminal symbol and A and B are non-terminal symbols. Regular grammars produce languages that are simple and limited in complexity because of this strict form. Regular languages are the result of regular grammars and are recognized by finite automata, which are computational models that handle simple language patterns by processing inputs sequentially with limited memory. Applications that need effective pattern recognition, like regular expressions in text processing and lexical analysis in compilers, frequently use these regular languages. Regular grammars are particularly helpful for tasks like pattern matching in software applications, tokenization in programming languages, and powering text search engines because of their speed and ease of use. Their capacity to manage recurring and distinct patterns makes them an essential tool in many branches of natural language processing and computer science.

Relationship Between the Types

Each type of grammar is a subset of the more general category above it in the Chomsky hierarchy, an inclusive framework that arranges grammars into a nested structure. The most limited type of grammars are regular grammars (Type 3), which fall completely under the larger category of context-free grammars (Type 2). The most general and potent class of grammars, unrestricted grammars (Type 0), in turn contain context-free grammars within context-sensitive grammars (Type 1). As one moves up the hierarchy, this tiered arrangement shows an increase in expressive and computational power.Every level of the Chomsky hierarchy has a distinct theoretical and applied purpose in the study of computational linguistics and formal languages. For instance, context-free grammars are essential for parsing programming languages and natural language syntax, whereas regular grammars are helpful for basic pattern matching and lexical analysis. More intricate structures and calculations are handled by context-sensitive and unrestricted grammars. The Chomsky hierarchy offers a fundamental framework for comprehending how various grammars work and how they are used in various fields of computer science and artificial intelligence by precisely defining these categories.

Parsing & Semantics

Parsing: The Process of Analyzing Language Structure

Parsing is the process of applying a grammar's rules to a string of symbols, usually a line of code or a sentence in natural language. It is essential to both formal and natural languages, allowing both machines and people to decipher the relationships and structure of a given input. Parsing aids in exposing the underlying structure of the content, which is frequently represented as a parse tree or syntax tree, by dissecting complicated inputs into smaller, more manageable parts. Programming parsing is an essential step in compilation or interpretation, where a parser validates code syntax and creates a structured representation using a formally defined grammar. For example, parsing guarantees that expressions such as x + y follow the proper grammar rules and order of operations. Similar to this, parsing aids in the identification of grammatical elements such as subjects, verbs, and objects in natural language processing (NLP), which helps determine the structure and meaning of sentences.

Lexical analysis and syntactic analysis are the two main stages of parsing. Finding the tokens—such as keywords, identifiers, or symbols—that function as the fundamental building blocks of the input is the main goal of lexical analysis. The arrangement of these tokens is then examined by syntactic analysis to see if it complies with the established grammar rules. This two-step procedure guarantees that the input's vocabulary and structure are both verified. Parsing is a fundamental process in language understanding and computational systems because its output serves as the structural foundation for later phases, such as semantic interpretation in natural language processing (NLP) or code generation in programming.

Semantics: Understanding Meaning

Beyond the surface-level structure revealed by parsing, semantics examines the meaning underlying linguistic or symbolic expressions. Semantics focuses on confirming that the content is meaningful within its context, whereas parsing makes sure that a sentence or piece of code complies with grammatical or syntactical rules. Stated differently, semantics examines what a statement truly expresses or accomplishes by interpreting the "what" behind the "how." This entails making sure that operations in programming languages follow the intended logic. For example, because division by zero is undefined, the expression 5 / 0 is semantically invalid even though it is syntactically correct. In programming, semantic analysis frequently involves type checking to ensure that operators, variables, and functions are used in ways that are appropriate for the context. For instance, adding a string to a number usually results in a semantic error even though it might pass a syntax check. Semantics examines the meanings of words, phrases, and sentences in the context of natural languages, addressing topics like ambiguity, metaphorical language, and contextual interpretation. Depending on the context, the word "bank" could refer to a financial institution or the edge of a river. Semantic networks, word embeddings, and ontologies are some of the techniques used by NLP systems to efficiently capture and analyze such meanings.

Parsing and Semantics: Interplay and Applications

The foundation of language comprehension in formal and human contexts is made up of the complementary processes of semantics and parsing. By locating appropriate syntactic structures in a sentence or code, parsing lays the groundwork and guarantees that the input complies with accepted grammatical or syntactic rules. By deciphering the meaning contained in these structures, semantics then expands upon this base, enabling systems to understand the purpose or logical connections present in the input. For machines to process and understand language efficiently, this dual strategy is essential. Semantic analysis checks for logical consistency, such as appropriate variable usage and type compatibility, while parsing confirms that code adheres to the correct syntax in programming. These processes are essential for creating dependable compilers and interpreters. Semantics converts grammatical relationships, such as subject-verb-object constructs, that are extracted by parsing into meaningful interpretations in natural language processing (NLP), allowing for intelligent applications like chatbots, machine translation, and question-answering systems. When combined, these procedures turn unprocessed input—whether code or plain text—into useful knowledge, which is essential for computational linguistics and contemporary software development.

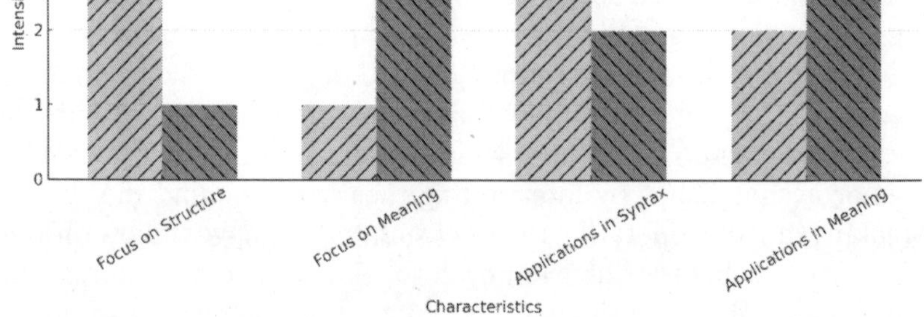

Figure 4.1: Comparison between parsing and semantics.

The four main features of parsing and semantics—focus on structure, focus on meaning, applications in syntax, and applications in meaning—are graphically compared in Figure 4.1. Parsing excels in areas that call for syntax validation and structural analysis, as evidenced by higher scores in "Focus on Structure" and "Applications in Syntax." Semantics, on the other hand, is very good at interpreting and determining meaning, as evidenced by higher scores for "Focus on Meaning" and "Applications in Meaning." This comparison demonstrates how semantics and parsing serve complementary functions, with semantics offering contextual understanding and parsing guaranteeing structural validity. When combined, they allow for thorough language processing.

Concept of Parsing Techniques

As the first step in comprehending structured input, parsing techniques are ways to examine a string's syntax using a particular grammar. By guaranteeing that the input complies with predetermined grammatical rules, these methods are crucial for interpreting both human and machine languages. Parsing is essential to computational systems for tasks like constructing compilers, interpreting programming languages, and enabling machines to accurately process natural language. Top-down and bottom-up parsing are the two primary categories into which these methods are typically divided. While bottom-up parsing starts with the input and works its way up to construct the start symbol, top-down parsing starts with the start symbol and tries to derive the input string by expanding grammar rules. Recursive descent parsing and shift-reduce parsing are two examples of variations within each category that are suited to various use cases and levels of complexity. Building effective language processing tools and systems requires an understanding of these techniques.

1. Top-Down Parsing

The process of top-down parsing starts with a grammar's start symbol and uses production rules to try and extract the input string. In accordance with the grammar's rules, the parser constructs the parse tree from the root down to the leaves. When working with complex or ambiguous structures, this method has limitations even though it is intuitive and effective for simple grammars.

a) Recursive Descent Parsing

Each non-terminal in the grammar is represented by a recursive procedure in recursive descent parsing, a simple type of top-down parsing. The parser recursively expands non-terminals to match the input string to production rules. Although this approach is simple to use, it has trouble with left-recursive grammars, which result in infinite recursion. A rule such as $A \to A\alpha$, for example, would result in an infinite loop. Recursive descent parsing is frequently utilized for small, manually created grammars, especially in educational settings or for straightforward domain-specific languages, despite its disadvantages. Rewriting the grammar or applying predictive parsing techniques are common ways to deal with left recursion.

b) Predictive Parsing

Recursive descent parsing is improved by predictive parsing, which uses a lookahead symbol to decide which production rule to apply, reducing the need for backtracking and increasing efficiency. A grammar that supports left-to-right input scanning with a single lookahead symbol is required for this method to function. Predictive parsing eliminates some of the difficulties associated with recursive descent parsing, but it necessitates modifying the grammar to eliminate left recursion and factor out common prefixes.

2. Bottom-Up Parsing

The parse tree is built using bottom-up parsing, which begins with the leaves of the input string and moves toward the root (start symbol). Compared to top-down parsing, this approach is more effective because it can handle a wider variety of grammars, including left-recursive and ambiguous ones. Reducing input substrings into non-terminals in accordance with grammar rules is the main goal.

a) Shift-Reduce Parsing

Shift-reduce parsing is a popular bottom-up method that stores grammar elements in a stack. The two primary functions of the parser are reduced, which substitutes a corresponding non-terminal for a sequence of symbols on the stack, and shift, which pushes the subsequent input symbol onto the stack. Until just the start symbol is left on the stack, this process is repeated. Shift-reduce parsing is effective for simple grammars, but it may run into problems in ambiguous grammars, like having to choose between shift and reduce actions. These disputes are settled by using sophisticated strategies or changing the grammar.

b) LR Parsing

LR parsing (Left-to-right scanning with Rightmost derivation in reverse) is the most powerful bottom-up parsing technique, suitable for a wide variety of context-free grammars, including those used in programming languages. LR parsers use a parsing table to guide the shift and reduce operations, making the process deterministic and efficient.

There are several variants of LR parsing:

- **SLR (Simple LR):** Simplifies table creation, though it has limited capabilities.
- **Canonical LR:** Can process the entire spectrum of LR grammars, but demands large tables.
- **LALR (Lookahead LR):** Strikes a balance between power and efficiency by merging similar states from Canonical LR, making it commonly used in practice.

- LR parsing is computationally demanding to implement manually, yet it is highly effective for large-scale applications, such as compiler construction.

3. Advanced Parsing Techniques

Complex grammatical structures and difficult linguistic situations are handled by sophisticated parsing techniques. Complicated problems like ambiguity, recursion, or irregular syntax are frequently difficult for traditional top-down or bottom-up approaches to handle. Advanced techniques like chart parsing, GLR (Generalized LR), or Earley parsers are used in these situations. These methods use probabilistic models, dynamic programming, or parallel parsing paths to more accurately and efficiently analyze and interpret complex linguistic structures. When dealing with ambiguous grammars or non-standard structures that defy accepted grammatical rules, these strategies are especially helpful. For example, sophisticated parsing guarantees improved understanding and more precise interpretations in natural language processing (NLP), where human language can be unpredictable and multi-interpretable. Therefore, advanced parsing techniques greatly increase the flexibility and capability of syntactic analysis systems by overcoming the drawbacks of conventional approaches.

a) CYK (Cocke-Younger-Kasami) Algorithm

The Cocke-Younger-Kasami algorithm, also known as the CYK algorithm, is a dynamic programming method that is specifically used to parse context-free grammars in Chomsky Normal Form (CNF). It creates higher-level grammatical structures by first segmenting the input string into substrings and then methodically joining these substrings. Its ability to take into account every potential parse tree is one of its main advantages; this makes it especially useful for examining ambiguous grammars, where a sentence may have more than one legitimate interpretation. But there is a price for this all-encompassing strategy. The computational complexity of the CYK algorithm is $O(n^3)$, where n is the input string's length. It is less appropriate for real-time or performance-sensitive applications due to its cubic time complexity. However, its capacity to investigate every syntactic possibility makes it an invaluable tool in natural language processing (NLP) and theoretical computer science, particularly for tasks requiring exhaustive parsing.

b) Earley Parser

A general-purpose algorithm called the Earley parser is made to parse any context-free grammar, including those with left recursion. It can produce one parse tree for ambiguous inputs or several parse trees for ambiguous ones, and it works well for unambiguous grammars. The Earley parser works well for real-time and streaming applications by processing the input incrementally using a dynamic approach. Because of this, it can be used in a variety of scenarios where parsing must happen instantly without waiting for all of the input. The Earley parser may perform more slowly when handling extremely ambiguous grammars, even though it provides greater flexibility than algorithms like CYK. It manages complicated and ambiguous grammatical structures with ease and is especially effective in natural language processing. It is a popular option for applications involving human languages, where ambiguity and structural variations are prevalent, due to its capacity to handle complex syntax patterns.

4. Comparison of Parsing Techniques

The methods and capacities of top-down and bottom-up parsing are very different. In order to match the input string, top-down parsing begins with the grammar's start symbol and moves down the parse tree. This category includes techniques that are straightforward and simple to use, such as predictive parsing and recursive descent. They are limited to particular grammars, like LL (1), though, and struggle with ambiguity and left-recursion. On the other hand, bottom-up parsing builds the parse tree backwards, starting with the input string and working upward toward the start symbol. This method includes techniques like shift-reduce parsing and LR parsing, which are renowned for their strength and adaptability. A greater variety of grammars, including left-recursive and some ambiguous structures, can be handled by bottom-up parsers. Because of its efficiency and resilience, many programming language compilers favor LR parsing in particular. Advanced algorithms like CYK and Earley parsing are used for even more complicated parsing requirements, but they have a higher computational overhead.

5. Applications of Parsing Techniques

In many different fields, parsing techniques are essential for processing and interpreting structured data. Parsing creates parse trees and verifies syntax in compilers and interpreters, which form the basis for code generation and optimization. Similar to this, parsing makes grammatical analysis easier in natural language processing, which makes it possible to perform important tasks like sentiment analysis, machine translation, and question answering. Additionally, parsing supports database query processing by ensuring the accuracy and efficiency of SQL queries by validating and optimizing them before they are executed. Additionally, parsing is necessary for code editors and integrated development environments (IDEs) to function properly. It drives features like intelligent code suggestions, error checking, and real-time syntax highlighting. The complexity of the grammar and the application's performance requirements determine the parsing method to be used, whether it be top-down, bottom-up, or another method. This demonstrates the technical adaptability of parsing techniques as well as their importance in a variety of contemporary computing domains.

Table 4.2: Different parsing techniques, including their approach, advantages, disadvantages, and applications.

Parsing Technique	Approach	Advantages	Disadvantages	Applications
Top-Down Parsing	Starts from the root and tries to rewrite it to the input string	Easy to implement; useful for syntax-directed translation	Struggles with left recursion; may require backtracking	Simple compilers, educational tools
Bottom-Up Parsing	Starts from the input and works up to the start symbol	Can handle a larger class of grammars; deterministic parsing	More complex implementation; harder to debug	General-purpose parsers (e.g., YACC, Bison)
Recursive Descent Parsing	Implements grammar rules using recursive functions	Intuitive; suitable for hand-written parsers	Backtracking can be inefficient; not suitable for left-recursive grammars	Small language interpreters, domain-specific languages
LL Parsing	Top-down parser that reads Left to right, constructs Leftmost derivation	Predictive; no backtracking with LL(1) grammars	Limited to LL(k) grammars; can't handle left recursion	Simple programming languages, parser generators (e.g., ANTLR for LL(*) parsing)
LR Parsing	Bottom-up parser that reads Left to right and constructs Rightmost derivation in reverse	Very powerful; can handle most programming languages	Complex to implement; requires parser generators	C, C++, Java compilers
SLR Parsing	Simplified version of LR parsing	Easier than LR; less state explosion	Less powerful; may fail for some valid grammars	Educational tools, smaller language parsers

LALR Parsing	Look-Ahead LR parsing	Balances power and simplicity; fewer states than LR	Still may have shift-reduce or reduce-reduce conflicts	Widely used in parser generators like YACC
CYK Algorithm	Bottom-up dynamic programming parser for CNF grammars	Guaranteed to find a parse if one exists	Inefficient for large grammars; requires CNF	Natural language processing, theoretical applications
Earley Parser	Handles any context-free grammar, top-down with dynamic programming	Can handle ambiguous and left-recursive grammars	Slower for unambiguous grammars	Speech recognition, NLP, general-purpose CFG parsers

Context-Free & Transformational Grammars

Context-Free Grammars (CFG)

Context-Free Grammars (CFGs) are crucial tools in linguistics and computer science that are used to model the structure of natural languages and define the syntax of programming languages. They are made up of production rules that substitute a series of terminal or non-terminal symbols for a non-terminal symbol. Because of the rule-based system's support for recursive and hierarchical patterns, CFGs can describe complex sentence structures and nested parentheses. The grammar rule $S \rightarrow (S) \mid \epsilon$, for instance, produces balanced parentheses, illustrating CFGs' proficiency in handling nested structures. CFGs are frequently used in compiler design, where they aid in the creation of syntax analyzers and parsers for interpreting computer code. They are also a fundamental component of natural language processing (NLP), which helps with syntactic analysis by dissecting sentences into their constituent nouns and verbs. CFGs do have some inherent limitations, though. In particular, they are unable to manage context-sensitive rules, like making sure that the subject and verb agree in a sentence, where the grammatical function of one word determines its correctness.

Transformational Grammars

Noam Chomsky developed transformational grammars in response to the shortcomings of more straightforward grammatical models, such as context-free grammars (CFGs), in capturing the complexity of human language. This method makes a distinction between surface structure, which represents the actual spoken or written form, and deep structure, which captures the underlying meaning of a sentence. This model explains complex linguistic phenomena like question formation, negation, and passive voice by employing transformations, which are rules that rearrange components within sentences. For instance, the change from "The boy is running" to "Is the boy running?" demonstrates a structural shift without compromising the main idea. Through the use of context-sensitive rules that take into account sentence variations and ambiguities, this grammar framework offers a more sophisticated understanding of syntax. It has contributed significantly to the advancement of contemporary linguistic theory by shedding light on universal grammar and the mental processes underlying language acquisition. Beyond theoretical linguistics, transformational grammar is useful in Natural Language Processing (NLP), especially in domains like dialogue systems and machine translation where more accurate and coherent syntactic and semantic interpretations are necessary, going far beyond what can be accomplished with surface-level analysis.

Comparison of CFG and Transformational Grammars

Although both transformational grammars and context-free grammars (CFGs) are instruments for language modeling, their scope and emphasis are very different.

CFGs define language syntax using basic production rules and are mainly interested in syntactic structure. Because of their simplicity, they are perfect for tasks like basic Natural Language Processing (NLP) and programming language design. CFGs are less appropriate for representing complex language phenomena because of their limitations in managing context-sensitive dependencies. They have trouble encapsulating the entire spectrum of linguistic nuances, but they are excellent at explaining hierarchical relationships. Transformational grammars, on the other hand, investigate the deeper connection between form and meaning by going beyond basic syntactic structure. Transformational grammars incorporate transformational rules that can explain complex linguistic phenomena by differentiating between deep and surface structures. They offer more potent insights into language structure, despite being more difficult to implement and computationally demanding. Because of their effectiveness and simplicity of use, CFGs are frequently employed in real-world applications such as compiler design. However, advanced linguistic studies and domains like artificial intelligence and cognitive science that demand a more sophisticated understanding of language are better suited for transformational grammars.

Applications of CFGs and Transformational Grammars

Context-Free Grammars (CFGs), which provide an organized and effective way to specify the grammatical structure of code, are essential in domains such as syntax analysis and programming language development. By clearly defining the rules governing the arrangement of programming constructs, they guarantee that programs are syntactically valid. CFGs are equally important in natural language processing (NLP), offering a transparent method for examining sentence structure. This is crucial for tasks like grammar checking and sentence parsing, which aim to make sure that language follows predetermined syntactic rules so that text can be understood and worked with more easily. However, transformational grammars perform exceptionally well in more complex linguistic applications, especially when dealing with context-sensitive rules and intricate linguistic structures. They make it possible to convert abstract representations into coherent, natural-sounding sentences and are essential for comprehending and simulating the complexities of natural languages. Because they provide insights into how people create and understand language, transformational grammars also have important ramifications for linguistic theory. They also facilitate more complex NLP tasks like sentiment analysis and machine translation, where it is essential to comprehend the connection between syntax and meaning. CFGs and transformational grammars work in tandem to address both the structural and transformational facets of language, and they are essential to artificial intelligence and computational linguistics.

Four essential features—syntax focus, context sensitivity, ease of implementation, and advanced linguistic analysis—are compared between Context-Free Grammars (CFG) and Transformational Grammars (TG) in Figure 4.2. CFGs are very useful for tasks like analyzing the syntax of programming languages because of their exceptional syntax focus and simplicity of use. Effective parsing and translation are made possible by their structure and simplicity, which is a fundamental advantage for computational applications. Transformational grammars, on the other hand, are superior in sophisticated linguistic analysis and context sensitivity. TGs are made to deal with more intricate linguistic phenomena, such as deeper semantic analysis and the subtle connections between sentence structures. Because of this ability, TGs are able to model complex linguistic features that CFGs find difficult to capture, like transformations and deep structures. The comparison demonstrates the complementary nature of these two grammatical frameworks, with TGs providing richer capabilities for sophisticated language modeling and CFGs being best suited for syntactic tasks.

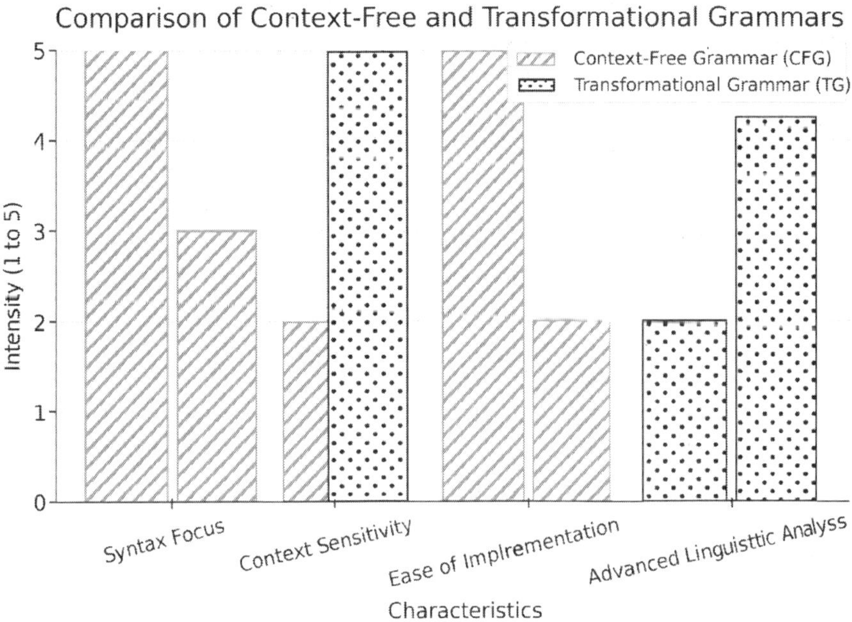

Figure 4.2: Comparison of context free and transformational grammars.

Recursive & Augmented Transition Nets

Recursive Transition Networks (RTNs)

Language syntax can be represented graphically using a formalism called Recursive Transition Networks (RTNs). They are perfect for modeling context-free grammars because they add recursion to the finite-state automata model. States are represented as nodes in an RTN, and transitions between them are represented by directed edges. Recursion and hierarchical structures are made possible by these transitions' ability to connect to other sub-networks. In natural language processing (NLP), RTNs are especially useful for identifying syntactic patterns, particularly those that contain recursive or nested elements. RTNs are more expressive than simpler finite-state automata because they can effectively capture the recursive nature of embedded clauses, such as in the sentence "The cat that the dog chased ran away," by enabling one network to call another.RTNs' visual clarity is one of their main advantages; linguists and computer scientists can use them to intuitively create and comprehend grammars. RTNs are nevertheless limited in their ability to manage context-sensitive dependencies, like word agreement. In these situations, RTNs by themselves are unable to sufficiently address these intricate relationships, necessitating the use of additional mechanisms or extensions.

Augmented Transition Networks (ATNs)

The capabilities of conventional Recursive Transition Networks (RTNs) are expanded by Augmented Transition Networks (ATNs), which add extra features like registers and procedural actions. Because these features allow the network to perform computations or store intermediate data during transitions, ATNs can process more complex language structures, such as context-sensitive dependencies. In order to resolve agreement or identify relationships within a sentence, registers serve as variables that store crucial information, such as the subject of a sentence. The combination of the computational power of procedural programming and the hierarchical structure of RTNs greatly enhances the ATN's capacity to parse natural languages with increased accuracy. Complex and ambiguous sentences, like "The boy who saw the girl smiled," are especially well-suited for ATNs because they store important components, like the subject ("The boy"), in a register and refer to it during the parsing process to ensure grammatical consistency. One of the main advantages of ATNs is their adaptability, which enables them to parse several sentence interpretations at once. However, when compared to simpler parsing models, the model's complexity makes it slower and more resource-intensive, so this flexibility comes at the expense of higher computational demands.

Differences Between RTNs and ATNs

Despite being graphical models for grammar representation, RTNs and ATNs have very different capabilities, as shown in Table 4.4. RTNs can only model hierarchical structures using recursive calls and are limited to context-free grammars. Because of this, they work well for basic syntactic analysis but are not flexible enough for more complicated linguistic tasks. By adding procedural actions and registers, ATNs expand on the framework of RTNs and can represent more complex linguistic phenomena and model context-sensitive languages. Syntactic structures interact with semantic or contextual information in natural language processing tasks, which is where ATNs excel. Although their increased expressiveness comes at the expense of higher computational demands, their capacity to manage these complexities makes them more expressive. RTNs are perfect for tasks that do not require context-sensitive analysis because they are more effective and easier to implement.

Applications of RTNs and ATNs

Natural language processing (NLP) and computational linguistics have made extensive use of RTNs and ATNs. Recursive Transition Networks, or RTNs, are mainly employed for parsing and syntax analysis tasks where context-free grammars can accurately represent linguistic structures. They serve as a fundamental tool in educational settings to teach formal language theory concepts, and they are crucial for tasks like recognizing parts of speech and fundamental sentence structures. However, more sophisticated NLP applications like speech recognition, machine translation, and dialogue systems use Augmented Transition Networks, or ATNs. They can deal with complicated sentence structures and ambiguities in language because of their special capacity to store contextual information. For conversational AI systems, this makes ATNs especially useful for parsing complex sentences, comprehending linguistic subtleties, and producing logical, context-aware responses.

Advantages and Limitations

Both ATNs and RTNs have unique disadvantages and advantages. Because of their well-known simplicity, effectiveness, and visual appeal, RTNs can be used for a wide range of tasks. But their main drawback is that they can't handle context-sensitive dependencies, which limits how well they can parse complex natural language. RTNs are less effective at capturing the subtleties of language that call for context-dependent understanding, even though they perform well on simpler tasks with clearly defined structures. However, by integrating sophisticated computational capabilities, ATNs overcome this constraint and are able to manage increasingly intricate, context-sensitive dependencies. However, the trade-off is that ATNs require more resources to design and implement because they are more complex. The particular language complexities involved and the available computational resources will determine whether to use RTNs or ATNs. RTNs are usually adequate for simple tasks with few contextual requirements, but ATNs offer a more reliable solution for parsing natural language with its complex dependencies.

Table 4.4: Comparison between the RTNs vs. ATNs.

Feature	RTNs (Recursive Transition Networks)	ATNs (Augmented Transition Networks)
Definition	RTNs are a type of formal grammar used to describe syntactic structures.	ATNs are an extension of RTNs that incorporate additional mechanisms such as predicates and features to allow for more expressive power.

Nature	Recursive, hierarchical structure.	Augmented with extra computational power for handling more complex syntactic and semantic rules.
Usage	Primarily used in syntax parsing, often for context-free grammars.	Used for more complex language parsing, including both syntactic and semantic analysis.
Complexity	Simpler, restricted to transition rules.	More complex, allowing for conditions, actions, and semantic constraints.
Transition Rules	Focus on simple transitions between states based on input symbols.	Transitions include conditions or actions that can alter the state or process more information.
State Representation	Each state represents a simple syntactic rule or phrase structure.	States can contain additional information such as semantic values or feature structures.
Flexibility	Limited flexibility; designed for simpler tasks.	More flexible, with the ability to represent more complex relationships and features.
Efficiency	More efficient for simpler parsing tasks.	Less efficient due to the added complexity and the use of additional computational features.
Applications	Used in early natural language processing systems for syntactic parsing.	Used in more advanced natural language processing tasks involving both syntax and semantics.
Predicates & Actions	No predicates or actions; transitions are purely syntactic.	Supports predicates and actions that can be executed during parsing, enabling complex rule evaluations.
Examples	Early parsing techniques for context-free languages.	Modern NLP systems where both syntax and semantic conditions are important.

Conclusion

This chapter explores the essential elements and processes of communication, emphasizing the grammatical differences between formal and natural languages. The Chomsky hierarchy of grammars is introduced, and key subjects like parsing, semantics, and different parsing strategies are covered. The chapter also looks at the distinctions between transformational grammars and context-free grammars, giving readers a thorough grasp of how language structure is represented. It also emphasizes how important Recursive and Augmented Transition Nets are for language analysis, highlighting their critical roles in natural language processing and syntax representation. Focusing on the development of artificial intelligence, the following chapter compares data-driven methods like machine learning and deep learning with symbolic AI. It examines the various uses of both paradigms, focusing on the increasing significance of AI that can be understood and explained. It also discusses the risks, advantages, and ethical ramifications of AI technologies, critically evaluating how they will influence how society and technology develop in the future.

Exercise:

- Explain the key elements and stages involved in effective communication, providing examples to illustrate each stage.
- Compare formal and natural languages regarding grammar, ambiguity, flexibility, and precision. How do these differences affect their respective uses?
- Describe the Chomsky hierarchy of grammars, offering examples for each grammar type (Type 0 through Type 3). Why is this hierarchy crucial for understanding language processing?
- Define parsing and semantics within the context of language processing. How do they work together to enhance the understanding of both natural and formal languages?
- Examine the differences between top-down and bottom-up parsing methods, providing examples of scenarios where each would be more appropriate.
- Develop a context-free grammar for a language that generates balanced parentheses and create a parse tree for the string ((())).
- Clarify the concepts of deep structure and surface structure in transformational grammar, explaining how transformational rules link the two.
- Construct a Recursive Transition Network (RTN) for simple sentences with embedded clauses, such as "The cat that chased the mouse ran away."
- Describe how Augmented Transition Networks (ATNs) expand upon RTNs, with an example illustrating how ATNs handle context-sensitive dependencies.
- Explore two applications of parsing techniques and grammars in natural language processing, and explain how these techniques allow machines to comprehend human language.

CHAPTER-5

AI THE PRESENT AND THE FUTURE

Introduction & Objective

With the ability to perform tasks that were previously only possible for humans, artificial intelligence (AI) is changing both industries and society. This change is a result of AI's development from its early roots in symbolic AI to the emergence of data-driven AI. As the field has developed, new developments such as Explainable AI and Machine Learning have increased the capacity of intelligent systems, allowing for more intricate and flexible decision-making procedures. AI is becoming more and more incorporated into commonplace applications, from banking to healthcare, improving scalability, accuracy, and efficiency. With a focus on important paradigms that have shaped its development, the chapter provides a thorough examination of AI's evolution. Along with highlighting the advantages of AI technologies—like greater automation and creativity—it also highlights the ethical ramifications of these technologies, recognizing their drawbacks, like biases and privacy issues. By looking at AI from a variety of angles, the chapter provides a comprehensive analysis of its effects both now and in the future, shedding light on both the obstacles to its widespread adoption and its potential to completely transform industries. This chapter aims to provide a thorough grasp of artificial intelligence's (AI) transformative role in the present and the future by examining the main approaches, applications, and ethical issues of AI. It explores the many methods that power AI systems, including neural networks, machine learning, and natural language processing, while showcasing the wide range of sectors in which AI is already having an effect. AI is changing how we work, live, and engage with technology in a variety of ways, from healthcare to driverless cars, demonstrating its enormous potential to boost productivity and advance human potential. Additionally, this chapter seeks to give readers a more thorough grasp of AI's advantages and disadvantages in order to promote a fair assessment of its potential. Even though AI has a lot of potential, there are ethical issues that need to be addressed given how quickly it is developing. In order to guarantee that AI benefits humanity as a whole, it is crucial to develop and implement AI responsibly, with an emphasis on building systems that are open, equitable, and consistent with social values. The chapter promotes critical thinking regarding AI's future and the moral frameworks that will be required to direct its advancement.

AI The Present and the Future

Around the world, artificial intelligence (AI) is drastically changing a variety of industries, including healthcare, finance, entertainment, and transportation. AI has fueled advances in fields like conversational agents, fraud detection, self-driving cars, and personalized medicine by analyzing enormous datasets, identifying patterns, and making defensible decisions. AI is also changing the creative industries by making it possible to create content, music, and art. Machine learning, natural language processing, and computer vision are key components of artificial intelligence (AI), which together imitate human intelligence and spur innovation and operational efficiency. But these developments also raise issues like decision-making bias, job displacement, and privacy risks. With advancements in quantum computing, neural networks, and general AI that seek to mimic human reasoning, the field of artificial intelligence is poised for even more significant advancements in the future. AI has the potential to transform industries like space exploration, education, and governance through its potential uses in advanced robotics, brain-computer interfaces, and predictive analytics. However, these opportunities also present important challenges, such as the need for moral standards, safeguarding against abuse, and making sure laws control the development of AI. The development of AI has enormous potential, but its success depends on striking a balance between creativity and moral obligation and preparing society for its revolutionary effects.

Concept of Symbolic AI

What is Symbolic AI?

Symbolic AI, also known as "Good Old-Fashioned Artificial Intelligence" (GOFAI), is a branch of AI that focuses on representing knowledge and reasoning through symbols and rules. Symbolic AI, which dates back to the middle of the 20th century, aims to encode data in a way that is both structured and comprehensible in order to mimic human cognitive processes. It seeks to support logical reasoning by employing human-friendly symbols, allowing machines to carry out intricate cognitive functions like planning, problem-solving, and decision-making. Developing systems that can work with abstract representations of the world and use rules to draw conclusions is the main goal of symbolic artificial intelligence. This method stands in contrast to more recent paradigms such as machine learning, which emphasize data-driven learning and pattern recognition. The strength of symbolic AI is its capacity for clear and precise reasoning, which makes it especially well-suited for tasks requiring formal reasoning, knowledge representation, and decision-making that is understandable by humans.

1. Representation of Knowledge

The foundation of symbolic artificial intelligence is structured knowledge representation, in which actual entities are represented as symbols with clearly defined relationships or characteristics. As an example, ideas like "dog" or "tree" are abstracted into symbols, and characteristics like "barks" or "has four legs" are connected to these things. Both humans and machines can more easily comprehend and interpret the data thanks to this methodical approach. This kind of knowledge organization made possible by symbolic AI enables the development of logical databases, or ontologies, in which concepts and facts are connected by relationships. These systems are based on frameworks such as frames or semantic networks, in which concepts are represented by nodes and their relationships are indicated by edges. This makes it possible for the system to use reasoning skills to deduce new information from the body of existing knowledge. Nevertheless, one drawback of symbolic AI is that it necessitates manual knowledge base curation, which can be resource- and time-intensive. Therefore, even though symbolic AI is effective at tasks requiring structured knowledge and reasoning, the effort required to maintain and update these systems limits its scalability.

2. Logic and Rules

Propositional and predicate logic are examples of formal logic that symbolic AI uses to reason with the data in its knowledge base. The "IF-THEN" rules and other logical expressions allow the system to draw conclusions from known facts. The system can gain new insights by connecting different rules, such as "If an animal is a dog, it is a mammal," for instance. Because symbolic AI is deterministic, all of its conclusions adhere strictly to predetermined rules, providing highly accurate reasoning. Nevertheless, this deterministic framework also presents a problem when handling ambiguous or incomplete data, a situation that probabilistic models such as machine learning are better suited to manage. Notwithstanding this drawback, symbolic AI's accuracy and explainability make it extremely useful in applications where exactitude and lucidity are crucial. In domains where precise and verifiable results are required, like law, healthcare, and formal decision-making, symbolic AI's structured reasoning capability is still essential.

3. Search and Planning

Symbolic AI searches for possible solutions by navigating through a problem space using search algorithms. Methods like depth-first search, breadth-first search, and heuristic-based approaches are frequently used to assess different routes. These algorithms, for example, enable the system to investigate several paths and determine the most effective one when trying to navigate a maze. One of Symbolic AI's main advantages is its ability to evaluate various options in an organized way, which helps it solve challenging issues where the best option must be chosen from a range of options. When it comes to planning, symbolic AI concentrates on decomposing a goal into more manageable sub-goals and figuring out the steps necessary to get there. Symbolic planners, such as STRIPS (Stanford Research Institute Problem Solver), model the starting state, the desired state, and the necessary actions using logical representations. Numerous industries, such as robotics, logistics, and automated scheduling, where accurate planning and decision-making are essential for productivity and success, have found value in this logical framework.

4. Explainability

Interpretability is a key characteristic that distinguishes symbolic AI from other AI paradigms and is one of its strongest points. Every choice the system makes can be linked to its underlying knowledge and rules because symbolic AI functions through deterministic and rule-based processes. Users are able to comprehend the exact logic behind each result thanks to this degree of transparency. In medical applications, for example, an expert system that diagnoses a disease can clearly state the reasoning process, for example, "Symptom A + Symptom B = Disease X," which offers a clear understanding of the reasoning behind the decision. This interpretability is especially helpful in high-stakes domains where understanding the reasoning behind conclusions is crucial, like healthcare, legal decision-making, and finance. Symbolic AI provides a solution that closely complies with ethical standards that require explainable outputs, in contrast to contemporary machine learning models, which frequently function as "black boxes" with opaque decision-making processes. Symbolic AI contributes to the preservation of trust and accountability by guaranteeing that every stage of the reasoning process can be tracked, which makes it appropriate for applications where transparency and clarity are essential.

5. Applications of Symbolic AI

Symbolic AI has been employed in various domains:

- **Expert Systems:** Systems such as MYCIN (for medical diagnosis) and DENDRAL (for chemical analysis) leverage encoded expert knowledge to make decisions and provide recommendations. These systems thrive in specialized fields where expertise can be translated into rules.
- **Natural Language Understanding:** Early NLP systems employed symbolic AI to parse sentences, identify grammatical structures, and interpret meaning. These systems were built on manually crafted rules and grammars.
- **Robotics:** Symbolic AI is applied in task planning for robots, enabling them to perform structured tasks like assembling products or following predefined routes.
- **Game Playing:** Systems like IBM's Deep Blue utilized symbolic reasoning to evaluate potential moves and strategies, ultimately defeating human chess champions.

6. Challenges of Symbolic AI

Despite its strengths, Symbolic AI faces significant challenges:

- **Scalability:** As the scope of a domain expands, it becomes impractical to encode all the required knowledge and rules. Updating the knowledge base to incorporate new discoveries demands significant manual effort.
- **Adaptability:** Symbolic systems face challenges when it comes to learning from new data or adjusting to unexpected situations. In contrast to machine learning, which can generalize from examples, symbolic AI necessitates explicit programming for each possible scenario.
- **Ambiguity in Real-World Data:** Due to the structured and deterministic nature of Symbolic AI, it is not well-equipped to manage noisy or incomplete data, limiting its effectiveness in dynamic environments.

Table 5.1: Overview of Symbolic AI.

Aspect	Description	Examples
Knowledge Representation	Symbols and logical relationships to encode facts and entities.	Semantic networks, frames, ontologies
Logic and Rules	Formal logic systems used to derive conclusions through reasoning.	Propositional logic, predicate logic
Search and Planning	Algorithms to explore solutions and plan sequences of actions.	STRIPS, heuristic search
Explainability	Transparent and interpretable decision-making processes.	Diagnosis in expert systems, reasoning in legal applications
Applications	Niche domains where explicit knowledge is essential.	MYCIN, DENDRAL, Deep Blue
Challenges	Scalability, adaptability, and inability to handle ambiguous or incomplete data.	Difficulty scaling to large domains or integrating with real-world noisy data
Future Potential	Hybrid systems combining symbolic reasoning with machine learning to address current limitations.	Neuro-symbolic AI, explainable AI (XAI)

This comprehensive breakdown captures the depth and breadth of Symbolic AI's methodologies, strengths, and challenges (Table 5.1).

Data-driven AI & Machine Learning

Data-Driven AI

With a focus on statistical techniques and algorithms, data-driven AI works by gleaning patterns, insights, and predictions from large datasets. Data-driven artificial intelligence (AI) learns on its own from the data, as opposed to rule-based systems like symbolic AI, which depend on explicitly encoded rules. It makes use of models that adapt and improve over time in response to the data they are fed, allowing for increasingly accurate results. The volume and quality of data that data-driven AI processes have a direct impact on its accuracy and resilience. The system's predictions get better as it absorbs more pertinent and carefully chosen data, demonstrating a greater comprehension of underlying patterns. The AI's ability to improve performance and adjust to changing circumstances is made possible by this cycle of continuous learning, which increases its value for applications requiring dynamic decision-making.

- **Core Principles**

Analyzing past data to find trends and patterns that can be applied to actual circumstances is how data-driven AI works. Large, varied datasets that faithfully capture the complexity of the environment it is intended to model are its foundation. AI systems can extract valuable insights from data by utilizing a range of algorithms, including classification, regression, and clustering. These insights form the basis of decision-making procedures. The ability of data-driven AI systems to extrapolate from the data in order to generate predictions and suggestions is their fundamental function. These algorithms give AI the ability to carry out tasks like sentiment analysis, recommendation generation, and fraud detection. Because recommendation engines, sentiment analysis platforms, and fraud detection systems all depend on the methodical examination of enormous datasets to produce precise results, data-driven AI has consequently emerged as a crucial instrument in many different industries.

- **Strengths**

The capacity of data-driven AI to continuously adapt and get better with more data is one of its main benefits. The ability of data-driven AI to generalize from real-world examples enables it to function well in dynamic environments, in contrast to traditional systems that require manual updates to account for new scenarios. This makes it especially useful in dynamic domains where new data is continuously generated and the system needs to change to remain relevant, like social media analytics or online retail. Furthermore, complex tasks that call for the identification of intricate patterns in sizable datasets are well-suited for data-driven AI. For instance, the underlying patterns in the data are frequently too complex to be manually encoded in domains such as image recognition, natural language processing, and predictive modeling. Data-driven AI is particularly well-equipped to recognize these patterns on its own, producing more precise forecasts and insights in situations that are challenging for traditional systems to handle.

- **Challenges**

Reliance on high-quality data is the main issue with data-driven models. Biased or incomplete data can produce biased results, posing serious risks in delicate areas where accuracy and fairness are crucial, such as criminal justice or hiring. In these situations, even minor biases in the data can lead to unfair decisions that hurt people or groups or perpetuate discrimination. Furthermore, a lot of data-driven models—deep learning models in particular—have interpretability issues that render them "black boxes." Applications that require accountability and transparency face significant challenges due to this opacity. Understanding decision-making processes is essential in these domains to guarantee that they comply with legal and ethical requirements, which makes many models' "black box" nature a significant challenge.

Machine Learning (ML)

Enabling systems to learn from data without explicit programming is the goal of machine learning, a subset of data-driven artificial intelligence (AI). Machine learning uses a range of algorithms and methods to help machines recognize patterns, predict outcomes, and enhance their performance as they are exposed to more and more data. Its gradual self-improvement makes it an effective tool for a variety of uses, including predictive analytics and speech recognition. Fundamentally, machine learning is predicated on the notion that systems can adjust and improve their behavior as they absorb more data. Machine learning models learn from examples rather than being explicitly programmed to carry out particular tasks, which improves their capacity to make precise decisions on their own. These models continuously improve as a result of being exposed to various data sets, which enables them to handle challenging tasks with greater accuracy and efficiency.

- **Core Principles**

Supervised learning, unsupervised learning, and reinforcement learning are the three primary categories into which machine learning (ML) is usually divided. Models are trained on labeled datasets in supervised learning, enabling them to classify or predict using the patterns they discover. When the model must generalize to new, unseen data and the result is known, this approach is frequently employed. Unsupervised learning, on the other hand, works with unlabeled data and aims to find hidden patterns or structures without knowing the results beforehand. Clustering, anomaly detection, and examining relationships within data are all aided by this kind of learning. On the other hand, reinforcement learning is a kind of machine learning in which agents pick up knowledge through interaction with their surroundings. The agents are taught to make choices that maximize cumulative rewards by using a system that penalizes undesirable behavior and rewards desirable behavior. In situations requiring dynamic decision-making, like autonomous systems, robotics, and gaming, this kind of learning is especially helpful. Depending on the type of data and the particular objectives of the model, each of these three types is essential in a variety of real-world applications.

- **Strengths**

Many advanced technologies, such as conversational AI, personalized medicine, and self-driving cars, are built on machine learning (ML). Machine learning (ML) can tackle difficult problems like speech synthesis, image recognition, and gaming by analyzing and learning from large datasets, frequently with superhuman accuracy. It is a driving force behind creative breakthroughs because of its strong algorithms, which enable systems to adapt and improve on their own. Furthermore, machine learning's modularity makes it possible for seamless integration across a range of industries. Because of its adaptability, machine learning (ML) can improve operations, maximize decision-making, and boost productivity in a variety of industries, including healthcare, finance, entertainment, and manufacturing. The potential uses of machine learning are therefore practically endless, influencing the course of innumerable industries and opening the door for ground-breaking solutions.

- **Challenges**

Machine learning (ML), like data-driven AI, is highly dependent on the caliber and volume of data used to train models. The availability of sizable and precise datasets, which form the basis for the algorithms' ability to generate predictions or classifications, has a direct impact on the efficacy of machine learning models. The model's performance may be seriously hampered by inaccurate, biased, or incomplete data. Furthermore, it can be difficult to comprehend how deep learning models, which are frequently employed in machine learning, arrive at their conclusions because they frequently lack interpretability. This opacity can cast doubt on the model's transparency and reliability, especially in high-stakes domains like medical diagnosis where making the wrong choice can have dire repercussions. Additionally, it takes a lot of computer power to train machine learning models, particularly for sophisticated algorithms like deep learning. These models require a lot of resources to develop and implement, including powerful hardware and a substantial time commitment. Because the computational cost of models rises with their complexity, organizations must obtain access to specialized infrastructure in order to meet the demands. To guarantee the efficiency and dependability of machine learning systems in crucial applications, the problems posed by the combination of high data requirements, opaqueness, and costly computational requirements must be carefully addressed.

Comparison of Data-Driven AI vs. Machine Learning, as mention in below Table 5.2:

Table 5.2: Data-Driven AI vs. Machine Learning.

Aspect	Data-Driven AI	Machine Learning
Definition	AI that uses large datasets to derive insights and make decisions autonomously.	A subset of AI that involves algorithms learning patterns from data.
Goal	To leverage data for automation and decision-making.	To create models that predict or classify data.
Methodology	Often relies on data collection, analysis, and rule-based logic.	Primarily focuses on training models using algorithms (e.g., regression, classification).
Data Dependency	Extremely dependent on large volumes of diverse data to function.	Relies on data, but can work with smaller datasets and specific features.
Complexity	Typically, more complex, involving the integration of multiple data sources and processes.	Focuses on model training and optimization, often using pre-defined data sets.
Adaptability	Can automatically adapt to new data over time, but often requires significant infrastructure.	Can adapt through continuous learning or retraining, depending on the model type.
Example Use Cases	Autonomous decision-making systems, smart cities, predictive maintenance, etc.	Spam filtering, image recognition, speech recognition, etc.
Tools & Techniques	Big Data analytics, Deep Learning, Neural Networks, Natural Language Processing.	Supervised, Unsupervised, and Reinforcement Learning algorithms.
Data Processing Needs	Often requires data preprocessing, cleaning, and normalization at a higher level.	Needs data preprocessing, but sometimes less complex compared to data-driven AI.
Interpretability	Can sometimes be harder to interpret due to complex algorithms used.	Can often be more interpretable, especially in simpler models like linear regression.
Scalability	Scalable but may face challenges when handling rapidly growing or unstructured data.	Highly scalable, especially with cloud-based machine learning platforms.

Examples of Data-Driven AI and Machine Learning

1. Examples of Data-Driven AI

Fraud Detection in Banking

- **Use Case:** Identifying fraudulent transactions based on historical data.
- **How It Works:** A dataset containing records of both fraudulent and legitimate transactions is analyzed to identify patterns, such as unusually large withdrawals or transactions from foreign locations.
- **Outcome:** The system flags suspicious activities for further review.

2. Recommendation Systems

- **Use Case:** Suggesting movies, books, or products to users on platforms like Netflix, Amazon, or Spotify.
- **How It Works:** Uses collaborative filtering or content-based filtering to analyze user preferences and recommend similar items based on historical data.
- **Outcome:** Personalized recommendations enhance user experience and increase engagement.

3. Market Analysis and Forecasting

- **Use Case:** Predicting stock prices or market trends based on historical economic data.
- **How It Works:** Models like time series analysis or regression identify trends, seasonality, and patterns to make future predictions.
- **Outcome:** Helps businesses and investors make informed decisions.

Examples of Machine Learning

1. Self-Driving Cars (Autonomous Vehicles)

- **Use Case:** Navigating roads safely without human intervention.
- **How It Works:** Machine learning models process sensor data, such as images, LiDAR signals, and GPS, to identify objects (e.g., pedestrians, other vehicles), predict their movements, and make real-time decisions.
- **Outcome:** Enables safe and efficient autonomous driving.

2. Image Recognition

- **Use Case:** Diagnosing medical conditions from X-rays or identifying objects in photos.
- **How It Works:** Deep learning algorithms, such as convolutional neural networks (CNNs), learn patterns in images to classify or detect objects.
- **Outcome:** Systems like Google Lens or AI-assisted medical tools can identify objects, landmarks, or diseases with high accuracy.

3. Chatbots and Virtual Assistants

- **Use Case:** Providing customer support or personal assistance (e.g., Siri, Alexa, or Google Assistant).
- **How It Works:** Natural Language Processing (NLP) models learn from large datasets of text to understand and generate human-like responses.
- **Outcome:** Enhances customer service by providing instant and accurate responses to queries.

Machine Learning and Deep Learning based AI

Machine Learning (ML) and Deep Learning (DL) have emerged as the key drivers of the remarkable advancements in artificial intelligence (AI) over the years. Without the need for explicit programming, these data-driven techniques allow systems to learn from enormous volumes of data, finding patterns, forecasting outcomes, and automating intricate decision-making procedures. While DL adopts a more specialized approach by concentrating on neural networks with multiple layers that replicate the structure and function of the human brain, machine learning (ML) provides the fundamental framework for artificial intelligence and encompasses a broad range of algorithms and techniques. ML and DL have had a significant impact on a number of industries, including healthcare, automotive, and entertainment. These cutting-edge AI techniques have fueled technologies like facial recognition, self-driving cars, and personalized medicine. AI will become a crucial component of our everyday lives and future innovations as ML and DL develop further because they have the potential to further transform industries, open up new opportunities, and solve difficult problems.

What is Machine Learning?

A subfield of artificial intelligence (AI), machine learning enables systems to learn from data and improve their performance over time as they process more data. It makes it possible for machines to recognize patterns, anticipate outcomes, and make decisions without the need for explicit programming by creating sophisticated algorithms. The fundamental tenet of machine learning is that systems are capable of evolving and adapting in response to experience, learning from past data to improve their performance. This area entails developing algorithms that can process input data and derive insightful information that can be applied to novel, untested situations. These algorithms can be anything from unsupervised learning methods that find hidden patterns in unstructured data to supervised learning models that use labeled data. Because of this, machine learning is essential to fields like autonomous systems, natural language processing, and predictive analytics, steadily increasing their accuracy and efficiency over time. ML is broadly categorized into three types:

- **Supervised Learning:** The model is trained using labeled data, where the input-output relationships are clearly defined. Examples include tasks like spam detection in emails and predicting house prices.

- **Unsupervised Learning:** The model identifies patterns and structures within unlabeled data. Common applications include clustering and dimensionality reduction, such as customer segmentation.
- **Reinforcement Learning:** The model learns by interacting with an environment, receiving rewards for desired actions through trial and error. This approach is widely used in game-playing AI and robotics

Predictive analytics, recommendation systems, and fraud detection are just a few of the fields that heavily rely on machine learning because of its proficiency with structured data analysis.

What is Deep Learning?

A subset of machine learning (ML), deep learning (DL) makes use of artificial neural networks that are modeled after the composition and operations of the human brain. Each layer of these neural networks contributes to the extraction of increasingly complex features from the data, hence the term "deep," which refers to the fact that these networks are built with multiple layers. For instance, in an image recognition task, the deeper layers concentrate on identifying particular objects within the image, while the initial layers may detect basic elements like edges. DL can efficiently identify complex patterns and relationships in big datasets thanks to this multi-layered approach. For training, DL models need a lot of data and a lot of processing power, unlike traditional ML models. Recurrent neural networks (RNNs) are used to solve sequence prediction problems, while convolutional neural networks (CNNs) are used for image processing tasks. Speech recognition, machine translation, and autonomous driving are just a few of the fields that have seen tremendous success thanks to deep learning's ability to handle complex, high-dimensional data. These developments show how DL can address difficult real-world issues that were previously outside the purview of previous AI models.

Differences between ML and DL

The basic goal of both machine learning (ML) and deep learning (DL) is to make predictions and automate tasks, but their approaches and applications differ greatly. In traditional machine learning, the most pertinent features for a task are determined by domain experts through manual feature extraction. Deep learning, on the other hand, automates this process so that the model can learn features straight from raw data without the need for direct human intervention. For handling unstructured data, like text, audio, and images, where traditional ML techniques might falter, DL is especially effective. A machine learning model may, for instance, use preprocessing methods to extract important characteristics like color and texture in image classification. A deep learning model, like a convolutional neural network (CNN), on the other hand, automatically picks up these characteristics during training. Deep learning models are more capable than traditional machine learning models, but this comes at a cost: they take longer to train and are more computationally intensive. Because of this, DL models require more resources but are ultimately more efficient for complicated tasks involving vast amounts of unstructured data.

Table 5.3: Differences between Machine Learning (ML) and Deep Learning (DL).

Aspect	Machine Learning (ML)	Deep Learning (DL)
Definition	A subset of AI that allows systems to learn from data without explicit programming.	A subset of ML that uses neural networks with many layers to learn from large amounts of data.
Data Dependency	Works with smaller datasets.	Requires large datasets for better performance.
Feature Engineering	Relies heavily on manual feature extraction and engineering.	Automatically performs feature extraction from raw data.
Model Complexity	Models are less complex, e.g., decision trees, SVMs, etc.	Models are more complex, consisting of deep neural networks.
Computational Power	Requires less computational power.	Requires high computational power (GPUs, TPUs).
Interpretability	Easier to interpret and explain the results.	Often considered a "black box," harder to interpret.
Training Time	Generally faster training time due to simpler models.	Longer training time due to deep networks and large data.
Applications	Suitable for problems with structured data like tabular data.	Ideal for unstructured data like images, audio, and text.
Examples	Regression, Decision Trees, Random Forest, SVMs, etc.	Convolutional Neural Networks (CNN), Recurrent Neural Networks (RNN), etc.
Performance with Data	Performance improves with moderate data sizes.	Performance improves significantly with large data sets.

The differences between ML and DL are evident in Table 5.3 above, which also highlights each technology's special advantages, disadvantages, and areas of application.

Applications of Machine Learning and Deep Learning along with advantages and challenges

Industries have been significantly impacted by machine learning (ML) and deep learning (DL), which have changed procedures and provided creative answers. Through the analysis of structured clinical data, machine learning (ML) plays a critical role in healthcare by predicting patient outcomes and diagnosing diseases, making it a vital tool for medical professionals. However, DL is particularly good at tasks involving unstructured data, like medical images like MRIs and X-rays, where it can spot patterns and abnormalities that human eyes might miss. While DL is used to develop more complex, individualized experiences like chatbots for customer service, machine learning (ML) is essential in the finance industry for identifying fraud and evaluating credit risks through the analysis of transactional data. While DL helps with complex tasks like natural language processing (NLP) for chatbots, machine translation, and even autonomous vehicles, where it processes sensor and camera data, ML also powers recommendation engines that offer customized shopping experiences for e-commerce platforms. Although ML and DL have both shown impressive potential, they work best with different kinds of data and applications. Although it frequently necessitates manual feature engineering and domain expertise to achieve optimal performance, machine learning is especially effective for structured datasets and smaller-scale problems. Although DL requires large datasets and significant processing power, it is more effective at handling large volumes of unstructured and complex data because it can automatically extract pertinent features from raw data. However, there are drawbacks to both technologies. As these technologies develop and become more integrated into different industries, they are vulnerable to problems like data bias, which can lead to unfair or skewed outcomes. This emphasizes the necessity of ethical considerations and fairness measures. DL is particularly well-suited for applications that are pushing the limits of automation and artificial intelligence because of its capacity to process unstructured data, such as text and images.

Future of ML and DL

The convergence of emerging technologies like edge computing, quantum computing, and neuro-symbolic artificial intelligence (AI) is becoming more and more important to the future of machine learning (ML) and deep learning (DL). Researchers are working hard to make models easier to understand, lower computational costs, and create solutions that are more broadly applicable. ML and DL will become more efficient as these developments progress, increasing their accessibility and influence across a range of industries. These technologies working together have the potential to speed up the creation of intelligent systems that can solve progressively more challenging issues. The potential of ML and DL is growing exponentially as a result of the quick expansion of datasets and the ongoing development of computing power. This development makes it possible to develop cutting-edge AI-powered solutions that revolutionize a number of industries. ML and DL are essential tools for influencing the direction of artificial intelligence and bringing about revolutionary change in a variety of industries because of their capacity to adjust to a variety of environments and solve real-world problems using scalable, flexible, and robust models.

Applications of symbolic & data driven AI

Expert Systems

The development of AI has been greatly aided by expert systems, especially in fields that call for specific knowledge. By processing data and making inferences based on a predetermined set of rules, these systems are intended to mimic the knowledge of human experts. Expert systems can simulate human decision-making in fields like engineering, law, and medicine because their logic is usually expressed as "if-then" rules. For example, an early medical expert system called MYCIN used a set of rules to identify bacterial infections and suggest treatments based on test results and patient symptoms. Expert systems' strength is their capacity to provide extremely dependable answers in domains with well-defined rules and expertise. In domains where accountability is crucial, their capacity to provide transparent justifications for decisions is invaluable. Expert systems have a number of drawbacks, despite their early success. Scalability is a significant issue because it can be challenging and resource-intensive to manage and update knowledge bases as the domain becomes more complex. The process of acquiring knowledge becomes a bottleneck for expert systems since they need a lot of domain-specific knowledge to work well. They also have trouble in areas where there is uncertainty, unclear data, or changing knowledge. Although expert systems work well for specialized, limited tasks, their rigid structure makes them less flexible in complex or quickly changing environments.

Natural Language Understanding (NLU)

One of the main areas where symbolic AI made a substantial contribution was Natural Language Understanding (NLU), which set the stage for increasingly complex natural language processing (NLP) systems. Rule-based techniques, such as parsing text using predefined grammars and mapping words to their meanings using lexicons, were used by early symbolic NLU systems. This made it possible for early AI systems to comprehend simple sentence structures and perform tasks like translating languages, responding to inquiries, and having simple conversations. Additionally, symbolic methods offered a straightforward and interpretable way to decipher sentence meaning. Systems like the early chatbot ELIZA, for instance, might react to user input according to pre-programmed patterns, showcasing the potential of symbolic AI for structured user interaction. But symbolic NLU found it difficult to deal with the ambiguities and complexity that come with human language. Significant difficulties were caused by idiomatic phrases, polysemy (words having multiple meanings), and contextual subtleties. Machine learning-based techniques that could learn from data and manage variability more skilfully gradually replaced symbolic systems because of their inflexible nature, which made it hard to adjust to such complexities. However, symbolic approaches continue to be employed in specialized fields where accurate language interpretations are necessary, like technical manuals or legal documents, where precise wording and meaning are crucial for precise analysis and decision-making.

Robotics and Task Automation

Symbolic AI is essential to robotics because it allows for intelligent decision-making and task automation. Robots can complete tasks like product assembly and environment navigation in a controlled and predictable way by using symbolic planners like STRIPS (Stanford Research Institute Problem Solver), which divide complicated tasks into smaller, more manageable actions. These systems use logical reasoning and a set of rules to decide what steps a robot needs to take in order to accomplish a particular goal. In structured environments with clearly defined tasks, observable constraints, and a system that can be closely monitored, symbolic AI performs especially well. Robots in warehouse automation, for instance, use symbolic reasoning to determine the best course of action when picking and positioning items. However, when used in dynamic, unpredictable environments where the system cannot rely exclusively on predefined rules, symbolic AI has limitations. Robots frequently face complex interactions, unforeseen changes, and incomplete information in real-world situations, which puts symbolic planners' strict logic to the test. Hybrid systems that blend machine learning and symbolic AI are becoming more and more popular as a solution to these problems. By utilizing the advantages of symbolic reasoning to preserve structure and logical planning abilities, these hybrid approaches enable robots to adjust to unpredictable or changing environments.

Game Playing

The field of gaming has been greatly impacted by symbolic AI, particularly in strategy games that call for the use of logical tactics and in-depth analysis of potential moves. One of the most prominent instances is IBM's Deep Blue, which defeated Garry Kasparov, the world chess champion, in 1997 using symbolic AI. Following the rigorous chess rules, Deep Blue evaluated millions of possible moves using a combination of symbolic reasoning and brute-force search. Deep Blue and other symbolic AI systems perform exceptionally well in games with clear rules and comprehensive information because they can methodically investigate every option in order to determine the best course of action. However, games that require dynamic, adaptive strategies or involve incomplete information, like poker, reduce the effectiveness of symbolic AI. Symbolic AI's dependence on preset rules and exhaustive search becomes a limitation in these circumstances. More sophisticated methods, like probabilistic models and reinforcement learning, are showing greater success with these kinds of games. These techniques enable systems to handle the uncertainty that symbolic AI finds difficult to deal with by learning from experience and modifying strategies based on the results of prior actions.

Applications of Data-Driven AI

Healthcare

By using enormous volumes of medical data to propel improvements in diagnosis, treatment strategies, and predictive health models, data-driven AI has completely transformed the healthcare industry. AI models, for instance, are able to analyze patient data, including genetic information, electronic health records, and medical imaging, in order to anticipate possible health risks and offer early interventions. Specifically, by spotting patterns that human physicians might miss, AI algorithms have emerged as a valuable tool for diagnosing diseases like cancer, diabetes, and cardiovascular disorders. Furthermore, AI-powered solutions such as IBM Watson Health evaluate enormous datasets to offer tailored treatment suggestions, improving the effectiveness and accuracy of healthcare delivery. AI is improving patient outcomes and lowering medical errors by assisting healthcare professionals in making better decisions by integrating large volumes of complex data. But despite their potential, these innovations come with drawbacks. Access to high-quality, representative datasets is essential for the success of data-driven AI in healthcare, but gathering them can be challenging because of concerns about patient privacy, data sharing, and consent. Furthermore, there is still a chance of false positives or negatives even though AI systems have demonstrated the ability to diagnose illnesses as accurately as human specialists, especially in less common conditions or unstructured data like medical imaging. Furthermore, ongoing discussions regarding the future role of AI in healthcare revolve around ethical concerns regarding the use and security of patient data.

Finance

Data-driven AI is being used in the financial industry in a number of ways to enhance decision-making, security, and efficiency. Fraud detection is one of the most common applications, where machine learning algorithms examine transaction data in real-time to spot unusual patterns or suspicious activity that might indicate fraud. By continuously learning from fresh data, these systems get better at identifying potentially dangerous transactions before they result in substantial financial loss. Furthermore, by evaluating a range of variables, such as a person's credit history, financial behavior, and even social media activity, AI plays a critical role in credit risk assessment by estimating the probability of default. This enables financial institutions to offer more specialized financial products and make more accurate lending decisions. Another game-changer is AI's role in algorithmic trading, which enables high-frequency, data-driven decisions that can respond nearly instantly to changes in the market. In order to predict stock movements, machine learning models examine both historical market data and current trends. This allows for faster and more accurate trades than human traders could. These applications have risks even though they have many advantages. For instance, discriminatory financial practices or erroneous forecasts may result from biased or insufficient data. Furthermore, questions concerning market manipulation and the moral application of algorithms are brought up by the quick development of AI in finance. Regulatory oversight will be crucial as AI continues to influence the sector in order to guarantee security, fairness, and transparency.

E-Commerce

With its dynamic pricing strategies and tailored recommendations, data-driven AI has emerged as a key component of contemporary e-commerce, improving the customer experience. In order to recommend goods or content that closely match user preferences, platforms such as Amazon and Netflix employ advanced machine learning models to examine user behavior, including browsing history, purchase patterns, and ratings. To make sure that suggestions are timely and pertinent, these recommendation systems combine collaborative filtering, content-based filtering, and hybrid techniques. By showing customers products, they are more likely to buy, this not only raises customer satisfaction but also boosts sales and engagement. AI's contribution to e-commerce also includes dynamic pricing, in which algorithms instantly modify prices in response to variables like inventory levels, rival pricing, and market demand. By doing this, e-commerce platforms can maintain their competitiveness in the market while optimizing pricing strategies to maximize profits. Additionally, chatbots and virtual assistants driven by AI are enhancing customer service by assisting customers in finding products, getting answers to their questions, and swiftly and effectively resolving problems. But the use of AI also brings up issues with data privacy and algorithmic bias in recommendation systems, which may have unanticipated effects on consumer behavior.

Autonomous Vehicles

The foundation of autonomous vehicles is data-driven AI, which enables them to process vast volumes of real-time data from sensors, cameras, and radar systems in order to navigate the environment safely and effectively. These cars can identify pedestrians, traffic signals, and other cars thanks to deep learning models. They can also decide whether to brake, accelerate, or steer in order to prevent collisions. Based on past and present data, machine learning algorithms further improve the system's capacity to forecast the actions of other road users, like cyclists or other drivers. This technology was invented by companies like Tesla and Waymo, and as self-driving cars gain experience in a variety of driving situations and environments, they are constantly enhancing their capabilities.

There are still important issues that need to be resolved in spite of the progress. One major issue is making sure autonomous cars are safe in uncommon and challenging driving scenarios. How should an autonomous car respond, for instance, when an accident is inevitable? Another significant challenge is making sure the system can adjust to novel situations, like changing weather patterns or road construction. The widespread use of self-driving cars raises ethical and regulatory concerns despite the ongoing advancements in data-driven AI, particularly with regard to liability in the event of an accident and public confidence in the technology.

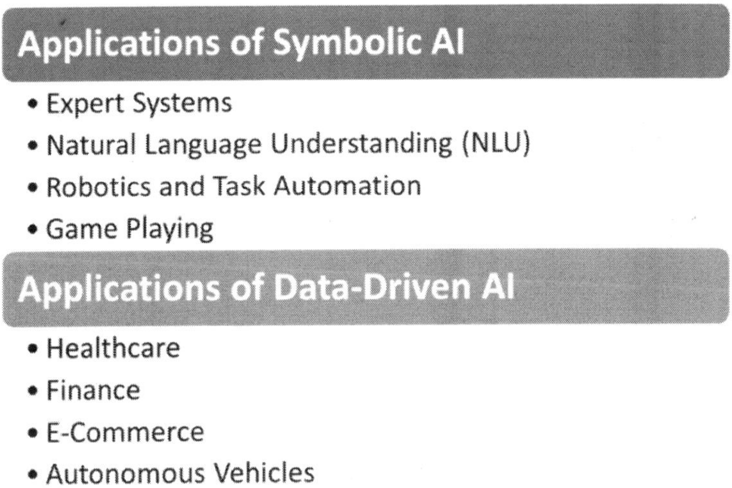

Figure 5.1: Applications of symbolic and data driven AI.

As shown in Figure 5.1, data-driven AI and symbolic AI each have special advantages and uses. Symbolic AI performs best in settings that call for logical problem-solving, structured knowledge representation, and explicit reasoning. This method works especially well in fields where accuracy and clarity are crucial, like expert systems and formal rule-based systems. However, data-driven AI excels in handling dynamic, unstructured environments such as image recognition and natural language processing, where patterns and trends are derived from massive amounts of data rather than preset rules. These two strategies work together to produce hybrid AI systems that capitalize on their respective advantages. While data-driven AI can improve flexibility and adaptability, symbolic AI can offer structure and reasoning. From financial modeling and customer service to healthcare and autonomous systems, this synergy provides a potent answer to a variety of real-world problems. Hybrid AI systems offer a promising future for resolving intricate, multidimensional issues by combining these complementary capabilities (Table 5.4).

Table 5.4: Comparison of Applications.

Aspect	Symbolic AI	Data-Driven AI
Definition	AI based on explicitly defined rules and symbols.	AI that learns patterns from data through algorithms.
Core Approach	Rule-based reasoning, logic, and knowledge representation.	Machine learning algorithms, neural networks, and statistical models.
Data Representation	Uses structured, explicit symbols and knowledge bases.	Uses large datasets to learn and infer patterns.
Explainability	High, as reasoning steps and rules are clear.	Often low, as models like deep learning are considered black-boxes.
Flexibility	Limited flexibility due to rigid rules and structure.	Highly flexible, capable of adapting to various problems.
Performance in Complex Tasks	Struggles with complex, uncertain, or incomplete data.	Performs well in handling complex, noisy, and unstructured data.
Use in Problem Solving	Best for tasks with clear rules and logical relationships (e.g., expert systems).	Best for tasks with large amounts of data or unclear rules (e.g., image recognition).
Applications	Knowledge-based systems, rule-based expert systems, decision support systems.	Image and speech recognition, natural language processing, recommendation systems.
Interpretability	High interpretability due to explicit rule-based logic.	Low interpretability, especially with complex models like deep learning.
Example Systems	Classic expert systems like MYCIN, SHAKEN, etc.	Deep learning models like GPT-4, Google's BERT, image classifiers, etc.

Interpretable & Explainable AI

Why Interpretable and Explainable AI are Important?

The growing use of AI in fields like criminal justice, healthcare, and finance emphasizes how crucial it is to comprehend how these systems make decisions. AI systems must give concise justifications for their decisions in order to win over users and stakeholders. To ensure patient and physician confidence in their dependability, AI-driven medical diagnosis systems, for instance, must provide explanations for their recommendations. In the financial industry, AI systems that reject loans are required to provide a clear justification in order to adhere to laws like the General Data Protection Regulation (GDPR) of the EU, which places a strong emphasis on the "right to explanation." Transparency is essential to making sure people understand the decisions that affect their lives, particularly in crucial areas like court rulings where ambiguity could encourage prejudice or mistakes. Explainability, which promotes equity and inclusivity by identifying biases in data and model design, is also crucial for the development of ethical AI. It is also useful for debugging and enhancing AI systems. Developers can optimize the system by examining the AI explanations and identifying any errors in the logic of the model or the data used. Understanding AI decision-making helps firms' lower risks and increase operational effectiveness while making sure AI systems meet ethical standards and intended results. The general effectiveness of implementing AI in high-stakes situations depends on the openness and confidence that explainability promotes.

Interpretable AI

Users can directly comprehend their decision-making processes thanks to interpretable AI models' inherent transparency. Because of their generally simpler structures, these models are perfect for applications where a high degree of accountability is essential. In the medical field, for example, a linear regression model can forecast a patient's recovery time while providing a clear picture of the ways in which age, comorbidities, and treatment type affect the result. This openness makes the model's recommendations more credible to patients and clinicians. In a similar vein, decision trees offer yet another illustration of interpretable AI. As in a loan approval system where certain thresholds like income and credit score determine the outcome, their branching structure demonstrates the path from input to output and precisely how certain conditions lead to particular decisions. Interpretable AI models have a lot to offer in terms of accountability and transparency, but in more complicated tasks, their simplicity may be a drawback. The complex patterns and unstructured data in fields like image recognition and speech processing, for instance, frequently call for more complex models—like deep neural networks—that are more difficult to interpret. These sophisticated models have less transparency even though they may be more accurate at handling challenging tasks. As a result, although interpretable AI is crucial in fields where consumer confidence and regulatory compliance are crucial, it might not always offer the degree of accuracy required for sophisticated applications that work with vast amounts of unstructured data.

Explainable AI

By providing insights into the decision-making processes of complex, opaque models, Explainable AI (XAI) improves transparency and tackles the problems they present. XAI aims to explain the decisions made by black-box models, like deep learning networks, which are frequently challenging to interpret because of their complex structure, in contrast to traditional interpretable AI, which concentrates on making models more understandable. Large and complicated dataset tasks, like language translation or object recognition in photos, are well suited for these models. However, particularly in crucial applications like healthcare or finance, their lack of transparency can be a major obstacle. Making these models more approachable is largely dependent on XAI techniques like SHAP (SHapley Additive exPlanations) and LIME (Local Interpretable Model-Agnostic Explanations). LIME provides a more straightforward explanation for individual predictions by locally approximating the behavior of a complex model. This is especially helpful in fields like medical imaging, where it can identify the features of an image that most helped with a diagnosis. By giving each feature an importance value, SHAP, on the other hand, offers a more mathematically based explanation, making it clear how each feature contributes to a specific prediction. Tools like Grad-CAM and saliency maps are especially useful for displaying the areas of an input image that had the biggest impact on the model's choice. Saliency maps, for instance, can highlight lung regions that the AI deems significant when diagnosing pneumonia from chest X-rays, helping medical professionals comprehend the reasoning behind the model's diagnosis. Notwithstanding the advantages of XAI, it is important to remember that these methods might only roughly represent the model's actual logic. This may cast doubt on the accuracy and comprehensiveness of these justifications, particularly when important choices are dependent on their insights.

Applications of Interpretable and Explainable AI

- Healthcare

Explainable AI (XAI) is significantly improving the precision and reliability of diagnostic and treatment planning systems in the healthcare industry. For instance, in order to identify diseases like cancer, AI models are being used to evaluate medical images from CT, MRI, and X-ray scans. But in order for these models to be really helpful, they need to be open about how they come to their conclusions. This implies that when an AI diagnoses cancer, it should not only display the outcome but also draw attention to the particular areas or patterns in the picture that supported the diagnosis. Because of this transparency, physicians are better able to trust the AI's results and confidently apply them to their clinical judgments. Furthermore, explainable AI models that forecast patient outcomes—like risk scores—provide insightful information about how a patient's prognosis is influenced by a variety of factors, including age, lifestyle, and pre-existing medical conditions, facilitating better informed medical decision-making.

- Finance

Explainable AI is in high demand in the finance industry due to regulatory requirements and the need to gain the trust of customers. AI is frequently utilized in fields where precise decision-making is essential, such as credit scoring, fraud detection, and investment advice. For example, if an AI system rejects a loan application, the consumer should be told about the main criteria that affected the decision, like income or credit history. Customers are given the chance to comprehend their financial situation and financial institutions are guaranteed to adhere to regulations thanks to this transparency. SHAP (Shapley Additive Explanations) values, which give various model features importance scores, are one of the most popular techniques for guaranteeing explainability in finance. By measuring each component's contribution, SHAP makes the financial ecosystem more accountable by assisting consumers and regulators in confirming and trusting the AI's judgments.

- Autonomous Vehicles

For safety and dependability in the field of autonomous vehicles, explainable AI is crucial. Autonomous vehicles need to be able to make quick, context-sensitive decisions in dynamic, complicated situations. A car must choose whether to stop at an intersection or use evasive maneuvers to get around an obstruction, for example. Manufacturers and regulatory agencies can track the logic behind these snap decisions with explainable AI. Saliency maps, which display which environmental factors—such as other cars, pedestrians, or traffic signs—influenced the car's behavior, are one method for accomplishing this. In addition to making, it easier to comprehend how the car makes decisions, this transparency guarantees that these systems function in a predictable, secure, and verifiable manner, fulfilling the safety regulations necessary for public roads.

- Legal and Criminal Justice

In legal and criminal justice contexts, artificial intelligence (AI) systems are being utilized more and more, particularly for risk assessments associated with parole, sentencing, or recidivism forecasts. However, these systems need to be comprehensible in order to be trusted and accepted. When it comes to delicate decisions that have the potential to impact people's lives, transparency is essential to ensuring that the AI does not reinforce preexisting biases. For instance, an AI system must provide a clear explanation of the criteria that led to the defendant's classification as high-risk, such as prior convictions, behavioral patterns, or socioeconomic status. This degree of explainability is crucial for protecting against potential biases or unfair outcomes that could result from opaque, black-box algorithms, as well as for fostering trust among legal professionals.

- Challenges in Implementing XAI

Explainable artificial intelligence (XAI) has many applications, but there are drawbacks to its deployment. The trade-off between accuracy and interpretability is one of the main challenges. Although they are simpler to comprehend, simpler models like decision trees or linear regressions might not always offer the level of performance needed for challenging tasks. More complex models, such as deep neural networks, on the other hand, provide greater accuracy but are frequently regarded as "black boxes," making it challenging to understand how they make decisions. For researchers and developers, balancing these conflicting priorities while maintaining high accuracy and interpretability in AI systems continues to be a significant challenge. Finding this balance is essential to promoting the use of AI in delicate and regulated domains where openness is essential to building credibility and guaranteeing equity.The subjectivity of explanations is another problem because different stakeholders, such as developers, regulators, or end users, frequently have different ideas about what makes an adequate explanation. For instance, an end-user without the technical background could easily become confused by a highly technical explanation that might satisfy the needs of a developer. This subjectivity complicates the task of effectively communicating complex model decisions by making it difficult to develop explanations that are universally understood or deemed adequate across diverse audiences. As a result, different parties may not find the same explanation satisfactory, leading to misunderstandings. Another major issue is scalability, especially when creating explanations for big datasets or real-time decision-making systems. Particularly as model complexity rises, the computational expense of producing these explanations may become unaffordable. Furthermore, although helpful, post-hoc explanation methods like LIME or SHAP might only provide estimates of the model's logic rather than a precise representation of the decision-making process. The underlying model's complexities may not be fully captured by these approximations, as seen in Figure 5.3, which could result in gaps in the precision or interpretability of the explanations offered.

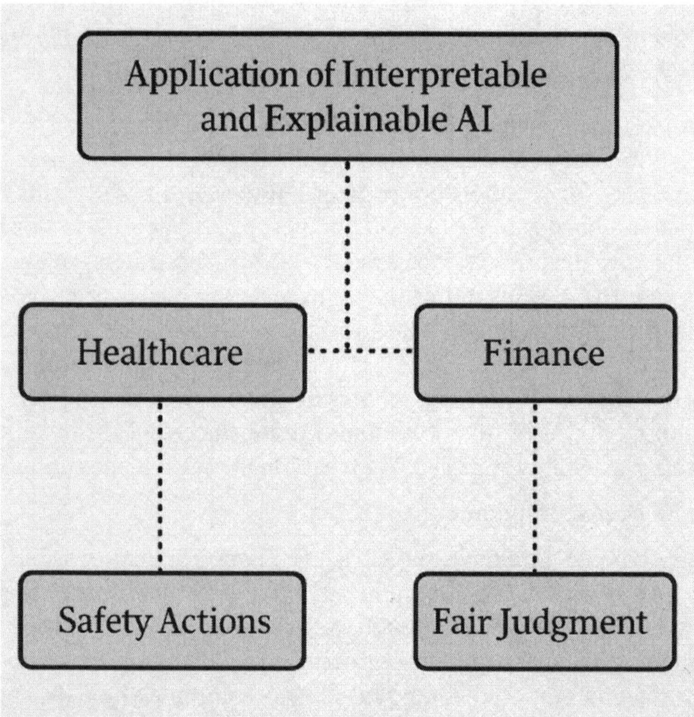

Figure 5.3: Applications of Interpretable and Explainable AI.

Future of Interpretable and Explainable AI

The development of hybrid models that blend the accuracy of more complex systems with the interpretability of simpler ones is the key to the future of Explainable AI (XAI). A promising field of study is neuro-symbolic AI, which combines data-driven learning and symbolic reasoning. In order to promote trust in AI applications, these hybrid systems seek to provide reliable performance while preserving transparency. In order to meet the increasing demand for more transparent AI solutions, researchers are attempting to make sure that AI systems are not only strong but also comprehensible and dependable by combining the advantages of both methodologies. C The accessibility and reliability of AI systems will greatly increase as long as developments in human-centered AI design, explainability theory, and visualization tools continue. These developments are essential to promoting the ethical and responsible development of AI. Fairness, openness, and conformity to social norms are becoming more and more important in society, and XAI will be essential in making sure AI systems incorporate these ideas. XAI will open the door for wider industry adoption and support the responsible use of cutting-edge technologies by making AI systems both transparent and accountable.

Ethics of AI

The ethical considerations, societal effects, and difficulties related to the creation and application of AI technologies are all covered in the field of artificial intelligence ethics. Fairness, accountability, and transparency become major concerns as AI becomes more ingrained in daily life. If these technologies are not properly controlled, they have the potential to violate privacy, reinforce prejudices, and even jeopardize job opportunities. In order to guarantee that AI systems are not only effective but also fair and just, promoting public trust and preserving individual liberties, ethical standards are crucial. Given the growing impact of AI systems on vital domains like healthcare, finance, governance, and law enforcement, ethical considerations guarantee that these technologies are developed and applied appropriately. To minimize possible harms and guarantee that AI's function in society is consistent with more general moral objectives, ethical frameworks place a high priority on human rights and values. Given their expanding potential, AI systems need to be developed under supervision to prevent escalating social injustices and to advance justice, inclusivity, and human dignity. For technology to benefit society as a whole in the future, ethical AI governance is essential.

Core Ethical Principles in AI

1. Fairness and Bias Mitigation

Critical decisions in a variety of fields, including hiring, lending, and law enforcement, are increasingly being made by AI systems. Regretfully, the biases present in the data that these systems are trained on may be reflected in them. An AI model may reinforce bias by favoring one gender over another, for instance, if it is trained on hiring data from the past that demonstrates a gender imbalance. Therefore, ensuring that AI models function equitably and make decisions that do not discriminate against particular groups presents an ethical challenge. Implementing tactics like using representative and diverse datasets, creating algorithms that are less susceptible to biased data, and carrying out routine audits are essential for identifying and reducing any potential biases. Organizations must give inclusivity top priority throughout the entire AI development process in order to address fairness. Correcting biased outputs after the fact is insufficient; proactive steps must be taken to guarantee that fairness is engrained in the system's architecture. This can involve working with a variety of stakeholders to assess the model's effects and adding fairness constraints to the algorithms. Furthermore, a more thorough examination made possible by process transparency can aid in the detection and correction of biases. AI developers can lessen unintended harm and contribute to the creation of systems that benefit everyone equally by concentrating on fairness and bias mitigation.

2. Transparency and Explainability

Deep learning-based AI systems in particular are frequently criticized for being "black boxes," meaning that it is difficult to understand or interpret how they make decisions. Because users and stakeholders might not fully understand how a particular decision was reached, this lack of transparency can erode trust in the system. In order to ensure that decisions are understandable and justified, AI systems must give explanations for their actions, according to the ethical principle of transparency. It promotes trust and guarantees that accountability can be allocated efficiently when users are able to follow the logic behind an AI's decision. AI researchers have created a number of methods to improve the interpretability of complex models in order to attain transparency and explainability. These include developing models that are more naturally explicable, like decision trees or linear models, or explaining the results of black-box models using tools like SHAP (Shapley Additive Explanations) and LIME (Local Interpretable Model-Agnostic Explanations). By highlighting the characteristics that had the biggest impact on the model's decision-making, these tools can shed light on how the AI behaved. Ensuring explainability promotes responsible and ethical AI deployment by empowering stakeholders to question and enhance AI systems in addition to increasing user trust.

3. Privacy and Data Protection

Large volumes of personal data are frequently used by AI systems in the big data era to produce insights and make decisions. This presents serious ethical questions about data security and privacy. AI developers need to make sure that people's right to privacy is upheld by handling personal data responsibly. Protecting privacy requires actions like encrypting data while it's being transmitted and stored, anonymizing sensitive data, and making sure that only the information that's required is gathered. AI systems should also abide by privacy laws, such as the General Data Protection Regulation (GDPR) of the European Union, which establishes precise rules for the use and security of personal data. In addition to meeting legal requirements, ethical data handling is essential for preserving public confidence in AI technologies. Users are more likely to accept AI-driven decisions when they have faith that their data is being handled responsibly. In order to establish this trust, it is also essential that data collection, storage, and use be transparent. Furthermore, obtaining users' informed consent about the data being collected is a crucial part of developing ethical AI. AI systems can function in a way that respects individual rights and fosters confidence in their use by adhering to privacy and data protection standards.

4. Accountability and Responsibility

AI systems have the potential to be harmful, either by making biased decisions like unfair loan rejections or by making mistakes like incorrect diagnoses in healthcare applications. This brings up significant accountability issues: who bears responsibility when an AI system makes a bad choice? According to ethical frameworks for AI development, developers, organizations, and legislators should all be held accountable for actions driven by AI. This involves making certain that the right systems, such as monitoring systems, fail-safes, and unambiguous documentation, are in place to handle errors and reduce risks. Furthermore, accountability and transparency go hand in hand. In addition to accepting accountability for their systems, AI developers must make sure that stakeholders and users can hold them responsible for any unfavourable results. Companies need to have well-defined procedures for handling problems, fixing errors, and paying people who have been harmed by AI decisions. Ethical AI practices can boost public trust in AI systems and guarantee their safe and advantageous deployment by fostering a culture of responsibility.

5. Safety and Security

A basic ethical concern is making sure AI systems are safe and secure, particularly in high-stakes applications like military systems, healthcare, and driverless cars. For AI systems to avoid endangering people or society, they must function dependably and without error. An additional source of worry is the possibility of adversarial attacks, in which malevolent actors take advantage of weaknesses in AI systems. The development of ethical AI places a strong emphasis on the necessity of thorough testing, such as stress tests and real-world simulations, in order to find and address any vulnerabilities prior to deployment. Furthermore, it is crucial to protect AI systems from cyberattacks and unauthorized access as they are increasingly integrated into sensitive domains. Businesses need to implement strong cybersecurity procedures, update their systems frequently, and create AI models that are difficult to manipulate. International collaboration is essential to establishing moral standards and preventing abuse in fields like military AI. AI developers can reduce risks, safeguard people, and guarantee that AI technologies benefit society without causing unforeseen consequences by maintaining safety and security.

Societal and Global Impacts

1.Job Displacement and Economic Inequality

Automation powered by AI is changing industries by increasing productivity, cutting expenses, and simplifying operations. But this change also poses a threat to job security, especially for employees in industries like manufacturing, retail, and customer service that rely significantly on manual or repetitive labor. A widening gap between workers with high-tech skills and those whose jobs are automated could result from the widespread adoption of AI, which could cause significant job displacement. Economic inequality may deteriorate as a result, making it more difficult for marginalized groups to adopt new technologies. It is imperative to fund upskilling and reskilling programs that equip workers for positions in cutting-edge industries, such as those involving artificial intelligence, in order to lessen these effects. Societies can better guarantee that the financial advantages of AI are distributed widely by placing a high priority on fair access to education and training. Addressing the economic inequalities brought on by AI automation requires proactive action from organizations and policymakers. Policies that promote universal basic income, retraining initiatives, and safety nets for displaced workers can be implemented by governments. Companies should also embrace ethical AI practices by providing career transition programs and cultivating a diverse workforce. The development of technology should not be the only focus; the wider societal impact should also be considered. Stakeholders can ensure that everyone has the chance to profit from the new economy by cooperating to create an atmosphere where AI developments spur economic growth while lowering inequality.

2. *Human Rights and Autonomy*

There are serious worries about how the quick development of AI technologies may affect human rights, especially those related to autonomy and dignity. For instance, without enough transparency or oversight, AI systems used in social services or law enforcement may make decisions that have an impact on people's lives, which could result in unfair or biased outcomes. People's capacity to make educated decisions and defend their rights may be compromised if life-changing decisions, like access to healthcare, justice, or financial services, are automated. In order to ensure that human oversight continues to play a crucial role in decision-making, ethical AI development necessitates a strong commitment to transparency, fairness, and accountability. The deployment of AI must be centered on a human-centric approach that puts the defense of individual liberties and dignity first in every situation. Governments and organizations must set up strong frameworks for AI governance in order to protect human rights. This includes explicit laws requiring AI systems to be equitable, explicable, and non-discriminatory. In order to stop damaging biases from being reinforced, it is also crucial to include a variety of viewpoints in the development and application of AI technologies. AI should be developed according to values that respect people's rights and liberties, and it should be viewed as a tool to improve rather than reduce human well-being. Society can optimize AI's advantages while lowering its risks to human rights by making sure AI systems are open, responsible, and respectful of human autonomy.

3. *Environmental Sustainability*

As the energy requirements for training and running large-scale models continue to increase, the environmental impact of AI development is becoming a more significant concern. For instance, deep learning model training frequently calls for enormous computational resources that use a lot of energy and increase carbon emissions. AI can have a significant impact on the environment, especially as more businesses spend money creating intricate models to spur innovation. To lessen AI's carbon footprint, ethical AI practices promote the use of renewable energy sources and energy-efficient algorithms. In order to ensure that AI advances global sustainability goals, it is crucial to strike a balance between the need to reduce its environmental impact and the desire for more potent AI as the technology develops. Collaboration among researchers, developers, and organizations is necessary to produce AI systems that use less energy. This entails using greener hardware, optimizing algorithms to lower computational demands, and taking the environmental effects of AI deployments into account at every turn. Governments can also support initiatives that encourage sustainability in AI development, such as grants for eco-friendly technology research and tax breaks for the use of renewable energy. AI can advance in a way that benefits society and the environment by incorporating sustainability into its design and application, addressing climate challenges and promoting innovation at the same time.

4. *Weaponization and Misuse*

There are significant ethical and security issues with the possible application of AI in weapon systems and mass surveillance. For instance, autonomous weapons might function without human oversight, possibly making decisions that could mean the difference between life and death without any accountability. This raises serious questions about the moral application of AI in military settings, where malevolent behavior or unforeseen consequences could cause extensive harm. Similar to this, surveillance systems driven by AI, like facial recognition software, have the potential to violate civil liberties and privacy rights, particularly when employed by businesses or governments without sufficient regulation. Establishing precise international standards and laws controlling AI's application in these delicate fields is crucial because its misuse could erode public confidence and cause instability in international relations. International cooperation is essential to addressing these risks by creating laws, regulations, and moral standards that control the application of AI in surveillance and weaponry. Governments and non-governmental organizations ought to collaborate to draft legally binding agreements that guarantee AI is applied sensibly and in accordance with humanitarian ideals. Care should be taken when developing AI in these domains, and precautions must be taken to avoid abuse and reduce damage. The world can endeavor to ensure that AI technology is used for peaceful purposes and does not contribute to the escalation of conflicts or human rights violations by fostering transparency, accountability, and international cooperation.

Frameworks and Guidelines

The principles of ethical AI have been codified in various frameworks to guarantee that AI is created and implemented responsibly. The Asilomar AI Principles, for example, stress that AI should be developed for the benefit of society as a whole and promote accountability, transparency, and shared benefits in AI development. These guidelines promote transparency in the development and application of AI systems, guaranteeing that their effects are beneficial and available to everyone. In addition, the EU Ethical Guidelines for Trustworthy AI make sure that AI systems respect basic human rights and societal values by emphasizing crucial components like privacy, fairness, and human oversight. Similarly, in order to guarantee moral AI practices internationally, UNESCO's AI Ethics Recommendations stress the necessity of international collaboration. These guidelines support the creation of global standards to mitigate AI's possible risks while promoting innovation. These frameworks work together to offer practical guidelines for the development and application of AI technologies that put ethics, accountability, and transparency first, guaranteeing that AI systems are in line with both societal demands and international ethical standards.

Challenges in Implementing Ethical AI

Job Displacement and Economic Inequality

Automation powered by AI is changing industries by increasing productivity, cutting expenses, and simplifying operations. But this change also poses a threat to job security, especially for employees in industries like manufacturing, retail, and customer service that rely significantly on manual or repetitive labor. A widening gap between workers with high-tech skills and those whose jobs are automated could result from the widespread adoption of AI, which could cause significant job displacement. Economic inequality may deteriorate as a result, making it more difficult for marginalized groups to adopt new technologies. It is imperative to fund upskilling and reskilling programs that equip workers for positions in cutting-edge industries, such as those involving artificial intelligence, in order to lessen these effects. Societies can better guarantee that the financial advantages of AI are distributed widely by placing a high priority on fair access to education and training. Addressing the economic inequalities brought on by

AI automation requires proactive action from organizations and policymakers. Policies that promote universal basic income, retraining initiatives, and safety nets for displaced workers can be implemented by governments. Companies should also embrace ethical AI practices by providing career transition programs and cultivating a diverse workforce. The development of technology should not be the only focus; the wider societal impact should also be considered. Stakeholders can ensure that everyone has the chance to profit from the new economy by cooperating to create an atmosphere where AI developments spur economic growth while lowering inequality.

Human Rights and Autonomy

There are serious worries about how the quick development of AI technologies may affect human rights, especially those related to autonomy and dignity. For instance, without enough transparency or oversight, AI systems used in social services or law enforcement may make decisions that have an impact on people's lives, which could result in unfair or biased outcomes. People's capacity to make educated decisions and defend their rights may be compromised if life changing decisions, like access to healthcare, justice, or financial services, are automated. In order to ensure that human oversight continues to play a crucial role in decision-making, ethical AI development necessitates a strong commitment to transparency, fairness, and accountability. The deployment of AI must be centered on a human-centric approach that puts the defense of individual liberties and dignity first in every situation. Governments and organizations must set up strong frameworks for AI governance in order to protect human rights. This includes explicit laws requiring AI systems to be equitable, explicable, and nondiscriminatory. In order to stop damaging biases from being reinforced, it is also crucial to include a variety of viewpoints in the development and application of AI technologies. AI should be developed according to values that respect people's rights and liberties, and it should be viewed as a tool to improve rather than reduce human well-being. Society can optimize AI's advantages while lowering its risks to human rights by making sure AI systems are open, responsible, and respectful of human autonomy.

Environmental Sustainability

With the rising energy costs associated with training and running large-scale models, the environmental impact of AI development is becoming a more significant concern. For instance, it frequently takes enormous computational resources to train deep learning models, which results in high energy consumption and carbon emissions. As more businesses invest in creating intricate models to spur innovation, artificial intelligence may have a significant negative impact on the environment. AI's carbon footprint can be decreased by using renewable energy sources and energy-efficient algorithms, which are encouraged by ethical AI practices. As technology advances, it is crucial to strike a balance between the need to reduce AI's environmental impact and the desire for more potent AI in order to make sure that AI helps achieve global sustainability goals. In order to develop AI systems that are more energy-efficient, researchers, developers, and organizations should collaborate. Using greener hardware, optimizing algorithms to lower computational demands, and taking into account the environmental effects of AI deployments at every stage are all examples of this. Governments can also encourage sustainable AI development through policies like tax breaks for renewable energy use and funding for environmentally friendly technology research. The design and application of AI can advance in a way that benefits society and the environment by incorporating sustainability, addressing climate issues and promoting innovation.

Weaponization and Misuse

There are significant ethical and security issues with the possible application of AI in weapon systems and mass surveillance. For instance, autonomous weapons might function without human oversight, possibly making decisions that could mean the difference between life and death without any accountability. This raises serious questions about the moral application of AI in military settings, where malevolent behavior or unforeseen consequences could cause extensive harm. Similar to this, surveillance systems driven by AI, like facial recognition software, have the potential to violate civil liberties and privacy rights, particularly when employed by businesses or governments without sufficient regulation. Establishing precise international standards and laws controlling AI's application in these delicate fields is crucial because its misuse could erode public confidence and cause instability in international relations. International cooperation is essential to addressing these risks by creating laws, regulations, and moral standards that control the application of AI in surveillance and weaponry. Governments and non-governmental organizations ought to collaborate to draft legally binding agreements that guarantee AI is applied sensibly and in accordance with humanitarian ideals. Care should be taken when developing AI in these domains, and precautions must be taken to avoid abuse and reduce damage. The world can endeavor to ensure that AI technology is used for peaceful purposes and does not contribute to the escalation of conflicts or human rights violations by fostering transparency, accountability, and international cooperation.

Benefits and Risks of AI

By improving decision-making, automating procedures, and facilitating previously unthinkable innovations, artificial intelligence (AI) has completely transformed a number of industries. AI's capacity to process enormous volumes of data at previously unheard-of speeds allows companies to enhance customer experiences, streamline operations, and create innovative solutions in industries like manufacturing, healthcare, and finance. AI is revolutionizing everything from sophisticated diagnostic tools to tailored recommendations, opening up new avenues for productivity and expansion. AI does have advantages, but it also has serious risks that need to be carefully considered and managed. To guarantee that AI is created and applied ethically, concerns like algorithmic bias, data privacy, and the possibility of job displacement must be addressed. AI technologies have the potential to worsen inequality, disseminate false information, or be abused for malevolent ends in the absence of adequate regulation. To properly utilize AI's potential and make sure that its developments maximize benefits to society while minimizing harm, it is essential to comprehend both its opportunities and challenges.

Benefits of AI

Enhanced Efficiency and Productivity:

By automating time-consuming and repetitive tasks, artificial intelligence has completely changed how businesses approach efficiency. This enables businesses to better allocate resources and streamline operations, which boosts productivity. AI-driven automation systems reduce human error and maximize workforce efficiency in sectors like manufacturing by ensuring consistent product quality and quicker production cycles. This results in increased output levels as well as cost savings. AI-powered solutions, like chatbots, are becoming more widespread in industries like customer service and provide round-the-clock assistance. By instantly responding to questions that would otherwise necessitate extensive human intervention, these systems enhance the overall customer experience. AI's capacity to automate a variety of tasks has also been crucial in allowing human employees to concentrate on more strategic and innovative facets of their jobs. Employee creativity and higher-level problem-solving are enabled by the removal of repetitive tasks, which eventually promotes organizational growth. Small and medium-sized enterprises that might not have large workforces also benefit from this trend toward automation. Businesses of all sizes can preserve competitive advantages by implementing AI to increase operational effectiveness and provide customers with better service.

Improved Decision-Making

The ability of AI to instantly analyze enormous volumes of data has revolutionized decision-making in a variety of industries. AI tools offer useful insights that assist businesses in making evidence-based, data-driven decisions by identifying patterns and trends in massive datasets. For instance, AI-powered algorithms can quickly examine medical images in the healthcare industry to spot possible illnesses or abnormalities that human physicians might overlook. Similar to this, predictive analytics models help predict market behavior in the finance industry, enabling businesses to identify new risks or make well-informed investment decisions. This improved decision-making process reduces dependence on intuition alone and increases accuracy, which produces better results. AI's accuracy and speed in processing data are especially useful in hectic settings where time is of the essence. AI-powered decision support systems, for example, can help physicians make more precise diagnoses, enabling quicker treatment. Artificial intelligence (AI) in financial services can identify fraudulent activity in real time, preventing significant losses. AI boosts operational efficiency and lowers the chance of errors by providing data-backed insights to support decisions. This improves organizational performance and service delivery across a range of industries.

Innovation and Problem-Solving

AI has emerged as a major force behind innovation in a wide range of sectors, resolving challenging issues that were once thought to be unsolvable. AI in robotics makes it possible for machines to carry out complex tasks accurately and effectively, which has led to advancements in manufacturing, healthcare, and even space exploration. For example, self-driving cars, which minimize the need for human intervention and have the potential to revolutionize the transportation sector, mainly rely on AI algorithms to navigate safely and make decisions in real time based on their environment. AI's developments in natural language processing have also greatly enhanced communication, enabling smooth interactions across international networks through automated content creation and real-time language translation. These AI-powered advancements also create new growth opportunities by promoting the emergence of completely untapped markets and business models. AI's capacity to tackle challenging issues has sparked innovative research in fields like cybersecurity, personalized medicine, and environmental sustainability. AI's contribution to solving societal issues is expanding, and its capacity for constant adaptation and development lays the groundwork for further developments. AI improves efficiency and transforms entire industries by solving long-standing issues, which encourages innovation and opens up new opportunities for both consumers and businesses.

Personalization

AI's capacity to provide incredibly customized experiences has fundamentally changed how customers interact with brands on a variety of platforms. AI helps businesses to customize their goods, services, and marketing campaigns to meet the needs of specific customers by examining user preferences, behavior, and previous interactions. To provide a more individualized shopping or viewing experience, companies such as Amazon and Netflix, for example, use AI algorithms to suggest goods and content based on user interests. In the end, this personalization promotes customer loyalty and retention by raising engagement, boosting customer satisfaction, and increasing conversion rates. Beyond entertainment and consumer goods, personalization has had a revolutionary impact on fields like healthcare and education. AI-powered personalized learning experiences give students access to specialized instructional materials that fit their learning preferences and pace, increasing engagement and results. AI can also be utilized in the healthcare industry to suggest individualized treatment programs based on a patient's medical records. By providing tailored solutions, AI assists businesses in building closer bonds with their clients, making sure that their products have a greater impact on them and resulting in long-term company growth.

Risks of AI

Bias and Discrimination:

Although AI systems are made to learn from enormous volumes of data, they have the potential to reinforce or even magnify societal biases if the data reflects them. Hiring algorithms that are trained on past employment data, for example, may give preference to applicants who fit specific demographics, like a specific gender or ethnicity, resulting in unequal opportunities for others. Discrimination may be strengthened as a result of these biased results, particularly in the criminal justice, lending, and employment sectors. It is crucial to make sure AI systems are trained on representative and varied datasets that span the wide range of society in order to reduce these risks. In order to determine fairness and take corrective action in the event that biases in the system's decisions are discovered, continuous audits and evaluations should also be put into place. In addition to being a technical problem, addressing bias in AI is also an ethical one. The active participation of ethicists, data scientists, and business executives is necessary to guarantee that AI systems do not reinforce discrimination. To guarantee AI fairness, transparent development procedures are essential, including precise instructions on data collection and model assessment. Companies should, for instance, conduct routine audits of their AI systems to look for discriminatory trends and take appropriate action to retrain models or modify algorithms as needed. A dedication to diversity, equity, and inclusivity in data and design will be essential as AI develops to reduce the possibility of bias and guarantee that AI benefits everyone equally.

Privacy Concerns:

The enormous volumes of data needed for training and decision-making present serious privacy issues as AI technologies become more pervasive in daily life. AI systems have the potential to violate people's right to privacy, especially those that depend on private information like facial recognition or surveillance tools. AI-enabled facial recognition technology used for mass surveillance, for instance, may track people without their consent, which could be abused and compromise personal liberties. The ethical ramifications of AI's data requirements underscore the necessity of strict laws and privacy safeguards to prevent the exploitation or misuse of people's personal information. An all-encompassing approach to data protection, encompassing anonymization, encryption, and transparency in data usage, is necessary to safeguard privacy in AI systems. Securing personal data and giving people more control over their own data should be the top priorities of ethical AI development. AI developers must be held responsible for the collection, storage, and use of data, and clear consent procedures should be put in place. Privacy laws that shield citizens from potential harm brought on by unregulated or unethical AI practices should be enforced by governments and regulatory agencies. To preserve public confidence and protect human rights in the digital age, it will be essential to make sure AI technologies are built with privacy at their core.

Job Displacement:

The labor market is facing serious challenges due to the quick development of AI and automation, especially in sectors like manufacturing, retail, and transportation. There is serious concern that many jobs may be replaced by AI systems, which would cause unemployment and economic disruption as these systems become more adept at tasks that have historically been performed by humans. For instance, self-checkout kiosks in retail establishments and automated systems in warehouses have already started to supplant human labor. Millions of workers who might not have the skills to move into new roles could be displaced if this trend continues. The shift to a more automated economy will necessitate significant investments in workforce reskilling and upskilling, even though AI has the potential to generate new employment opportunities in industries like technology, data science, and AI development. Governments, corporations, and academic institutions must work together to create curricula that give workers the skills required for new industries. Furthermore, during this transitional phase, policies like wage subsidies or universal basic income (UBI) could lessen the financial strain on displaced workers. To guarantee that the advantages of AI are widely distributed and that workers are not left behind in the changing labor market, proactive measures to address job displacement through education and retraining will be crucial.

Lack of Transparency:

Artificial intelligence (AI) systems, particularly sophisticated models like deep learning, frequently function as "black boxes," which means that humans cannot readily comprehend or interpret their internal decision-making processes. In high-stakes applications where knowing how decisions are made is essential, like healthcare, criminal justice, and finance, this lack of transparency can be problematic. People who are impacted, for example, have a right to know the rationale behind an AI system's decision to reject a loan application or decide on sentencing in a criminal case. These systems' opacity can raise questions about accountability and bias and undermine confidence in their fairness. To promote trust and guarantee that these systems are used responsibly, it is imperative that AI become more transparent. One strategy is the creation of explainable AI (XAI), which aims to improve human accessibility and interpretability of AI systems. Developers can contribute to making sure AI decisions are impartial, accountable, and devoid of unconscious biases by building models that provide concise justifications for their choices. External audits and the release of information about the data used to train models, the algorithms used, and the evaluation procedures are further ways to improve transparency. In addition to enhancing public confidence, increased transparency in AI will facilitate improved ethical and regulatory oversight.

Security Risks:

AI systems are vulnerable to malicious exploitation and cyberattacks, just like any other technology. Hackers can reverse-engineer systems to obtain sensitive data without authorization, or they can alter AI models to generate inaccurate results. Adversarial attacks on machine learning models, for instance, may entail covertly changing input data to lead the AI system to make incorrect judgments, thereby jeopardizing security in applications like cybersecurity or driverless cars. Such flaws could have serious repercussions, from monetary losses to bodily injury, as AI becomes more intricately incorporated into vital infrastructure. Strong cybersecurity measures must be put in place at every stage of the AI development lifecycle in order to reduce security threats. To protect sensitive data, this entails frequent vulnerability assessments, ongoing monitoring, and the application of cutting-edge encryption techniques. Additionally, AI models should be built to withstand adversarial attacks, and their effectiveness should be evaluated in a range of possible threat scenarios. Ensuring the security of AI systems will be crucial to their safe and moral implementation as they become more and more common. Organizations can lower the risks of malicious exploitation and contribute to preserving public confidence in these technologies by investing in AI security and working with subject-matter experts.

Balancing Benefits and Risks:

While AI has revolutionary potential in a variety of domains, including healthcare and education, it is important to be aware of its possible drawbacks. As AI technologies develop, they have the potential to solve challenging issues, increase productivity, and transform entire industries. Nevertheless, these advantages entail the need to control the risks involved, including prejudice, privacy issues, and job displacement. Achieving a balance between ethics and innovation is crucial to ensuring that AI advances in a way that maximizes benefits to society while reducing potential risks. This calls for careful regulation, stakeholder cooperation, and a dedication to design that is focused on people. In order to adopt a responsible approach to AI, governments, corporations, and researchers must collaborate to develop moral standards and legal frameworks that encourage openness, equity, and responsibility. To make sure that society is aware of both the advantages and dangers of artificial intelligence, public education and awareness campaigns will be essential. By cultivating a culture of responsible AI development and promoting innovation within a well-defined ethical framework, we can leverage AI's potential to bring about positive change while protecting against any potential negative effects. This cooperative endeavor will be essential to guaranteeing that AI plays a role in a sustainable and just future.

Because AI has both advantages and disadvantages, its development and application require a balanced approach (Table 5.5). On the one hand, AI has the potential to revolutionize industries, improve workflows, and spur innovation in a wide range of fields, providing hitherto unthinkable solutions. However, its quick development raises questions about moral conundrums, security flaws, and the possibility of social harm. Addressing these risks while encouraging responsible development and application is essential to fully utilizing AI's potential. We can guarantee that AI's development benefits all of humanity by utilizing its advantages while tackling ethical, security, and societal issues. To establish a setting where AI responsibly serves humanity, proactive steps like strict laws, moral standards, and ongoing education are crucial. By minimizing risks and optimizing AI's beneficial effects, these initiatives can guarantee that AI's potential is fully realized without sacrificing core human values.

Table 5.5: Benefits vs. Risks of AI.

Benefits of AI	Risks of AI
Automation of Repetitive Tasks	**Job Displacement**
AI can handle repetitive, mundane tasks, improving efficiency and allowing humans to focus on more complex work.	Automation could lead to job losses, particularly in industries reliant on routine tasks.
Improved Decision Making	**Bias and Discrimination**
AI can analyze vast amounts of data, providing insights that lead to better decisions in various fields like healthcare, finance, and business.	AI systems can reflect and perpetuate existing biases present in data, leading to discriminatory outcomes.
Enhanced Personalization	**Privacy Concerns**
AI enables personalized experiences in areas like e-commerce, education, and entertainment, enhancing customer satisfaction.	AI systems often require access to personal data, raising concerns over privacy and data protection.
Advancement in Healthcare	**Security Threats**
AI can aid in diagnosing diseases, drug discovery, and personalized medicine, improving health outcomes.	AI systems can be vulnerable to hacking, misuse, or manipulation, posing a security threat.
24/7 Availability	**Loss of Human Control**
AI can work tirelessly without breaks, increasing productivity and availability of services.	Over-reliance on AI may result in reduced human oversight, potentially leading to unintended consequences.
Efficiency and Cost Savings	**Ethical Concerns**

AI can optimize processes, reduce errors, and save costs in many industries, making operations more efficient.	Ethical questions arise, such as how AI systems make decisions and the potential for abuse in areas like surveillance and military use.
Assistive Technologies	**Impact on Social Interaction**
AI can improve accessibility, such as through assistive technologies for people with disabilities, offering new opportunities for independent living.	Increased reliance on AI could reduce human interaction, leading to social isolation or weakened interpersonal skills.

Conclusion

The evolution of AI from symbolic AI to data-driven methods like machine learning is summarized in this chapter, along with the challenges and applications of each. It explores how early AI systems relied on logic and rule-based models, whereas more recent methods use enormous volumes of data to build more predictive and adaptive systems. In addition to discussing the necessity of accountability and transparency in machine learning models, the chapter highlights the significance of Explainable AI. In order to guarantee AI's beneficial effects on society, it emphasizes the significance of responsible development and delves deeper into ethical issues, describing the advantages and dangers of the technology. In the following chapter, the idea of learning in AI is presented, with a focus on its importance in creating intelligent systems. It examines supervised, unsupervised, semi-supervised, and reinforcement learning, among other forms of learning, to give readers a thorough grasp of how computers learn from data. The chapter addresses the fundamental algorithms for each type of learning, such as clustering and regression techniques, and goes over the fundamentals of reinforcement learning with an emphasis on the roles of environments and agents. It also covers strategies for assessing and improving learning models, including hyperparameter tuning, cross-validation, and approaches to common problems like overfitting and underfitting.

Exercise

- Define Symbolic AI and discuss its primary applications. How does it differ from Data-driven AI?
- What are the major types of Machine Learning, and how do their approaches to learning from data vary? Provide examples for each type.
- Identify two real-world applications for Symbolic AI and two for Data-driven AI. What characteristics make each approach suitable for its respective application?

- What is Interpretable and Explainable AI (XAI)? Why is it important in high-risk sectors like healthcare and finance?
- Examine the ethical challenges of AI. How can issues such as bias, lack of transparency, and accountability be effectively addressed?
- Identify and explain three advantages and three risks of AI. How can organizations manage these risks while maximizing AI's potential?
- Compare and contrast the roles of Symbolic AI and Machine Learning in autonomous systems, such as self-driving cars.
- How does Explainable AI foster trust and accountability in AI systems? Provide examples of tools or techniques used for making AI more explainable.
- What are the environmental impacts of training large AI models? Suggest strategies to reduce the carbon footprint of AI technologies.
- In your view, what role should governments play in regulating AI development and deployment? Provide examples of existing frameworks or guidelines..

CHAPTER-6

LEARNING AND ADAPTATION IN AI

Introduction & Objective

In artificial intelligence, learning entails creating systems that can adjust, forecast, and get better over time with the help of data and feedback. This feature enables AI systems to improve their performance and accuracy as they are exposed to new data, allowing them to grow through experience. A key component of artificial intelligence, machine learning, powers these procedures by utilizing algorithms that find patterns and connections in data, enabling machines to learn and develop on their own. Learning is a fundamental component of contemporary AI that allows machines to solve intricate issues, identify patterns, and make wise decisions without the need for explicit programming. Large datasets allow AI systems to extract strategies and insights that would be too complex or time-consuming for human programmers to manually encode. This ability to self-improve is essential for the creation of autonomous technologies that can continuously learn and adapt in changing environments, like predictive analytics, intelligent assistants, and self-driving cars.This chapter's goal is to give readers a basic understanding of the various forms and approaches to learning in artificial intelligence, such as supervised, unsupervised, and reinforcement learning. These fundamental paradigms, which provide unique methods for problem-solving and algorithm training, serve as the foundation for the creation of AI models. Unsupervised learning finds patterns in unlabeled data, supervised learning uses labeled data for training, and reinforcement learning uses agents to learn by making mistakes. This chapter establishes the foundation for comprehending how AI systems learn and develop by exploring these techniques. By the end of this chapter, readers will have a solid understanding of important algorithms, including Q-learning, decision trees, support vector machines, and clustering techniques, as well as an awareness of how these algorithms can be used to solve practical issues. The chapter will also present methods for assessing and optimizing AI models, assisting readers in understanding how to improve their strategies in order to produce more precise and effective results. Readers will be equipped to interact with AI models and help create more efficient problem-solving techniques thanks to this thorough overview.

Introduction to Learning in AI

In artificial intelligence (AI), learning is the process through which machines pick up new information or become more proficient at tasks over time without the need for explicit programming. The foundation of artificial intelligence is learning, which gives computers the ability to recognize patterns, decide, and adjust to changing conditions by using data-driven insights. In contrast to traditional programming, which involves human programmers setting specific rules and commands, AI models use algorithms that allow them to learn from large datasets, enhancing their capacity for autonomous prediction, classification, and decision-making. Learning involves more than just committing information to memory; it also involves extrapolating knowledge to deal with novel and unfamiliar circumstances. Although machine learning (ML), the most well-known type of AI learning, involves algorithms that automatically modify their parameters in response to input data, it also includes a number of other methods, each with a unique methodology and set of applications, including deep learning, reinforcement learning, and unsupervised learning. Supervised learning, unsupervised learning, and reinforcement learning are the three subcategories of machine learning. The model learns from labeled data in supervised learning, where each input is matched with an appropriate output. The model learns from these examples and uses that knowledge to classify or predict new data. Unsupervised learning, on the other hand, looks for hidden patterns or structures, like clusters or associations, in data by learning from it without explicit labels. In a different paradigm known as reinforcement learning, an agent learns by interacting with its surroundings and getting feedback in the form of rewards or penalties. Over time, it refines its approach to accomplish a specific objective. These learning paradigms are applied in a variety of contexts, from robotics and autonomous vehicles to computer vision, speech recognition, and natural language processing.

In addition to automating tasks, AI learning creates new opportunities in domains like creativity, problem-solving, and decision-making that were previously believed to be exclusively human. But there are drawbacks to this learning process as well, like data bias, moral dilemmas, and the requirement for a lot of labeled data in order to properly train models. Learning algorithms will get more effective as AI develops, enabling machines to learn in real-time, from fewer examples, and in more complex ways. There is a lot of promise for the future of AI learning, including areas like explainable AI, which aims to make the decision-making process of AI models transparent and intelligible to humans, and transfer learning, which allows a model trained on one task to be modified for a different but similar task. These developments will make it possible for more intelligent, moral, and flexible systems to address challenging, ever-changing issues in a variety of fields.

Definition and Importance of Learning in AI

The ability of machines to learn, recognize patterns, and make decisions based on information and experiences rather than just explicit programming is known as learning in artificial intelligence (AI). AI systems are capable of analyzing large volumes of data, learning from it, and using what they have learned to tackle challenging issues thanks to methods like machine learning and deep learning. In order to improve the system's capacity to adjust to novel and varied inputs, this process entails developing models that can generalize from observed data, meaning they can identify patterns even in situations that are not visible. AI systems can get better over time without constant human assistance by implementing learning mechanisms. These systems can operate intelligently and independently in dynamic environments because they can recognize patterns, forecast outcomes, and adapt to deal with unforeseen circumstances. AI applications are becoming more and more effective, efficient, and adaptable across a range of industries, including healthcare, finance, education, and more, as they continue to learn. AI can handle increasingly difficult tasks and provide creative solutions thanks to its ability to continuously improve.

Importance

The importance of learning in AI lies in its ability to enable machines to handle complex, data-driven tasks that would be challenging or impossible to program manually. Unlike traditional programming methods, where each step must be explicitly defined, AI systems can learn from vast amounts of data, identifying patterns and relationships without human intervention. This ability allows AI to solve intricate problems, adapt to new environments, and handle diverse scenarios, making it an invaluable tool in various industries. As AI continues to evolve, its capacity for learning ensures that machines can become more efficient and accurate over time. By learning from data, AI systems can adapt to new situations, improve over time, and provide accurate results in diverse scenarios. This adaptability is critical in addressing real-world challenges that require constant updates and refinements. For example, AI's ability to predict market trends can help businesses make informed decisions, while its capacity to diagnose diseases can assist healthcare professionals in providing more accurate treatments. Similarly, AI's recognition of speech or images has revolutionized customer service, security, and accessibility, making it clear that learning is at the heart of AI's potential to transform industries and improve lives.

Advantage of learning in AI is its capacity for generalization

A machine learning model can apply its learned patterns to new, unseen data by generalizing what it has learned from training on a dataset. This implies that direct supervision is not necessary for the model to solve issues or make predictions. An AI that has been trained to recognize cats in pictures, for instance, can correctly identify new pictures of cats even if it hasn't seen those particular pictures before. One of the main features of machine learning technology is its capacity to adjust to novel situations. The ability of AI to use the fundamental ideas discovered from the training data to address a broad range of tasks, from language processing to image recognition, is what gives it its versatility. Because of its versatility, AI can be used in a wide range of industries, including healthcare, finance, and customer service, offering solutions in domains that call for intricate pattern recognition and judgment. As a result, after a machine learning model is created, its possible uses go well beyond the parameters of the initial training dataset.

Another aspect of its importance is scalability

A machine learning model can apply its learned patterns to new, unseen data by generalizing what it has learned from training on a dataset. This implies that direct supervision is not necessary for the model to solve issues or make predictions. An AI that has been trained to recognize cats in pictures, for instance, can correctly identify new pictures of cats even if it hasn't seen those particular pictures before. One of the main features of machine learning technology is its capacity to adjust to novel situations. The ability of AI to use the fundamental ideas discovered from the training data to address a broad range of tasks, from language processing to image recognition, is what gives it its versatility. Because of its versatility, AI can be used in a wide range of industries, including healthcare, finance, and customer service, offering solutions in domains that call for intricate pattern recognition and judgment. As a result, after a machine learning model is created, it's possible uses go well beyond the parameters of the initial training dataset.

Table 6.1: Benefits of Learning in AI.

Benefit	Description
Enhanced Problem-Solving Skills	AI encourages analytical thinking and the development of solutions to complex problems.
Job Opportunities	AI skills are in high demand across industries, offering various career paths.
Automation of Repetitive Tasks	AI knowledge helps in automating tasks, improving efficiency and reducing human error.
Increased Innovation	AI enables the creation of innovative products and services, improving industries.
Data-Driven Decision Making	AI helps analyze large data sets, enabling better, more informed decision-making.
Improved Efficiency and Productivity	AI optimizes workflows and processes, leading to higher productivity.
Personalized Learning and Solutions	AI can create customized educational experiences and solutions based on user needs.

Global Impact and Contribution	AI can be applied to solve global challenges, such as climate change, healthcare, and more.
Interdisciplinary Knowledge	Learning AI often involves knowledge across various fields, fostering a well-rounded skill set.
Adaptability to Future Technologies	As AI becomes more integrated into society, learning it ensures adaptability to future tech trends.

The above Table 6.1 summarizes the key benefits of learning in AI, highlighting its role in driving intelligent, adaptive, and efficient solutions.

Categories of learning: Supervised, Unsupervised, Semi-supervised, and Reinforcement Learning

Types of Learning in AI

Supervised learning, unsupervised learning, semi-supervised learning, and reinforcement learning are the four primary categories of AI learning. Depending on the type of data and the intended results, each type has a distinct function.

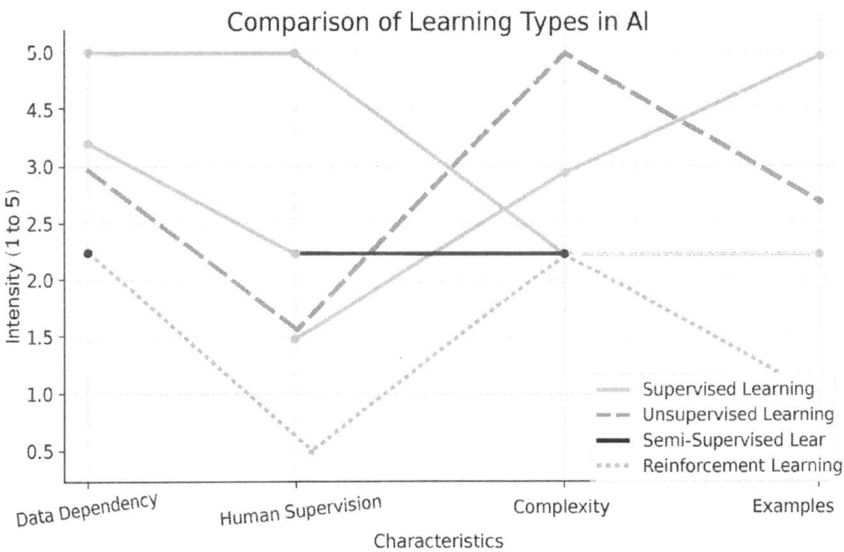

Figure 6.1: Compares different types of learning in AI.

The different forms of AI learningsupervised, unsupervised, semi-supervised, and reinforcement learningare contrasted in Figure 6.1 according to attributes like complexity, examples, data dependency, and human supervision. While reinforcement learning is particularly complex, supervised learning is ranked highest in terms of human supervision and examples. Because unsupervised learning necessitates less human oversight, it is ideal for exploratory analysis.

1. Supervised Learning

In supervised learning, each input is connected to a known output, and the model is trained using labeled data. In order to enable the model to forecast the output for novel, unseen data, the goal is to understand the relationship between inputs and outputs. Classification (like identifying spam emails) and regression (like predicting home prices) are common tasks in supervised learning.

- **Examples:** Linear Regression, Decision Trees, Support Vector Machines (SVM), Neural Networks.
- **Advantages:** Highly accurate for well-labeled datasets and straightforward to interpret.
- **Challenges:** Requires large, labeled datasets, which can be costly and time-consuming to obtain.

2. Unsupervised Learning

Unsupervised learning operates on unlabeled data, where the model aims to identify patterns or structures within the data without direct supervision. It is typically employed for tasks like clustering (grouping similar items) and dimensionality reduction (simplifying the data representation).

- **Examples:** K-Means Clustering, Principal Component Analysis (PCA), Hierarchical Clustering.
- **Advantages:** Does not require labeled data, making it useful for exploratory data analysis.
- **Challenges:** Results can be harder to interpret, and it requires domain expertise to validate the discovered patterns.

3. Semi-Supervised Learning

Semi-supervised learning blends elements of both supervised and unsupervised learning. It utilizes a small set of labeled data in conjunction with a larger set of unlabeled data. The labeled data steers the learning process, while the unlabeled data aids the model in achieving better generalization.

- **Examples:** Techniques that combine supervised algorithms with unsupervised methods like clustering or self-training.
- **Advantages:** Reduces the need for extensive labeled data while improving model performance.
- **Challenges:** Balancing the influence of labeled and unlabeled data can be complex.

4. Reinforcement Learning

Reinforcement learning is a process where an agent learns to interact with its environment and identify optimal actions by maximizing cumulative rewards.

Unlike other learning methods, it emphasizes sequential decision-making and learning through feedback.

- **Key Concepts:** Agents, environments, rewards, actions, and states.
- **Examples:** Q-Learning, Policy Gradients.
- **Advantages:** Effective for tasks requiring long-term planning, such as robotics and game AI.
- **Challenges:** Computationally expensive, requires careful design of reward structures, and can be unstable.

Common algorithms

Common Algorithms in AI Learning

1. Linear Regression

A basic machine learning algorithm, linear regression is frequently used for regression tasks in which the objective is to predict a continuous output variable from one or more input variables. The approach is predicated on the idea that the independent variables (features) and the dependent variable (target) have a linear relationship. By fitting a line, as shown by the equation $y=mx+c$, where m indicates the line's slope, c is its intercept, and y is the expected value, it tries to model this relationship. In order to determine the best-fitting line, thc model minimizes the sum of squared differences between the observed and predicted values. Because it is simple to understand and intuitive, linear regression is a great option for novices and a good starting point for more complicated regression problems. But it has a drawback: it presumes that the variables have a linear relationship, which may limit its applicability to more complicated or non-linear datasets. Although it works well for straightforward linear relationships, more sophisticated methods may be needed when the data exhibits interactions or non-linear patterns that linear regression is unable to sufficiently capture.

A linear regression model fitting a line to a collection of observed data points is shown in Figure 6.2. By minimizing the sum of squared differences between the actual data points (blue dots) and the predicted values on the line, the best-fitting linear equation ($y=mx+c$) is represented by the red line. A useful tool in statistical analysis, this visualization clearly illustrates how linear regression captures linear relationships in data in an easy-to-understand and interpretable manner. Numerous applications, including sales forecasting, home price prediction, and relationship analysis in scientific research, heavily rely on this algorithm. Linear regression can be sensitive to outliers, multicollinearity among features, and non-linear patterns in data, despite its simplicity and ease of use. When using linear regression models, these variables can skew the model's predictions and lower its accuracy, highlighting the significance of meticulous feature selection and data preprocessing.

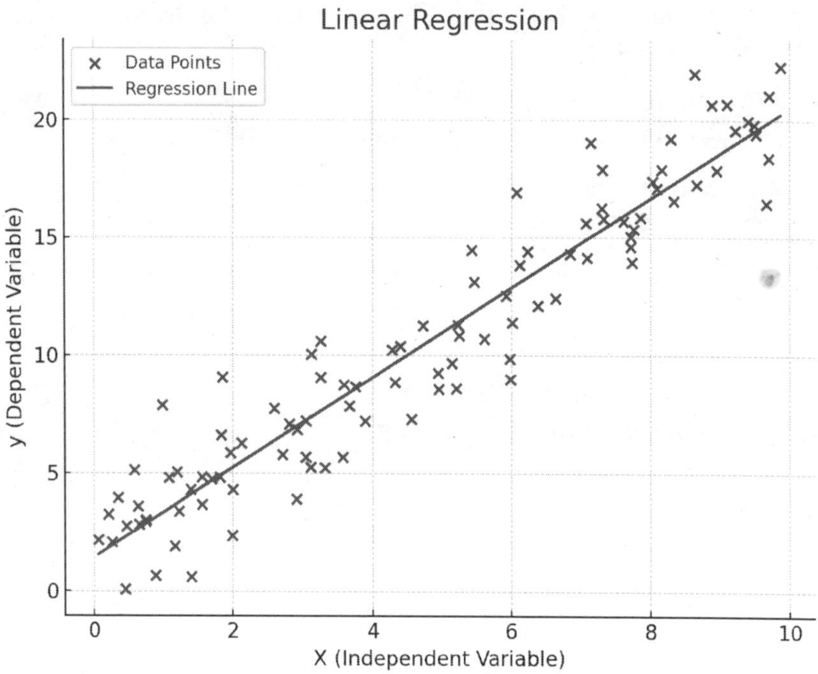

Figure 6.2: Linear Regression.

2. Decision Trees

A flexible non-parametric model for classification and regression applications is the decision tree. They create a tree-like structure by recursively dividing the dataset into subsets according to the values of input features. The predicted outcome or target variable is represented by the tree's leaves, while each node in the tree represents a decision rule that divides the data into smaller groups. Decision trees are very useful for comprehending decision-making processes because they are simple to understand and visualize. They provide flexibility in a variety of fields, including marketing, healthcare, and finance, by handling both numerical and categorical data. Despite their advantages, decision trees can overfit, especially if they get too deep and complicated. Poor generalization on unseen data results from overfitting, which happens when the model picks up noise or small details from the training set. Pruning (removing portions of the tree that don't contribute much value), limiting the tree's depth, and using ensemble approaches like Random Forests are some strategies that can be used to counteract overfitting. These modifications strengthen the model and enhance its functionality, particularly in practical applications where accurate and explicable decision-making processes are required, like fraud detection, risk assessment, and medical diagnosis.

3. Support Vector Machines (SVM)

A potent class of supervised learning algorithms, Support Vector Machines (SVM) are mostly employed for classification tasks. In a multi-dimensional feature space, SVM finds the best hyperplane to divide the data points of various classes. SVM maps the input features to higher-dimensional spaces, where a linear separation can be accomplished, in situations where the data is not linearly separable. SVM can handle intricate, non-linear classification problems thanks to this transformation. For tasks like text classification and bioinformatics, it works especially well in high-dimensional spaces and with datasets that have a distinct margin of separation. SVM can be computationally demanding, though, especially when working with big datasets. The model's performance depends on the selection of kernel functions and the adjustment of hyperparameters (such as the kernel parameters and the regularization parameter). Making a bad decision can result in either overfitting or underfitting. SVM is still among the strongest and most dependable algorithms for classification tasks in spite of these difficulties. It is indispensable in fields like image recognition and bioinformatics because of its capacity to operate effectively with smaller datasets, concentrate on support vectors (the most instructive data points), and deliver high accuracy in challenging classification problems.

4. Neural Networks

Neural networks are made up of layers of connected neurons that process and change input data; they were inspired by the structure of the human brain. By using weighted sums and activation functions to apply a number of transformations at each layer, these networks are intended to model intricate relationships. Neural networks are well-suited for tasks requiring high predictive accuracy, such as image recognition, natural language processing, and autonomous systems, because they are adept at identifying complex patterns in data and can learn from enormous volumes of information. They excel in situations where conventional machine learning algorithms might falter due to their capacity to learn from massive datasets. Neural networks have certain drawbacks despite their efficiency. They require substantial resources for training, making them computationally costly, especially for deep learning models with several hidden layers. Furthermore, in the absence of suitable regularization strategies like dropout or early stopping, they may be prone to overfitting and require sizable labeled datasets for optimal performance. Nonetheless, neural networks are the foundation of deep learning due to their capacity to represent extremely intricate patterns in data. Significant advances in AI have resulted from this, allowing systems to carry out tasks like medical image analysis, real-time language translation, and autonomous driving.

This Table 6.2 reviews the key characteristics of each algorithm, highlighting their strengths, limitations, and applications for a comprehensive understanding.

Table 6.2: Comparison of Common Algorithms.

Feature	Linear Regression	Decision Trees	SVM (Support Vector Machine)	Neural Networks
Type	Supervised Learning (Regression)	Supervised Learning (Classification/ Regression)	Supervised Learning (Classification/ Regression)	Supervised Learning (mostly Classification)
Use Cases	Predicting continuous values (e.g., house prices)	Classification, regression, feature selection	Text classification, image recognition	Image recognition, NLP, time series
Model Complexity	Simple	Moderate to Complex	Moderate to High	High
Interpretability	High (coefficients are easy to understand)	Medium (can be visualized)	Low to Medium	Low (black box model)
Training Time	Fast	Fast to Moderate	Moderate to Slow	Slow (depends on layers/ size)
Handling Non-linearity	Poor (assumes linearity)	Good (can handle non-linear data)	Excellent (with kernel trick)	Excellent
Overfitting Tendency	Prone to underfitting	Prone to overfitting (can be pruned)	Can overfit with improper tuning	High (requires regularization/dropout)
Scalability	Excellent	Good	Poor to Moderate	Moderate to High (with GPUs)
Feature Scaling Needed	No	No	Yes	Yes
Handling Missing Data	Poor	Handles well	Poor	Poor to Moderate

Common Algorithms: K-Means Clustering, Principal Component Analysis (PCA), Hierarchical Clustering

1. K-Means Clustering

An unsupervised learning technique called K-Means Clustering is frequently used to divide a dataset into a predetermined number of clusters, represented by the letter k. By repeatedly allocating data points to the closest cluster centroid and then recalculating the centroids using the newly assigned points, the algorithm seeks to minimize the variance within each cluster. The algorithm begins by choosing k initial centroids, which can be done at random or with the aid of tools like K-Means++. The algorithm allocates each data point to the cluster linked to the nearest centroid, usually determined by the Euclidean distance metric, after the centroids have been initialized. Following point assignment, the centroids are modified to reflect the cluster's mean of the data points. Until convergence, when the centroids and point distributions among clusters stay the same, this process is repeated.

Notwithstanding its ease of use and effectiveness, K-Means Clustering has certain drawbacks. Choosing the ideal number of clusters, k, is one of the main difficulties. The elbow method, which plots the sum of squared distances between data points and centroids for various values of k and chooses the value at which the curve flattens, is a popular technique for figuring out k.Furthermore, clusters are assumed to be uniformly distributed in the feature space and spherical in shape by K-Means. This assumption might not apply to all datasets, especially if clusters have different densities or irregular shapes. Additionally, K-Means may be sensitive to the centroids' initial placement, which could result in less-than-ideal solutions if the centroids are not initialized properly. K-Means is still a popular and effective clustering algorithm in spite of these drawbacks, particularly for big datasets.

- **Applications:** Customer segmentation, image compression, and pattern recognition.
- **Strengths:** Simple, scalable, and computationally efficient.
- **Limitations:** Sensitive to outliers, initialization, and non-globular clusters.

2. Principal Component Analysis (PCA)

A potent dimensionality reduction method called principal component analysis (PCA) is intended to convert high-dimensional data into a lower-dimensional space while retaining the greatest amount of variance. PCA simplifies complex data structures by determining the principal components, which are orthogonal axes that capture the most significant variance in the dataset. This transformation lessens the redundancy that is frequently found in high-dimensional datasets and aids in more effective data visualization. By eliminating noise and superfluous features from the data, PCA is essential to machine learning workflows and data preprocessing. It makes it possible to comprehend the structure and underlying patterns of high-dimensional data more clearly. By making algorithms faster and more effective, PCA not only improves visualization but also improves model performance. PCA reduces data complexity without sacrificing important information by projecting data onto these principal components.

- **Applications:** Image compression, financial modeling, and bioinformatics.
- **Strengths:** Effective for high-dimensional data and improves model efficiency.
- **Limitations:** Sensitive to scaling, assumes linear relationships, and may lose interpretability of original features.

3. Hierarchical Clustering

An unsupervised algorithm called Hierarchical Clustering uses either an agglomerative (bottom-up) or divisive (top-down) method to create a hierarchy of clusters. The agglomerative approach begins with individual data points and gradually combines the closest clusters in an iterative manner. The divisive method, on the other hand, starts with every data point in a single cluster and divides it into smaller groups in a recursive manner. A dendrogram, which shows the hierarchical relationships between clusters, is frequently used to visualize the merging or splitting process. In some applications, Hierarchical Clustering is more flexible than K-Means because it does not require the user to predetermine the number of clusters. It provides a more thorough and comprehensible clustering structure and works especially well with smaller datasets. Its computational complexity, however, may be a drawback because it can slow down and become ineffective with larger datasets, which makes it less appropriate for big data applications. Notwithstanding these difficulties, it is a useful tool for examining data across a range of domains due to its capacity to disclose intricate cluster hierarchies.

- **Applications:** Gene expression analysis, document clustering, and social network analysis.
- **Strengths:** Does not require predefining k, produces a detailed clustering hierarchy.
- **Limitations:** Computationally intensive, sensitive to noise and outliers.

Agents, Environments, Rewards

1. Agents:

The agent is the primary decision-making unit in reinforcement learning, interacting with its surroundings to accomplish a predetermined goal. It is the agent's responsibility to observe its surroundings, act, and modify its behavior in response to the results of those actions. Through this process, the agent can gradually learn and improve its behavior to maximize the total rewards. The ability of an agent to create and improve a policy—a tactic that links observed states (or circumstances) to actions—is a crucial feature. Whether it's a straightforward rule-based method or a sophisticated machine learning-based algorithm like deep reinforcement learning, a policy aids the agent in making decisions. Success in dynamic, complex environments depends on the agent's capacity to adjust and enhance its performance. An effective agent strikes a balance between exploitation and exploration, with exploitation concentrating on applying known actions that have produced favorable outcomes in the past and exploration experimenting with new actions to find more effective strategies. The way the agent interacts with its surroundings is greatly influenced by its sensors and actuators. In autonomous cars, for instance, sensors like cameras and LIDAR enable the agent to sense its environment, and actuators like the brakes and steering wheel enable it to act on those observations. Depending on the task at hand, an agent's design changes; more complex tasks call for more sophisticated algorithms and techniques to ensure optimal decision-making.

2. Environments:

In reinforcement learning, the external system that the agent interacts with is called the environment. It defines the rules and dynamics of the task and acts as the context that determines how the agent's actions will result in outcomes. The agent's actions are received by the environment, which interprets them and reacts by producing new states and feedback, usually in the form of rewards or penalties. The loop created by this interaction enables the agent to continuously modify its behavior in response to input from the surroundings. Environments can be either stochastic or deterministic, depending on the task. The same action taken by an agent under the same circumstances will always result in the same outcome in deterministic environments. In chess, for instance, every move is subject to a set of predetermined rules that dictate the result. However, in stochastic environments, there is uncertainty because outside variables like the weather or human behavior can affect how an action turns out. The environment's complexity has a direct impact on an agent's capacity for learning and task performance. While more complex environments with high-dimensional spaces, like those found in robotics or self-driving cars, require sophisticated navigational techniques like deep reinforcement learning, simple environments with few variables enable the agent to rapidly discover optimal policies. In order to cope with dynamic and frequently unpredictable changes, the agent may need to learn intricate patterns and strategies in these environments. To guarantee that the agent can successfully complete the intended tasks while learning by trial and error, the environment's rules, states, and reward system must be carefully designed.

3. Rewards

Rewards act as feedback signals that direct an agent's behavior in reinforcement learning. The agent's main goal is to choose actions that result in desired outcomes in order to maximize the total reward it receives over time. The environment indicates whether an action was successful or unsuccessful in reaching the agent's objective by rewarding the agent after each action. Rewards can be either delayed, where the agent must assess the long-term effects of a series of actions, or immediate, where the agent receives feedback right after completing an action. An agent might, for instance, get a small reward for killing an enemy in a video game (an immediate reward) but a larger reward for finishing the level (a delayed reward). The difficulty with delayed rewards is that more complex learning strategies are needed because the agent has to learn to link actions to results that might not be obvious right away. The way the agent behaves is greatly influenced by the reward function's design. While a poorly designed reward function may result in unexpected behaviors, a well-designed reward function guarantees that the agent learns to take actions that are consistent with the overall goal. A robot might learn to move aimlessly without accomplishing its intended task, like navigating a maze, if it is rewarded for simply moving. In order to promote effective learning and prevent suboptimal behavior, the reward function must be carefully designed to motivate the agent to act appropriately at the appropriate times. The success of a reinforcement learning agent depends on striking a balance between short-term and long-term rewards and making sure that the rewards accurately reflect the task at hand.

Markov Decision Processes (MDPs)

A mathematical framework for simulating decision-making problems with partially random and partially controllable outcomes is offered by Markov Decision Processes (MDPs). The decision-maker selects actions that affect the system's state in an MDP, which represents a system as a collection of states, actions, and transition probabilities. Because of the inherent randomness in the environment and the decision-maker's actions, the state changes over time, making the process dynamic. Transition probabilities capture the randomness, and the choices made to maximize the intended results reflect the decision-maker's control. When decisions must be made gradually over time and the system's evolution is uncertain, MDPs are especially helpful. The cumulative reward, which is usually modeled as a function of the current situation and the action performed, is what the decision-maker seeks to maximize. Given the probabilistic nature of state transitions, the best course of action is one that maximizes long-term rewards, which can be found by solving MDPs. MDPs are used in a variety of domains were making strategic decisions in the face of uncertainty is essential, including robotics, economics, artificial intelligence, and reinforcement learning. An MDP is defined by four key components:

- **States (S):** The possible situations or configurations the system can be in.
- **Actions (A):** The set of choices available to the agent in each state.
- **Transition Probabilities (P):** The probability of transitioning to a new state given the current state and action.
- **Rewards (R):** The feedback signal that indicates the value of being in a particular state or taking a specific action.

Working of MDPs

Based on the transition probabilities, the agent selects an action after observing the current state at each step. It is rewarded for the action that was performed. As the agent engages with its surroundings and gains knowledge from each choice and result, this process keeps going. The agent's objective is to determine the best course of action in each state to maximize the cumulative reward over time, which is known as an optimal policy. This long-term view enables the agent to make choices that will maximize its overall benefit over the course of its experience, rather than just focusing on short-term gains. The future state depends only on the current state and action, not on the order of past states, according to the Markov Property, which is assumed by MDPs. By lowering the quantity of information, the agent must constantly take into account, this feature streamlines the decision-making process. This simplification makes MDPs effective instruments for resolving intricate decision-making issues in a variety of fields, including artificial intelligence, robotics, finance, and game theory.

Applications of MDPs

The ability of MDPs to model decision-making in uncertain environments makes them useful in a variety of domains, including robotics, game AI, and finance. When a robot has to figure out the best way to get somewhere while avoiding obstacles and controlling movement uncertainty, for example, MDPs can be used to simulate navigation tasks in robotics. In a similar vein, MDPs are used in finance to optimize investment strategies by forecasting the results of different decisions over time and modeling market dynamics. Figure 6.3 depicts a basic MDP consisting of four states and a variety of actions link them. An action and its associated reward are labeled on each edge of the graph, illustrating the connections between the states. An MDP's core idea—that the agent transitions between states based on actions and the rewards that go along with them—is illustrated by this representation. Following an ideal policy derived from this structure, the agent navigates the state space efficiently with the goal of selecting actions that result in the highest cumulative reward.

MDPs are essential to reinforcement learning because they form the basis of algorithms that tackle difficult sequential decision-making problems, such as policy gradients and Q-learning.

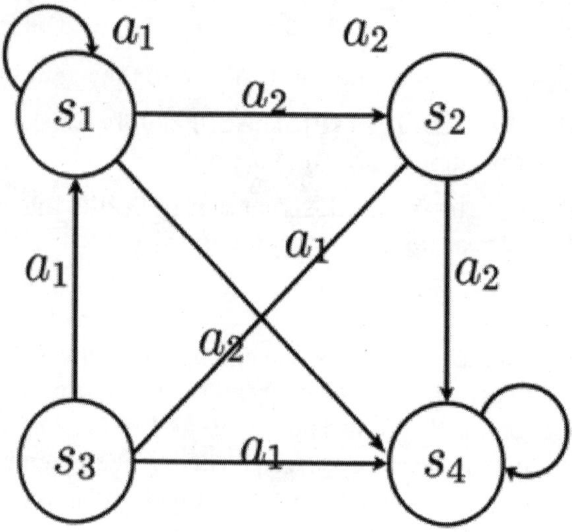

Figure 6.3: simple MDP Four States.

Q-learning and Policy Gradients

Q-Learning

The core goal of the model-free reinforcement learning algorithm Q-Learning is to estimate the value of actions in particular states, or Q-values. The agent can monitor the expected utility of performing a specific action in a given state by using a Q-table, where each cell represents a distinct state-action pair. Because the algorithm doesn't require an environment model, it can be used to solve problems with complex or unknown dynamics. The agent gradually improves its comprehension of which actions result in the best long-term outcomes by updating the Q-values and receiving rewards for interactions with the environment. Q-Learning's iterative update process, which strikes a balance between expected future returns and immediate rewards, is its fundamental concept. The Bellman equation is used to accomplish this, and the reward received and the maximum Q-value of the subsequent state are used to modify the Q-value. The Q-table improves with learning, enabling the agent to determine the best course of action—a mapping from states to actions that optimizes cumulative rewards. In the end, Q-Learning enables agents to make wise choices in unpredictable and changing situations without needing to know anything about the system beforehand. The core equation is:

$$Q(s,a) \leftarrow Q(s,a) + \alpha[r + \gamma \max_{a} Q(s',a) - Q(s,a)]$$

- **States (s)**: Current state of the agent.

- **Actions (a)**: Choices available in the state.
- **Reward (r)**: Feedback received after taking an action.
- **Learning rate (α)**: Determines how much new information overrides old information.
- **Discount factor (γ)**: Balances immediate rewards against future rewards.

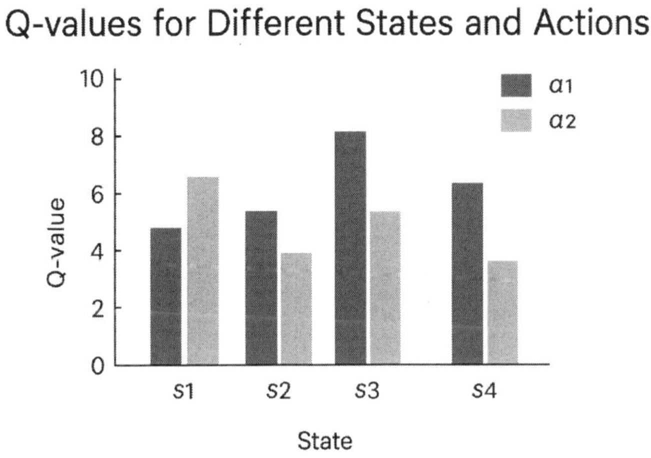

Figure 6.4: Q-values for Different States.

The bar chart above displays Q-values for different states and actions (Figure 6.4). These values influence the agent to select actions with the highest.

Policy Gradients

In reinforcement learning, a class of algorithms known as policy gradients optimizes a policy directly as opposed to using value functions. These approaches usually use a parameterized function to represent the policy, mapping states to the likelihood of choosing each potential course of action. This method makes learning more adaptable and efficient in settings with continuous or high-dimensional action spaces. The policy allows agents to make probabilistic and flexible decisions based on their current observations by mapping states to probabilities of performing each action. Policy gradient methods use gradient ascent to maximize the cumulative expected reward in order to gradually improve the policy's performance. These algorithms modify the policy in a way that maximizes long-term gains by computing the gradient of the expected reward with respect to the policy parameters. Particularly effective in situations where value-based approaches falter, like in partially observable or non-Markovian environments, is this direct optimization technique:

$$\nabla J(\theta) = \mathbb{E}\left[\nabla \log \pi_\theta(a|s) \cdot G_t\right]$$

Policy ($\pi_\theta(a|s)$): The probability of taking action a in state s, parameterized by θ.

Gradient ($\nabla J(\theta)$): Adjusts policy parameters to improve expected rewards.

Return (G_t): Total discounted reward from time t.

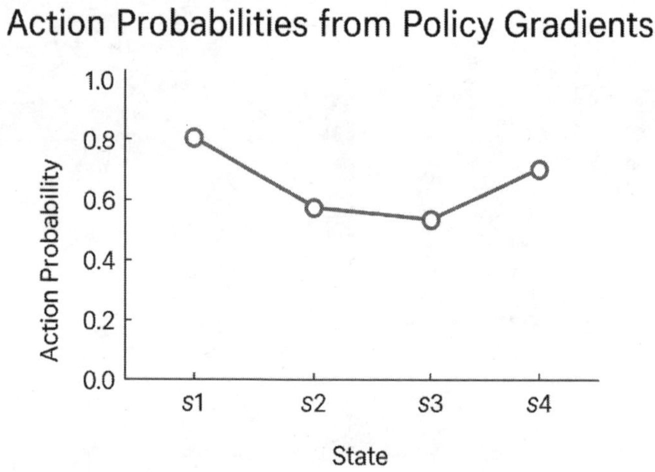

Figure 6.5: Policy Gradients

The line chart above illustrates the action probabilities derived from policy gradients. In contrast to Q-Learning, which deterministically selects the optimal action, policy gradients sample actions according to learned probabilities, facilitating stochastic exploration (Figure 6.5).

Comparison and Applications

- **Q-Learning:** Suitable for discrete action spaces and environments where value-based learning is effective. Commonly used in robotics and game AI.
- **Policy Gradients:** Preferred for continuous action spaces and environments requiring stochastic policies, such as autonomous driving or complex robotics.

Both strategies are crucial for reinforcement learning, and they offer unique benefits for handling various sequential decision-making problems.

Evaluation and Optimization of Learning Models

When developing and implementing machine learning models, evaluation and optimization are essential phases. These procedures measure a model's performance using relevant metrics, which aids in determining how well it generalizes to new, unseen data. Models run the risk of overfitting to training data without careful assessment, which would lead to subpar performance in the real world. Sentence summary: Assessment confirms the dependability and efficiency of machine learning models in real-world settings. In contrast, optimization aims to improve performance and efficiency by fine-tuning model parameters, algorithms, and data preprocessing methods. Developers can increase accuracy, lower errors, and make sure the model works within the intended constraints by methodically modifying these components. To put it succinctly, optimization turns a good model into a high-performing one that is suited for particular environments and tasks.

1. Model Evaluation

Analyzing a model's performance on a dataset that wasn't used for training is called evaluation. This stage is essential to comprehending how well the model predicts outcomes when presented with unknown data. We prevent overfitting and guarantee a more accurate indicator of the model's performance by keeping the training and evaluation datasets apart. This stage aids in assessing the model's ability to generalize to fresh data. A model may not be able to adjust to real-world situations if it only performs well on the training set and poorly on evaluation data. As a result, assessment is a crucial sign of a model's dependability and usefulness in various contexts. Common evaluation metrics depend on the type of task:

- **For regression:** Metrics like Mean Squared Error (MSE), Mean Absolute Error (MAE), and $R2$ score are used.
- **For classification:** Metrics include accuracy, precision, recall, F1-score, and Area Under the Curve (AUC).

One common method for robust evaluation is cross-validation. It entails splitting the dataset into multiple folds or subsets of equal size. Until each fold has been used as the test set once, the model is trained on a combination of these folds and tested on the remaining fold. The risk of skewed performance estimates is reduced by the repeated training and testing, which guarantees that every data point is used for both training and validation. Cross-validation's primary advantage is its capacity to offer a trustworthy assessment of a model's capacity for generalization. It lessens the variability that could arise from a single train-test split by averaging the performance metrics across all folds. Because of this, cross-validation is particularly helpful when dealing with sparse data, ensuring that the evaluation results are more reliable and consistent.

2. Hyperparameter Tuning

A crucial stage in machine learning model optimization is hyperparameter tuning, which entails changing parameters that have an immediate effect on the model's performance but are not discovered during training. These hyperparameters regulate a number of learning-related factors, including the number of layers and nodes in a neural network and the learning rate, which establishes how quickly the model updates in response to fresh data. Techniques like grid search, which tests every possible combination of the parameters, and random search, which chooses combinations at random to find the best configuration, are popular methods for adjusting these parameters. Although these techniques can be useful, they can also be computationally costly, particularly when dealing with large datasets and complex models. More advanced hyperparameter optimization methods have been created to overcome these obstacles. For example, Bayesian optimization focuses on promising regions of the search space rather than blindly examining every possibility by using probabilistic models to direct the search for hyperparameters more effectively. Such techniques are also used by automated machine learning (Auto-ML) platforms to automate the hyperparameter selection and tuning process, making it easier for users who are not as skilled in machine learning to understand. Models can improve performance and generalization while reducing the computational expense of manual tuning by utilizing such techniques.

3. Addressing Overfitting and Underfitting

Two basic issues that come up during machine learning model training are overfitting and underfitting. When a model gets too complicated and begins to learn the noise or erratic variations in the training data instead of the underlying patterns, this is known as overfitting. Because of this, the model performs poorly on test data even though it does remarkably well on the training set. This is because the model's capacity to generalize to new, unseen data is impaired. By penalizing excessively complex models and validating the model's performance on several subsets of the data, regularization techniques like L1 or L2 regularization and cross-validation can help reduce overfitting. Conversely, underfitting occurs when the model is too basic to adequately represent the underlying structure of the data. This frequently happens when the model is unable to adequately fit the data due to a lack of features or inadequate training. As a result, the model performs poorly on both unseen data and the training set. Adding more features, increasing the number of layers in a neural network, or modifying the model's ability to better capture the patterns in the data are all crucial ways to address underfitting. Building successful machine learning models that generalize well to new data requires striking the correct balance between overfitting and underfitting.

Techniques to address overfitting include:

- **Regularization:** Adding constraints like L1 (Lasso) or L2 (Ridge) regularization to the optimization process.
- **Dropout:** Randomly dropping neurons in neural networks during training.

- **Pruning:** Reducing the complexity of decision trees.

Using more intricate models, extra features, or longer training periods can help prevent underfitting.

4. Monitoring and Optimization

Optimization involves improving the model's performance iteratively. Key strategies include:

- **Learning Rate Schedules:** Adjusting the learning rate dynamically during training.
- **Data Augmentation:** Increasing dataset diversity using transformations like rotations or flips for images.
- **Early Stopping:** Halting training when the validation performance stops improving, preventing overfitting.

Additionally, monitoring metrics during training, such as loss and validation error, provides insights into the model's learning dynamics, helping identify potential issues early.

Cross-validation

A reliable assessment technique for gauging a machine learning model's capacity for generalization is cross-validation. For training and testing, it divides the dataset into multiple subsets, or folds, and employs different combinations of these folds. Compared to a single train-test split, this method guarantees that the model is evaluated on several data segments, providing a more reliable performance estimate. The data is separated into k equal-sized folds for k-fold cross-validation, the most popular type of cross-validation. The remaining fold is used for testing after the model has been trained on $k-1$ folds. Each fold serves as the test set once during the k repetitions of this process. The bias that could arise from a single split is lessened by averaging the overall performance over all k iterations. By revealing how the model functions on unseen data, cross-validation aids in addressing issues like overfitting or underfitting. By enabling comparisons of model performance under various configurations, it also improves hyperparameter tuning. However, because the training process is repeated several times, cross-validation can be computationally demanding, especially for large datasets or complex models. Stratified cross-validation is frequently used for unbalanced datasets in order to maintain the class distribution across folds. This guarantees that every fold accurately represents the features of the entire dataset, producing evaluation metrics that are more precise, particularly in classification tasks.

Hyperparameter Tuning

Optimizing a machine learning model's hyperparameters to attain optimal performance is known as hyperparameter tuning. Hyperparameters that cannot be learned from the data, like the learning rate, regularization strength, number of layers in a neural network, or *k* in k-nearest neighbors, are predetermined. "Better tuning, better learning" is a popular expression in machine learning that highlights the significance of this procedure. Grid search is the most straightforward method, in which every possible combination of hyperparameter values is thoroughly tested. Grid search is thorough but computationally demanding, particularly when working with a large number of parameters. By randomly selecting combinations, random search provides a quicker option that frequently produces comparable results with a lot less processing power. Advanced techniques like Bayesian optimization, which use probabilistic models to concentrate on the most promising hyperparameter regions, are employed for more effective tuning. This method eliminates pointless calculations and is more strategic. "Smart search saves time and power," as the saying goes. Intelligent search algorithms are incorporated into the modeling workflow by automated machine learning (AutoML) frameworks, which further streamline tuning. To ensure optimal performance, hyperparameter tuning is essential for striking the correct balance between underfitting and overfitting. Inadequate selection of the hyperparameters can cause even the most advanced models to malfunction. Therefore, to fully realize a model's potential, careful tuning and regular evaluation are necessary.

Overfitting & Underfitting

Overfitting

When a machine learning model learns the noise or unimportant details in the training data rather than the underlying patterns, this is known as overfitting. This phenomenon frequently results in a model that performs exceptionally well on the training dataset but struggles to generalize to new, unseen data. The essence of overfitting, in which the model concentrates too much on particular data points rather than capturing the broad trends or relationships, is encapsulated in the phrase "memorizing the training data instead of learning from it." As a result, when used on test datasets or real-world situations, its predictions lose their accuracy. When the model is overly complicated in relation to the caliber and volume of the training data, the risk of overfitting rises. Overfitting can occur, for example, when training an unpruned decision tree, using an excessive number of features, or building a deep neural network with an excessive number of layers. In these situations, the model can't account for even the slightest variations in the data. Techniques like cross-validation, regularization, model simplification, or expanding the training data set are frequently used to avoid overfitting.

Overfitting can be mitigated through various techniques:

- **Regularization:** Imposing constraints on the model, like L1 (Lasso) or L2 (Ridge) regularization, to prevent overfitting by penalizing overly complex models.

- **Dropout:** Randomly deactivating neurons during training in neural networks to minimize dependency on specific paths.
- **Pruning:** Simplifying decision trees by reducing their depth or complexity, emphasizing the most significant patterns.
- **Data Augmentation:** Expanding the variety of training data by generating new samples through transformations such as rotations, flips, or scaling.

Although overfitting presents challenges, it shows that the model has enough capacity to recognize patterns, implying that with careful optimization, performance can be improved.

Underfitting

Poor performance on both the training and test datasets results from underfitting, which happens when a model is too basic to capture the underlying structure of the data. This usually indicates that the model is unable to identify significant relationships and patterns in the data. Underfitting is aptly described as "failing to learn enough from the data," in which the model's simplicity keeps it from understanding how complex the task at hand is. Consequently, whether the model is tested on known or unknown data, the predictions continue to be erroneous. Underfitting frequently occurs when the input features are insufficient to describe the target variable, the model is excessively constrained, or the training procedure is inadequate. Underfitting can be caused, for instance, by feeding in few or irrelevant features, training for too few epochs, or using a linear model for a nonlinear problem. Techniques like making the model more complex, lengthening the training period, or creating more informative features are frequently employed to solve this problem.

To address underfitting:

- **Enhance Model Complexity:** Implement a more advanced algorithm or increase the number of parameters in the model (e.g., adding additional layers in a neural network).
- **Extend Training Duration:** Train the model for additional epochs or iterations to achieve improved convergence.
- **Refine Feature Selection:** Introduce relevant features or transformations that more effectively capture the relationships in the data.

While underfitting is easier to detect, it indicates that the model needs further refinement to become useful.

Balancing the Two

Finding the ideal balance between overfitting and underfitting is the main difficulty in machine learning. This can be achieved by selecting a model complexity that is appropriate, making sure the training data is adequate and varied, and evaluating the model's performance using techniques like cross-validation. It is possible to determine whether the model is overfitting or underfitting by continuously monitoring training and validation errors during the training process.

Table 6.3: Overfitting vs. Underfitting

Aspect	Overfitting	Underfitting
Definition	The model is too complex, capturing noise and irrelevant details in the training data.	The model is too simple, failing to capture underlying patterns in the data.
Model Complexity	Very high complexity, many parameters.	Very low complexity, too few parameters.
Training Data	Performs well on training data but poorly on new, unseen data (test data).	Performs poorly on both training and test data.
Bias	Low bias (accurate on training data).	High bias (underestimates the complexity of the data).
Variance	High variance (sensitive to small changes in the training data).	Low variance (too generalized and inflexible).
Example	A decision tree that splits too many times or a very deep neural network on small data.	A linear regression model trying to fit a complex dataset.
Performance on Test Data	Poor generalization; test error is high.	Poor performance on both training and test data.
Mitigation	Use simpler models, regularization techniques, or more data.	Increase model complexity or use more relevant features.

The above Table 6.3 summarizes the key differences, causes, and solutions for overfitting and underfitting, emphasizing their importance in building well-generalized models.

Conclusion

The importance of learning in AI was emphasized in this chapter, with a focus on how it supports the creation of intelligent systems. It examined the fundamental algorithms and applications of the four main categories of machine learning: supervised, unsupervised, semi-supervised, and reinforcement learning. Every strategy makes a distinct contribution to AI's capacity for data analysis, pattern recognition, and well-informed decision-making. Phrase sentence: To understand how AI evolves and gets better with experience, one must have a solid understanding of these learning styles. The chapter covered fundamental techniques as well as more complex ideas that are essential to reinforcement learning, like Markov Decision Processes, Q-learning, and policy gradients. Additionally, it emphasized how important model evaluation and optimization methods like cross-validation, hyperparameter tuning, and overfitting and underfitting mitigation techniques are. These methods guarantee the accuracy and generalizability of AI models. To put it simply, mastering these cutting-edge techniques is essential to creating reliable and effective AI systems that can be used in the real world.

Exercise

- Clarify the concept of learning in AI and explain its significance in the development of intelligent systems.
- Contrast supervised, unsupervised, semi-supervised, and reinforcement learning, providing a real-world example for each type.
- Outline the working principles of Linear Regression and Support Vector Machines (SVM). In which situations would you prefer one over the other?
- Highlight the differences between K-Means Clustering and Hierarchical Clustering. How do you determine the optimal number of clusters in K-Means?
- Define agents, environments, and rewards within the context of reinforcement learning. Illustrate their interaction with an example from a self-driving car system.
- Explain the components of a Markov Decision Process (MDP) and describe how the Markov property simplifies decision-making.
- Differentiate between Q-learning and policy gradients, and discuss the advantages of using policy gradients for continuous action spaces.
- Define cross-validation and explain its importance in model evaluation. Compare k-fold cross-validation with stratified cross-validation.
- Describe grid search and random search as techniques for hyperparameter tuning. What are the advantages of Bayesian optimization over these methods?
- Define overfitting and underfitting. Discuss two techniques for addressing each problem and their impact on model performance.

Book for Further Reading

- **Artificial Intelligence:** A Modern Approach by Stuart Russell and Peter Norvig
- **Artificial Intelligence:** Foundations of Computational Agents" by David L. Poole and Alan K. Mackworth
- Pattern Recognition and Machine Learning" by Christopher Bishop
- Deep Learning by Ian Goodfellow, YoshuaBengio, and Aaron Courville
- **Machine Learning:** A Probabilistic Perspective" by Kevin P. Murphy
- **Artificial Intelligence:** Structures and Strategies for Solving Complex Problems" by George F. Luger
- Introduction to Artificial Intelligence" by Wolfgang Ertel
- The Elements of Artificial Intelligence" by S. N. Sivanandam and S. Sumathi
- Artificial Intelligence: A New Synthesis" by Nils J. Nilsson
- The Age of Em: Work, Love, and Life when Robots Rule the Earth" by Robin Hanson

Bibliography

- Russell, S. J., &Norvig, P. (2021). Artificial intelligence: A modern approach (4th ed.). Pearson.
- Nilsson, N. J. (2010). The quest for artificial intelligence: A history of ideas and achievements. Cambridge University Press.
- Kaplan, J. (2016). Artificial intelligence: What everyone needs to know. Oxford University Press.
- Domingos, P. (2015). The master algorithm: How the quest for the ultimate learning machine will remake our world. Basic Books.
- Turing, A. M. (1950). Computing machinery and intelligence. Mind, 59(236), 433–460. https://doi.org/10.1093/mind/LIX.236.433
- Goodfellow, I., Bengio, Y., &Courville, A. (2016). Deep learning. MIT Press.
- Poole, D., Mackworth, A., & Goebel, R. (1998). Computational intelligence: A logical approach. Oxford University Press.
- Bostrom, N. (2014). Superintelligence: Paths, dangers, strategies. Oxford University Press.
- Chollet, F. (2019). Deep learning with Python (2nd ed.). Manning Publications.
- Mitchell, M. (2019). Artificial intelligence: A guide for thinking humans. Farrar, Straus and Giroux.
- Haenlein, M., & Kaplan, A. (2019). A brief history of artificial intelligence: On the past, present, and future of AI. California Management Review, 61(4), 5–14. https://doi.org/10.1177/0008125619864925
- McCarthy, J., Minsky, M. L., Rochester, N., & Shannon, C. E. (2006). A proposal for the Dartmouth summer research project on artificial intelligence, August 31, 1955. AI Magazine, 27(4), 12–14.
- Floridi, L., &Chiriatti, M. (2020). GPT-3: Its nature, scope, limits, and consequences. Minds and Machines, 30(4), 681–694. https://doi.org/10.1007/s11023-020-09548-1
- Dignum, V. (2019). Responsible artificial intelligence: How to develop and use AI in a responsible way. Springer.

- LeCun, Y., Bengio, Y., & Hinton, G. (2015). Deep learning. Nature, 521(7553), 436–444. https://doi.org/10.1038/nature14539
- Brynjolfsson, E., & McAfee, A. (2014). The second machine age: Work, progress, and prosperity in a time of brilliant technologies. W.W. Norton & Company.
- Wang, F. Y., Zeng, D., & Wang, J. (2007). Artificial intelligence in the 21st century. IEEE Intelligent Systems, 22(2), 88–95. https://doi.org/10.1109/MIS.2007.36
- Marcus, G. (2020). The next decade in AI: Four steps towards robust artificial intelligence. arXiv preprint. https://arxiv.org/abs/2002.06177
- Kurzweil, R. (2005). The singularity is near: When humans transcend biology. Viking.
- Tegmark, M. (2017). Life 3.0: Being human in the age of artificial intelligence. Alfred A. Knopf.
- Wang, P. (2019). On the conceptual foundations of artificial general intelligence. Springer.
- Shneiderman, B. (2020). Bridging the gap between ethics and practice: Guidelines for reliable, safe, and trustworthy human-centered AI systems. ACM Transactions on Interactive Intelligent Systems (TiiS), 10(4), 1–31. https://doi.org/10.1145/3419764
- Ethem, A. (2010). Introduction to machine learning (2nd ed.). MIT Press.
- Siau, K., & Yang, Y. (2017). Impact of artificial intelligence, robotics, and automation on higher education. Twenty-Third Americas Conference on Information Systems (AMCIS 2017).
- Vardi, M. Y. (2012). The consequences of machine intelligence. Communications of the ACM, 55(1), 5. https://doi.org/10.1145/2063176.2063177
- Searle, J. R. (1980). Minds, brains, and programs. Behavioral and Brain Sciences, 3(3), 417–424. https://doi.org/10.1017/S0140525X00005756
- Buchanan, B. G. (2005). A (very) brief history of artificial intelligence. AI Magazine, 26(4), 53–60.
- Jordan, M. I., & Mitchell, T. M. (2015). Machine learning: Trends, perspectives, and prospects. Science, 349(6245), 255–260. https://doi.org/10.1126/science.aaa8415
- Amodei, D., Olah, C., Steinhardt, J., Christiano, P., Schulman, J., &Mané, D. (2016). Concrete problems in AI safety. arXiv preprint. https://arxiv.org/abs/1606.06565

- Moor, J. H. (2006). The Dartmouth College artificial intelligence conference: The next fifty years. AI Magazine, 27(4), 87–91.
- Anderson, M., & Anderson, S. L. (2011). Machine ethics. Cambridge University Press.
- Walsh, T. (2016). Machines that think: The future of artificial intelligence. Prometheus Books.
- Boden, M. A. (2016). AI: Its nature and future. Oxford University Press.
- Zeng, Y., Lu, E., &Huangfu, C. (2018). Linking artificial intelligence principles. arXiv preprint. https://arxiv.org/abs/1812.04814
- Shoham, Y., & Leyton-Brown, K. (2009). Multiagent systems: Algorithmic, game-theoretic, and logical foundations. Cambridge University Press.
- Schmidhuber, J. (2015). Deep learning in neural networks: An overview. Neural Networks, 61, 85–117. https://doi.org/10.1016/j.neunet.2014.09.003
- Minsky, M. (1986). The society of mind. Simon & Schuster.
- Pearl, J. (2000). Causality: Models, reasoning, and inference. Cambridge University Press.
- Legg, S., &Hutter, M. (2007). Universal intelligence: A definition of machine intelligence. Minds and Machines, 17(4), 391–444. https://doi.org/10.1007/s11023-007-9079-x
- Lake, B. M., Ullman, T. D., Tenenbaum, J. B., &Gershman, S. J. (2017). Building machines that learn and think like people. Behavioral and Brain Sciences, 40, e253. https://doi.org/10.1017/S0140525X16001837